CADFAN'S CHURCH

A History with Digressions

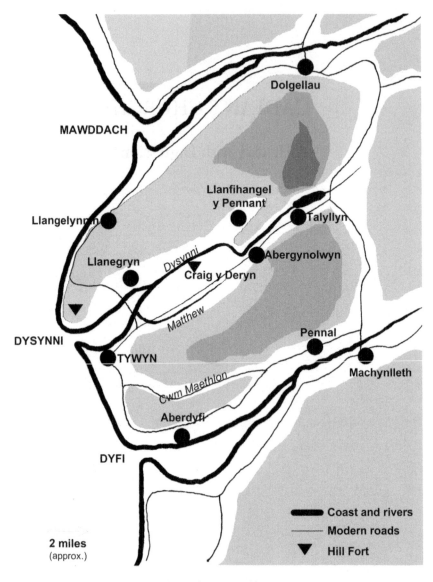

Cantref Meirionydd

CADFAN'S CHURCH
A History with Digressions

Meryl Gover

Matador
9 Priory Business Park
Wistow Road
Kibworth
Leicester LE8 0RX, UK
Tel: (+44) 116 279 2299
Email: books@troubador.co.uk
Web: www.troubador.co.uk/matador

ISBN 978 1784622 909

British Library Cataloguing in Publication Data.
A catalogue record for this book is available from the British Library.

Printed and bound in the UK by TJ International, Padstow, Cornwall
Typeset in 12pt Minion Pro by Troubador Publishing Ltd, Leicester, UK

Matador is an imprint of Troubador Publishing Ltd

To the Glory of God
and in joyful remembrance of all those who,
over the centuries,
have worshipped in the areas
visited by Cadfan and his followers.

Church of fair Cadfan, brilliant to behold,
Church of faith and devotion and belief and communion
As though it had been fashioned by God Himself.

Canu Cadfan, Llewellyn Fardd I

The publication of this book has been partially funded by a grant of £1000 from the Peter Saunders Trust, Tywyn, whose support is much appreciated.

ACKNOWLEDGEMENTS

By permission of Llyfrgell Genedlaethol Cymru/the National Library of Wales, extracts from Bangor Diocesan and Welsh Church Council records and from the *Aberystwyth Observer* are quoted in this book.

I also acknowledge, with gratitude, permission from the Editors of the *Cambrian News* and *Archaeologica Cambrensis* to include quotations from their publications.

Thanks

This could not have been written without the help of a number of people and institutions.

My thanks are due to the staff of Tywyn Library for early suggestions and to Gwynedd Libraries for supplying a range of books. *The History of Merioneth (Volumes 1 & 2)*, produced by the Merioneth Historical and Record Society, were invaluable both for the information they contained and for their pointers to a wide range of references. The National Library of Wales (NLW), and especially the staff in the South Reading Room, kept me supplied with many original sources, and the NLW Welsh Journals Online and Welsh Newspapers Online were very helpful.

Much of the information on the later history of the church came from the church safe where, thankfully, a box full of documents had not been discarded as out of date. Its contents have now been transferred to the Merioneth Records Office, Dolgellau, which also holds the past church registers and other interesting sidelights on life in Tywyn.

I owe an immense debt of gratitude to Professor Catherine McKenna of Harvard University for allowing me to include her translation of *Canu Cadfan*. My thanks also to Professor Nancy Edwards of the University of Bangor and to J. Potter for emailing me the relevant portions of their books before publication.

I should particularly like to thank my brother and sister-in-law, Bill and Lesley Gover, for their detailed study of the book, identifying inconsistencies and assumptions, correcting errors and making suggestions for rewording. Their help has been invaluable. Thanks, also, to Sue Whitehouse for proof-reading the book. All remaining errors, whether of fact or expression, are all my own.

CONTENTS

1. THE COMING OF CADFAN

THE STORY

It was not a big estuary. Not like the great estuaries of the Mawddach to the north and the Dyfi to the south. Its mouth was south of its present position and may have been quite wide, as the great shingle bank that formed it had not yet spread far north. Within the estuary, beyond Craig y Deryn, water stretched upstream at high tide but the strength of the current was much less than that of the great estuaries which carried so much more water.

On either side the land rose quite steeply for a few dozen yards before levelling off to provide a wide area for crops; the north bank was protected from the bitter north winds by the hills behind. Uncultivated areas were covered by scrubby bush and stunted trees, kept small by the salty west wind. There was little of the forests of inland areas. The main channel of the river passed close to the north bank at all stages of the tide and provided a good place to bring in the fishing boats and coastal traders. Ffordd Ddu, an ancient trackway running over the hill from Llwyngwril, came down to the water here and, on the hill behind, an old hill fort showed that the area had been inhabited for many centuries[1].

On the south side of the estuary the river was divided into several small channels and there was less water except towards high tide. Instead, sand bars spread over that part of the estuary. There were channels to the shore navigable by the

1

fishing boats but it was not so easy to reach as the north bank. On the other hand, there was much more flat land suitable for cultivation stretching south around the edge of the hill and east into the valley of the River Matthew[2].

Fish from the sea and river, well watered but not marshy level ground for crops, the forest for wood; the two shores of the Dysynni provided a better place to live than many inland settlements.

Far offshore the trading ships passed, some from as far away as Lyons and even the Eastern Mediterranean[3]. Having come so far they needed rich areas with which to trade their goods, places like eastern Ireland, South Wales and Anglesey with its fertile croplands. The shores of Cardigan Bay had little to offer them and they kept well out at sea for fear of the lee shore. Some goods and passengers for this area might have come with them from the continent but they would have been put ashore in South Wales to find one of the smaller vessels that traded along the coast to complete their journey. The arrival of a coastal trader at the northern landing of the Dysynni was a time of excitement, of greeting old friends, wondering at travellers, trading for the goods on the ship.

It was here, in the spring[4], about 516 AD, that Cadfan and his companions arrived. Seeking solitude, a "desert place", they may even have been told, "You need the sandy shore, the *tywyn*." Leaving the north shore they were taken with their belongings in a small fishing boat across the estuary, up a channel through the sandbanks to a small mound rising 6 feet or so above the main shoreline. It was a special place; at its lower edge a spring of fresh water flowed[5], making it a suitable place to settle, yet there was no sign of the land around being cultivated already.

The group had come from "Llydaw" seeking peace and solitude to worship God. They intended to settle for a long time, perhaps for life, and needed to be self-sufficient. They had brought seeds, enough grain and dried pulses to last until their first harvest, tools, perhaps some livestock and, if they were very fortunate, also a gospel.

After erecting a rough cross and giving thanks to God for their new home, their first action was to erect a small hut made from branches woven and tied together and covered by sods of turf, just big enough to protect all of them from the weather and to be used for their worship initially.

Even on that first day there were children peeping out from the underbrush watching the strangers[6]. It was important for the newcomers to make contact with those who already lived in the area, and Cadfan made his way along what looked like a narrow track between bushes until he came to an area under cultivation. Nearby was a small cluster of huts, built much as he and his companions were building theirs.

Here he had his first stumbling talk with those who were to become their neighbours. Latin was of no use; although the Romans had penetrated towards the area they had never had much effect on the local culture or language. Breton, and even South Welsh, had some similarities with the local language but there were many different words and differences in pronunciation. Slowly he managed to communicate the basic information that he and his companions had come to settle in the area, that they did not want to cause any problems for those who lived here, that he would come and talk again.

A message was sent to the local leader about the new arrivals and he came to find out more about the strangers. Christianity had hardly reached this area of Wales and Cadfan's reply may have been the first he heard of Christ.

Meanwhile, between times of worship, Cadfan and his companions hastily cleared an area for their crops, dragging up the bushes and putting them aside for future use, using mattocks to break the ground and then sowing the seed, while one or two fished to help eke out their limited provisions. To keep out marauding deer and wild pigs they built a stockade around the cultivated land partly by using existing bushes and partly by piling uprooted bushes and stones between them. Once their future crops were safe their next building was a small place for worship, the first church to be built at what was to become Tywyn.

As time went by, Cadfan and his companions got to know more about their neighbours who lived in small groups, or hamlets, often containing related families. A number of these hamlets had a common leader – perhaps one might call him a lord or chieftain – who had a more elaborate dwelling known as a *llys*; the local *llys* was quite possibly at Craig y Deryn[7].

Whether Cadfan and his companions had come as evangelists or whether they had come seeking a quiet contemplative life, they soon saw the necessity to spread the gospel to these people who had little or no knowledge of it. Occasionally local people came to watch and listen to the strangers who, several times a day, stood around a cross praying and singing. As time went by Cadfan and his companions began to use these opportunities to teach and preach.

As the local people began to believe in Christ, some of Cadfan's companions began to travel further afield, some seeking the solitude and silence that had been their original goal, others spreading the message. They started to name the place each had settled after the settler – "I'm going to Celynin's", "see you at Cadfan's" – and sometimes the name stuck, much later becoming the place name or being used as the dedication of a church.

Cadfan himself travelled up the southern side of the valley of the Matthew, pausing for a drink from Pistyll Cadfan before resting on Eisteddfa Cadfan. He continued along the edge of the hill, passing Bryneglwys[8], where he is said to have built a chapel, or perhaps a cell for meditation, before walking over the hill to Corris on his way to Llangadfan[9], a place both for retreat and for preaching.

Eventually, as Cadfan grew older, he once more felt the need to retreat from the work that had come upon him as the needs of Tywyn and the area become apparent. With some of his original companions, he moved to Ynys Enlli (Bardsey Island) where, with Lleu as co-founder and successor, he established a group known as Bangor Cadfan[10]. There he died and was buried.

THE EVIDENCE

How much of the first part of the chapter is really true? The earliest record that mentions Cadfan actually dates from the 12th century (and that's about going to Bardsey) so what can we really know about what happened in the early 6th century?

Mapping the locations of archaeological finds and sites shows that there has been movement between western Gaul and both sides of the Irish Sea as far back as about 3000 BC[11]. Imported pottery reveals sea-borne connections not only with Gaul but as far away as the Eastern Mediterranean – the area in which Christianity first spread[12]. In Wales, the lack of remains around Cardigan Bay suggests that landfall was mainly confined to the southern and northern peninsulas. (Professor Pierre-Roland Gist warns against over-simplified views of the amount of long-distance sea traffic, one factor being limited navigational aids[13]. However, the Norse made voyages to Iceland and Greenland across treacherous seas with no sight of land many years before the compass reached northern Europe in the 13th century.)

The Celtic ships that made these voyages were described by Timaeus in the 4th century BC as being made of wickerwork covered with hide[14], and even in the 9th century similar vessels sailed to Iceland. Local fishing and coasting boats were probably a smaller version of the same design. Just as nowadays we may fly from Britain to a major airport in another country and then change to a smaller plane to reach our destination, so the long-distance trading ships would carry passengers to main trading ports.

Sea travel was also seasonally dependent, as St Paul found on his way to Rome, with little or nothing moving between autumn and spring. Cadfan and his followers probably originally came ashore in South Wales at the mouth of the River Taf on the south coast[15]. After the winter – or even after several years – they would have walked the transpeninsular route to the estuary of the Gwaun to board the first of the small coasting boats that would eventually land them in Tywyn.

On land we think of travelling along valleys but in the 6th century these were filled with marshes; along the sides of the hills there would have been banks of forest with some scrub between the marsh and the woods. Longer-distance paths were normally above the tree line and through passes rather than along the river valleys[16].

Migration

Various factors may have influenced the movement of Christians. From the beginning of the 3rd century, individuals and small groups moved into the Egyptian desert, most famously St Anthony, who moved there in 270/1 AD and became known as the Father of Desert Monasticism[17]. By the end of the 4th century, his influence had moved into southern Gaul and St Martin founded a monastery near Tours, which was "outside the dominion of any bishop". This combination of Eastern mysticism, asceticism and the urge to seek a "desert place" for contemplation and worship took root and flourished – but its followers faced hostility from the Gaulish episcopal establishment[18]. Where better to go than northwards? (Although there is also the possibility that the Gaulish church authorities may have directed a deliberate evangelisation of Cornwall, Wales and beyond.)

In addition, there was external pressure. In the 5th century, the withdrawal of Roman troops from the provinces, followed by the fall of Rome, led to increasingly disturbed conditions in Western Europe. Without the protection of the legions, "barbarians" – migrants – could move westwards into and across Europe from the East. Many Christians, with their families, left their homeland in the Lyons-Vienne area and took the sea routes northwards[19].

Which of these would apply to Cadfan and his followers? We cannot know for sure, but the most likely seems to be that they were seeking a lonely place. By the late 5th or early 6th century there seem to have been three orders, or types, of holy men[20]: bishops who had a roving commission, those in charge of the great monastic houses (mainly in southern Wales at first) and the wandering saints – the *pererini* – who sought lonely places for prayer, praise and meditation, sometimes alone, sometimes with a band of followers. The *pererini* spread furthest afield, taking Celtic Christianity far and wide. They would start with one or two beehive cells, and possibly a preaching cross, and in time a little church would grow up, first in wattle and daub, then in wood and eventually in stone. It might ultimately become one of our parish churches of today.

Geography

The basic shape of the Dysynni Valley has not changed much since Cadfan's time although, like the Mawddach and Dyfi, silting has occurred[21]. It is likely that, before the draining of the southern marshes by the owners of the Ynysymaengwyn Estate in the 18th and 19th centuries, the south side of the Dysynni resembled the south sides of the Mawddach and Dyfi with more sandbanks, saltings and marshes than on the northern side. It is thought that 700 years ago, before the silting and the drainage, the river was tidal up to Craig y Deryn (Bird Rock).

St Cadfan's Church is on land about 6 feet above the surrounding roads. The solid geological foundations beneath the area are mainly composed of glacial moraine[22]. To the north of the vestry, natural deposits are sandy gravel with large rounded boulders[23], while to the south of the chancel the subsoil is mainly shale[24].

The St Cadfan's Wells baths (now filled in and under a building) were at the end of the road between the Market Hall and the NatWest Bank. The spring itself was within the north-west boundary of the current churchyard[25].

Infrastructure

There was a well-used prehistoric mountain trackway, the Ffordd Ddu[26], which ran south-west from the area of Dolgellau along the flanks of Cadair Idris round to Friog/Llangelynnin and then across the hill to the north-west shore of the Dysynni. This was probably a port and haven for shipping before the excessive silting and the extension of the south shingle bank northwards. The main line of the track was followed by a Roman road which, however, crossed the Dysynni further east and skirted the hill south-east of Tywyn, possibly reaching Pennal.

To the north of the estuary Castell Mawr, a hill fort small enough to have been built quickly by one or two boatloads of incomers, commanded the open valley of the Dysynni from a height of about 400 feet[27].

Inland, Craig y Deryn was crowned by another hill fort[28] with an elaborate inturned entrance and a double line of defences. It was still inhabited in the Roman period as shown by Romano-British pottery remains found there. Below it, the Dysynni was deep enough at high tide to allow easy transfer of goods by small boats.

In the area around Abergynolwyn, the names Pistyll Cadfan (Cadfan's Waterfall), Eisteddfa Cadfan (Cadfan's Seat) and Llwybr Cadfan (Cadfan's Path) are recorded. It is thought that Eisteddfa Cadfan is the outcrop opposite Tan y Coed Farm on the B4405 (SH662055) and Pistyll Cadfan is the stream coming down to the west of it[29].

Llwybr Cadfan pathway is not marked on Ordnance Survey maps but it has been suggested that it probably ran from Tywyn along the northern flank of the hills of the River Matthew valley as far as Eisteddfa Cadfan. It may then have gone via Abergynolwyn and Pen Eisteddfa to Dolgellau[30] or via Bryneglwys to Corris and then by Aberllefenni and Mallwyd to Llangadfan.

There seems no obvious reason why the area of Bryneglwys (Church Hill), after which the slate quarry was named, should be associated with a church. St David's Church at Abergynolwyn (1871) post-dates Bryneglwys quarry (1840s). It is at least feasible to suggest that the name does indeed reflect a time when someone, if not Cadfan, had a chapel or hermitage there (although it was not uncommon for a small church to be built in such an area with occasional services for the isolated community).

Society and housing

After the departure of the Romans, society was made up of two major social groups: freemen and bondmen[31]. Bondmen were settled in small hamlets, often of closely related people, near the fields they would be working; their houses are thought to have been of wood, turf and thatch.

Groups of hamlets were attached to the *llys*, or court, of a local lord to whom they rendered dues and service. The *llys* was probably a rectangular wooden-built home and very often it would be situated within the ramparts of an Iron Age hill fort such as that at Craig y Deryn.

Genealogy and names

Cadfan's parents are given in *Canu Cadfan*[32] as Eneas and Gwenn. In *Bonedd y Sant*[33] they are given as Eneas Ledwic from Brittany and Gwen Teirbron daughter of Emyr Llydaw. His importance is indicated by others – Padarn, Tydecho, Trunyaw and Maelrys – being defined as cousins to Cadfan. Memories can go back a very long way but the time span suggests some 'improvement' in the genealogy over time!

Cadfan is reputed to have been a warrior saint but this may be due to confusion with the 7th century Cadfan ap Iago, King of Gwynedd in the early 7th century[34].

The names of fourteen Celtic saints associated with St Cadfan are found in three genealogies of pre-16th century date[35] – 900 years after they arrived! It is interesting that, apart from saints otherwise accounted for, these names are those of church dedications in the Merioneth area[36]:

St Bodfan (or St Bodfan and St Mary) at Llanaber
St Brothen at Llanfrothen
St Celynnin at Llangelynnin
St Derfel at Llandderfel

St Dwywe at Llanddwywe Is-y-craig/Uwch-y-craig
St Enddwyn at Llanenddwyn
St Mael and St Sulien at Corwen
St Madryn at Trawsfynydd
St Tanwg at Llandanwg
St Trillo at Llandrillo
St Twrog at Maentwrog
St Tydecho at Llanymawddwy

Some of these are coastal churches, which could have maintained communication with Tywyn by sea[37].

Did the churches and their dedications exist first and was the legend of these being the names of Cadfan's companions made up later? Or was it the other way round – were these really Cadfan's companions who spread out from the initial settlement to find their own lonely places and to preach the gospel? Certainly St Cadfan's Church became one of the "mother churches" of Wales with daughter chapels recorded at Talyllyn, Llanfihangel-y-Pennant and Pennal.

Perhaps some of the names given in the manuscripts were indeed companions of Cadfan. *Bonedd y Sant* includes Mael, Sulien, Tanwg, Tecwyn and Tydecho with those who travelled to Enlli (Bardsey) with Cadfan[38].

Egryn does not appear in the list of those who came with Cadfan even though Llanegryn is so close to Tywyn. He is said originally to have been a monk of Llanilltyd, which was founded about 500 AD[39]. If Egryn was already settled on the north side of the Dysynni, that might explain why Cadfan and his companions settled on the more exposed and less promising south side.

Cadfan is now much less well known, even in North Wales, than David but A. W. Wade Evans[40] noted that among the ancient foundations of North Wales and North Cardiganshire there were no dedications to David; however not only did Tywyn have St Cadfan's Church but also Capel Cadfan within the churchyard. There were also Capel Cadfans in Llangedris and Llangathen, while there were church dedications to St Cadfan at Llangadfan and Llangathen.

Dates

Bishops, such as Deiniol, may have been associated with kings, which enables their dates to be at least approximately known. (There is a legend in Tywyn that Deiniol visited Cadfan and spent some time with him before he became Bishop of Bangor in approximately 546 AD. If true, this would at least give a latest date for Cadfan's arrival; there is, however, no evidence for such a visit.)

For the *pererini* there were no such links to provide any dating. The earliest record of 516 AD as the time of Cadfan's arrival seems to be in a report of a visit by the Cambrian Archaeological Society in 1896[41]. This has been repeated in the list of abbots, rectors and vicars dated 1930 and displayed in the church. The majority of the other information in that list can be independently corroborated, which suggests there may, somewhere, be a source for the 516 date. The best we can say is that, based on the movements that took place around then, Cadfan probably arrived in the late 5th or early 6th century.

2. THE DARK AGES

Evidence for the way the church developed during the Dark Ages is scanty. There is the *Life of St Samson of Dol* (5th century)[1], the report from Gildas on his visits[2], and there is what Giraldus Cambrensis found (and was surprised and somewhat shocked by) when he travelled through Wales in 1188[3].

Christianity in Wales had not been founded by missionaries from Rome and it did not follow the ways of the Roman church. The native ("Celtic") churches of Britain (chiefly those following the traditions of Iona) agreed at the Synod of Whitby in 664 AD to follow the Roman method of calculating the date of Easter. However, the churches in Wales did not actually alter their calculations until 768 AD, a change credited to Bishop Elfoddwy of Gwynedd[4]. There were many other differences from the observance of the Roman church.

MONASTERIES

Monasteries were already well established, at least in South Wales, by the early 6th century and more continued to be founded[5]. These were very different from monasteries in the Middle Ages. Because of its isolation and the early date at which it developed, the organisation of the Celtic Church differed from that established in Europe and most of England.

In Wales, as in Ireland which is only eighty-five miles from Tywyn across the Irish Sea, the kin group was the very ground of all inheritance. A man giving land to an ecclesiastical foundation could not separate that land from the rights of his kindred in regard to it. In Ireland this resulted in the kin of the founder or major donor of the site controlling appointments to the post of abbot[6], while in Welsh religious communities both property rights and monastic offices tended to go by inheritance[7].

Contrary to our expectations – and those of the Normans – monks and clerics in the Celtic Church were not necessarily celibate. Married clergy had been acceptable in the early church and many of those who were members of Tywyn's ecclesiastical community would have lived with their wives and children. This way of life continued for many hundreds of years.

Did the post of abbot, or any other post, pass by inheritance[8] at Tywyn? We cannot know. The idea shocked the Normans and yet, apart from the kin-group issue, there was another practical purpose. In an era when literacy was unusual, leadership in the community required the leader to be literate[9]. In addition, knowledge of Latin for reading the Bible and an ability to move freely among the upper classes of society without difficulty would have been important for the abbot. Care could be taken to see that an heir was suitably prepared for the job. There is a record of a son being adopted who was to be trained as heir[10].

The monastic rules, vows and codes of behaviour, at least in South-East Wales, were outlined by Gildas in the 6th century[11]. Manual labour, which would include growing crops and caring for livestock as well as carrying out necessary building work and repairs, was expected of most monks. As well as food crops, herbs were also grown specifically for medicinal purposes[12].

THE CHURCH AND ITS SURROUNDINGS

The original wattle and daub church building – lasting perhaps twenty-five years between rebuilds – would have been replaced, as soon as enough labour was available, with a wooden building, perhaps in rectangular form along the lines of the *llys*. At some time this could have been replaced by a stone building.

Burials inside and around the church began, perhaps because of a general belief that the nearness of bodies to the holy men would help the soul. Some wished to mark the burial spot with a stone. A stone carved with the name of Pascent and dating from the 5th or 6th century was in Tywyn churchyard until the early 18th century. One man in the Tywyn area inscribed an epitaph to his wife in Welsh on a stone that was subsequently reused for other burials; this is now known as the Cadfan Stone. Over time, these burials raised the ground around the church even further above the surrounding plain.

It has been suggested that curvilinear boundaries and being above the level of the surrounding land are signs of an old burial ground[13]. St Cadfan's churchyard is about 5 to 6 feet (nearly 2 metres) above its surroundings with the earth now held back by walls. Until the late 19th or early 20th century there was no definite demarcation to north and west. In addition, a curve in the wall facing College Green to the south is known to have been altered in the early 20th century[14], and the 1891 edition of the OS map has indications of a much larger curvilinear enclosure to the north where the well dedicated to Cadfan was situated[15].

Among the treasured belongings of the church at Tywyn would have been one or more relics of St Cadfan; not mortal remains but items reputed to belong to him, such as a bell or crozier. These were especially important because legal oaths were normally only valid if they were sworn on a relic; perhaps surprisingly to us, such oaths were far more important than those sworn on a gospel[16].

As the establishment grew, in the 8th or 9th century a sundial (or "mass clock") was commissioned, to regularise the times of services and to enable people to arrive on time[17]. Only two such sundials survive in Wales: one in Tywyn and the other at Clynnog Fawr.

As St Cadfan's original settlement developed into a monastery and its influence spread, it is likely that the local lord and others would gift it with hamlets with bondmen, part of whose produce would provide some of the establishment's food[18]. Other grants of tenanted land might come from the local prince or the Prince of Gwynedd; such land might be quite a distance from Tywyn itself. Eventually the church would receive more than was needed for its community but it seems that this surplus was not transferred into lasting forms of wealth as it would have been elsewhere in Europe. Some may have been stored locally, ensuring that in times of famine the local people would not starve, some displayed in alms-giving or hospitality and some used as payment for labour[19] (for example, making the mass clock) or the construction and repair of buildings.

This lack of portable wealth did not save Tywyn from being "ravaged by the Gentiles" – sacked and burnt by Irish-based Vikings – in 963[20]. However, in company with the majority of Welsh churches that suffered the same fate in the later 10th century, there was only the one attack. Unlike English and Irish churches, Welsh churches apparently did not provide enough loot to warrant a return visit!

NAWDD

An important aspect of the legal status of churches, from Roman legislation and even "barbarian" codes, was their right to extend protection to people fleeing from their enemies – the right we would call sanctuary[21]. Welsh law books use the word *nawdd* (protection) and *noddfa* (place of protection) and that of Tywyn is celebrated in *Canu Cadfan*, the mid-12th century poem by Llewelyn Fardd I in praise of Tywyn. The person claiming *nawdd* was allowed to go about in the churchyard and enclosure, and his livestock could go with the community livestock as far as they could go out and back in a day; for Tywyn, perhaps as far as Bryncrug. It has been suggested[22] that the cross-marked stone said to have stood on Bryn y Paderau (now built into the church tower) and the prehistoric pillar known as *Croes Faen* on Hendy Farm (SH 5968 0154) may have marked the extent of this sanctuary.

   Nawdd was one sign of status. Breaking *nawdd* of a church was sacrilege and anyone doing so had to pay a fine as a compensation payment for injury to the honour of the saint and his church. For ordinary churches the sum was £7 (over £3000 today); for mother churches such as Tywyn double that, with half going to the Abbot "if holy and literate" (i.e. not a lay abbot) and the other half being shared between the priests and *claswyr*[23].

CLAS

The *clas* consisted of a community associated with the church. The members had hereditary rights, which probably were clerical in origin. By the 12th century the *clas* may have been partly, or even completely, made up of laymen. These were referred to as the *claswyr* (men of the *clas*)[24]. *Canu Cadfan* describes the *clas* as lying outside the dyke surrounding the church, a description which may indicate a lay community dependent on the church.

We do not know the limit of the surrounding ditch, but there may be a hint in the name of a building. At the junction of College Green and National Street stands *Porth Gwyn*. The name, which pre-dates the current building, is usually translated as "White Door" or "White Porch", and the door is always painted white. But *porth* can also mean gate and *gwyn* may mean holy or blessed. Was *Porth Gwyn* the Blessed Gateway, the entrance to the grounds of the church, the *noddfa*, with its sanctity and promise of *nawdd*, protection?

EVIDENCE FOR TYWYN'S STATUS

A combination of archaeological and historical evidence, plus evidence of its status in the 12th and 13th centuries, identifies Tywyn as one of the high-status native churches of Wales[25].

- The church was unusually large for North Wales. Internally it was about 109 feet in length. In comparison Llandaff Cathedral was only 40 feet in 1120 (though it was subsequently rebuilt). In addition, the church was cruciform, with a tower over the crossing, and an aisled nave and clerestory, a combination found in few other non-cathedral churches of Wales.

- The Pascent stone (5/6th century) is thought to have been a gravestone and the cross-inscribed "Cadfan Stone" (8/9th century) once marked several graves.

- The sundial (8/9th century) indicates the presence of a community concerned to make the times of worship regular and recognisable, and rich enough to afford such a dial.

- The implication of the Viking raid in 963, referred to in *Brut y Tywysogion*, is that this church (as well as others in North Wales from Holyhead in 961 to Bangor in 1073) was thought to be wealthy enough to be worth raiding and therefore, presumably, important[26].

- Many high-status churches had a mortuary chapel or *capel-y-bedd*, traditionally built over the site thought to be the burial place of the founder. A free-standing chapel, known as *Capel Cadfan*, was recorded in the north-west of the churchyard in 1806, "some of whose walls were standing within memory and the site still discernible" although it is no longer visible[27].

- A principal characteristic of the high-status churches was the presence of *claswyr* (probably canons or portioners) ruled by an abbot[28]. The Abbot of Tywyn is praised in the mid-12th century *Canu Cadfan* of Llywelyn Fardd I, while the *Taxatio* of Pope Nicholas IV in 1291 records that Tywyn had its revenue divided into portions.

3. INTO A NEW MILLENNIUM

As mother church of the *cantref* (not County) of Meirionydd well into the 12th century, Tywyn's influence extended from the Dyfi to the Mawddach and inland as far as the Corris/Cross Foxes/Dolgellau corridor[1]. It would have been responsible for all the other churches within that region[2], ensuring that the spiritual needs of the people in each area were met[3].

To the local people, Bangor and St David's may have been thought of as important cathedrals but their direct effect on the day-to-day life of the *clas*, the church and the daughter churches was minimal. For all of the Welsh Church, Rome was a distant pilgrimage centre, acknowledged as being a source of ultimate authority but having hardly any impact on the practical matters of church life, a situation which was to change dramatically over the next couple of centuries[4] – although changes to Tywyn came more slowly than elsewhere.

The late 11th and the 12th centuries were times of continual upheaval as rulers and their descendants vied for land, control and influence, but initially Tywyn was saved from the direct influence of the Norman Conquest. By 1086 the Normans had penetrated North Wales from Chester and controlled at least as far as Conwy[5]. By 1092 they had imposed their first nominee, Hervé, as Bishop of Bangor. From Chester, Norman control reached to Montgomery. Beyond both lay Tywyn, protected by mountains and by the fierce opposition to the Normans of the Princes of

Gwynedd and Powys. By 1098 the Normans were pulling back from the northern corridor[6] and by 1114 Henry I had recognised Gruffudd ap Cynan as Prince of Gwynedd[7].

THE STONE CHURCH

We do not know at what stage the church at Tywyn was first built in stone. It could have been a long time before the end of the first millennium or, perhaps, soon after the Viking sack in 963 AD. J. F. Potter suggests that there are signs of pre-Norman construction in the spacing of the clerestory windows and the thickness of the walls above the pillars[8]. J. Prichard, architect for the 1880s restoration, wrote that he was "not prepared to say that the building was not erected at an earlier period than the 11th century"[9].

In northern France much rebuilding of churches took place in the first part of the 11th century; most building or

The church in the late 12th century (computer simulation)

The 12th century nave pillars and clerestory windows

rebuilding in Wales was from the late 11th to the early 12th century[10]. Pevsner[11] gives 12th century as the date of the church and, from his observation of the fenestration, Andrew Davidson suggests the second half of the 12th century[12], while Potter sees the same windows as pre-Norman[13]. Tradition in

Tywyn holds that the work was started in the third quarter of the 11th century and took about fifty years to complete – dates suggested are 1065 and 1116, no doubt to fit in with the "foundation date" of 516 AD!

Could Tywyn's traditional dates make sense? Tywyn would probably still have been in contact with northern and western France via the sea routes, as it had been in Cadfan's day. Could they have been inspired to 'get started' ahead of others in Wales? If the building really did take place over a long period of time, the design might well have been modified as it went along, so that later additions would have a later style. A long building period would also fit a conjecture that the work was financed year by year from the ordinary income of the *clas*. The total absence in Tywyn Church of such features as dog-tooth mouldings may reflect a monastic situation, or an early date, or just limited finances. The description in *Canu Cadfan* suggests that the building had been completed before the poem was written shortly after 1147.

THE ALTARS

The church had three altars dedicated to St Mary, St Peter and, presumably, St Cadfan. It also owned a crosier attributed to Cadfan and probably also a gospel[14], which would have been essential if boundary disputes arose involving ecclesiastical laws. Such disputes were settled by swearing on "crosier and gospel book"[15].

The dedication of the altars is of interest. It was becoming increasingly common to dedicate new churches to universal saints such as Mary and Peter and, earlier,

Michael; these saints were even replacing, or being joined with, less well-known local saints in the dedications of existing churches[16]. In his account of his church following the redevelopment in 1880-4 the vicar, the Reverend Titus Lewis, wrote "Above the chancel steps… are the figures of St Peter and St Mary who, together with St Cadfan, are the patron saints of the Church."

The *capel y bedd* (relic chapel) mentioned as existing "as late as 1620"[17] may already have been built to house these relics. Its site was still discernible in the early 19th century when it was said that "some walls were still standing in living memory"[18].

MORFRAN, ABBOT OF TYWYN

In 1137 on the death of Gruffudd ap Cynan, Owain ap Gruffudd (Owain Gwynedd) succeeded his father as Prince of Gwynedd and his younger brother, Cadwaladr, had charge of Meirionydd[19]. He was expected to be subordinate to Owain but Cadwaladr sought autonomy, perhaps based at his new-built earthwork castle of Cynfal near Rhydyronnen, Tywyn, where its *motte* can still be seen.

Cadwaladr was exiled but returned with a fleet from Ireland to help him. In 1147 Owain sent his sons, Hywel and Cynan, to attack Cadwaladr, concentrating on the castle at Cynfal. The brothers found it in the keeping of its steward, Morfran, who was the abbot of Tywyn. Presumably Morfran was a lay abbot who could give his time to the care of the castle. It was not unknown for an abbot to be a fighting man; Giraldus Cambrensis (Gerald of Wales) in 1188 described the Abbot of Llanbadarn Fawr as a layman who "strutted about in armour accompanied by a retinue of warriors"[20].

Lay or ordained, Morfran was a sturdy warrior who kept faith with his current employer and refused to yield the castle, narrowly escaping death when Hywel and Cynan succeeded in taking it by force. This event is recorded historically[21] and was the inspiration of Llewelyn Fardd I's *Canu Cadfan*.

GIRALDUS CAMBRENSIS

In 1188, forty years after Morfran's defence of Cynfal, the Archbishop of Canterbury, Baldwin of Forde, toured Wales for six weeks "preaching the cross" – that is, seeking volunteers to go on the Third Crusade. He was escorted by Giraldus who described their travels in *The Journey Through Wales*. Giraldus came from South Wales and wrote in detail about what they did, saw and heard in their five weeks there. Then they started to travel north[22]. They spent one night at Llanbadarn Fawr and "attracted many persons to the service of Christ on the following morning". Giraldus recorded a lengthy criticism of the situation there, including that the church "like many others in Wales and Ireland" had a lay abbot whose sons officiated at the altar. He ended by writing that he thought it prudent, for the time being, not to mention the subject again[23].

Later that day they headed north again, were ferried across the Dyfi, probably to Aberdyfi where there was an important ferry throughout the Middle Ages[24], and "slept that night in Tywyn. Early next morning, Gruffudd son of Conan [ap·Cynan] came to meet us, humbly and devoutly asking pardon for having so long delayed his attention to the archbishop." And that's it! No description of Tywyn, nothing about the church nor its people, just that they went on to Llanfair. Perhaps he was tired after the intensive days and did not write up his diary that night; perhaps he was angry that Gruffudd, son of the Cynan who attacked Cynfal, had not met them as they arrived (or perhaps he just had a cold). The one person who might have told us something about Tywyn and its church at that time says nothing.

BOUNDARIES AND ORGANISATION

Although Gruffudd ap Cynan was the lord of the *cantref* of Meirionydd, by this time the area was already probably administered as two separate *commotes*: Tal-y-bont and Ystumanner. The division between them was the line of the Afon Dysynni up the valley and then through the gorge to Abergynolwyn and north-east to the Corris valley, leaving the area around Llanfihangel-y-Pennant in Tal-y-bont. Tal-y-bont does not seem to have had a mother church and its *maerdref* or commotal centre was at Rhydycriw in Llanegryn. Tywyn may have remained mother church for the whole *cantref* or may have been restricted mostly to Ystumanner, which had the prince's court and *maerdref* at Pennal[25].

Meanwhile the organisation of the church was changing. The boundaries of the Diocese of Bangor began to be defined in the first part of the century and were completed with the establishment of a new diocese in north-east Wales based at St Asaph. The archdeaconry of

Meirionydd was set up by 1195[26] and this was divided into the two rural deaneries of Ardudwy and Ystumanner/Tal-y-bont (the deanery now known as Ystumanner), which are first mentioned in 1254 and 1291 respectively. Parishes were gradually established up until the late 13th century by devolution of parochial rites from the mother church to local churches. Fundamental to this was the transfer to the local churches of tithes, burial fees etc. which had previously gone to the mother church. A parish became that area from which tithe was due to the parish church[27].

However, Tywyn still managed to remain 'different' as is shown by the much later *Valor Ecclesiasticus* (Valuation of Churches) of 1535. This shows thirty-five churches in the County of Merioneth and thirty-two parishes. Unlike the other daughter churches, Pennal, Talyllyn and Llanfihangel-y-Pennant were specifically said to be chapels of Tywyn[28].

CANU CADFAN

A full translation by Catherine McKenna will be found in Appendix F.

The poem *Canu Cadfan* (Cadfan's Song), otherwise known as *Canu i Gadfan* (Song to Cadfan), was composed by Llewelyn Fardd I while Morfran was still abbot at Tywyn, probably shortly after his defence of Cynfal for Cadwaladr. It links traditions and praise of Cadfan with praise of Morfran and also of Cadfan's Church at Tywyn and its wonders. Cadwaladr, who named his son Cadfan (suggesting wholehearted support for the *clas* of Tywyn), had been expelled from the *cantref* of Meirionydd by Cynan.

Possibly Morfran's position as abbot was at stake or even the whole future of the community at Tywyn[29]. In such a situation the poem may have been intended, at least partly, to assert Tywyn's temporal privileges and religious renown[30], speaking of it as "the noble country of Cadfan" (49) and ending with a plea to God to protect Cadfan's domain.

The poet describes the church as "near the edge of the blue sea", which seems strange to us as the present seashore is about three-quarters of a mile from the church.

In the 12th century the tide would have reached to the fence in the background

However, it was not until the draining of the marshes in the 18th century that the fields we now see to the north of the church were created. In the 12th century the whole area would have been covered at high tide, with water coming to the foot of Gwalia Road just a few dozen yards from the church. The church on its small mound would have towered above it.

The poem almost seems to challenge anyone wanting to downgrade the church and *clas* as it celebrates Cadfan's power which, under God, defends and protects Tywyn, making it a place "where violence dares not go", "where no man dares carry off a necessity from the church", "where no one dares constraint of its revenues" (18, 19, 21) and

> There is not lost of its land nor of the strength of its dwelling a foot because of war, difficult to avoid.
> No one dares violence over its wall, no one contemplates the treachery of piercing its door. (71-74)

Cadfan is also credited with God-given supernatural powers:

> He performed miracles by his [God's] permission setting fire here in clothing.
> He relieved plague and want and denial. (109-111)

Tywyn is described:

> A fair hill is Tywyn, it is not right to be silent about it. Like the fair abode of heaven its dwellings. (125-126)

There is also much about the church itself:

> There is a church fully fair to describe in the land of
> Meirionydd, good to praise it.
> ... much visited church of Cadfan of fair dwellings.
> (143, 144, 147)

The church has three altars, the third one of which is presumably Cadfan's altar:

> Mary's altar of the Lord, trustworthy sacred relic;
> The altar of Peter in his authority which should
> be praised;
> And the third altar which was bestowed by heaven –
> Blessed is its dwelling because of its hospitality.
> (25-28)

Morfran is praised for "guarding the rood [crucifix] and the tribute and the wood and the choir [chancel]..." (65, 66)

The poem says the church has precious relics, which are "heard of widely" (81)[31]. Another line refers to "a properly arrayed relic as excellent as itself" (156). The relics include:

> The noble gospel, humble guide, with the fair
> precious crozier of new miracles, which prevents the
> enemy from killing his opponent. (50-52)

The church was made "like Dewi's church" (St David's[32] cathedral) (32). This suggests that its cathedral-like cruciform design with side aisles and clerestory, like St David's, had been completed by the middle of the 12th century at the latest.

In addition: "Our hangings are superior to Llanddewi's" (158)!

There is also comparison with the cathedral of the diocese: "The lofty church of Cadfan's flock, like Bangor…" (80). This may refer to similarities in the two buildings. However, Tywyn is within the Diocese of Bangor and McKenna suggests that, by this comparison, Llewelyn Fardd I is probably asserting the church's independence of diocesan authority.

There is also mention of services although these seem entwined with both God and everyday life:

Praiseworthy is the one God, he is the one defender,
to Meirionydd he gives continual gifts.
Its choir and its liturgy are praised and its music and
its warriors and its sea and its ale and its church near
the sea, near the tide bank too. (95-99)

and

And the circle of the floodtide filling the river mouth
[estuary], and at vespers the order of service. (161-2)

Morfran was clearly a lay abbot. He "arranges battle with the Lord's consent" (59), he is a "stout lord" (69) who "does not tolerate cowardice in conflict" (75) and he supports "warriors from beside the sea" (165). As was fitting in a leader he was "Morfran flowing with gifts, pride of a day's entertainment"(60).

Giraldus wrote that, for the Welsh, generosity and hospitality were the greatest of all virtues[33] and these are also praised for Tywyn:

And neither is there want therein, only beautiful things and poets and poetry, only peace and mead in vessels, only easy discourse, exchange with a poet, and fine men without shame, without hardness, and a treasure house and talent and goodness, and a properly arrayed relic as excellent as itself, and craft and song and cheerful singing... (150-157)

But perhaps the most telling lines are those we hope may still apply today:

Church of fair Cadfan, brilliant to behold... church of faith and devotion and belief and communion, as though it had been fashioned by God himself. (33, 35-36)

4. CONFLICT AND CHANGE

THE CHURCH AT TYWYN

In 1198/9 the *clas* at Tywyn faced a possible threat to its influence with the founding of a Cistercian abbey at Cymer near Dolgellau with the support, and possibly the original initiative, of Gruffudd ap Cynan. Initial benefactions came from Gruffudd himself, his son Hywel and also Maredudd ap Cynan[1]. The danger, if danger it was, would be the effect of the abbey on the people of Dolgellau and the surrounding area who had previously looked to Tywyn as mother church. Tywyn's influence was, however, still great. Although Gruffudd and his son were buried at the Cistercian Abbey of Aberconwy, the elegy to Maredudd who died rather later includes "the resting place of a king… the one of generous heart above the land of Cadfan", which suggests that he may have been buried in Tywyn[2].

Another elegy by an Anglesey poet about the same time laments Nest ferch Hywel who was probably buried at Tywyn:

> The candle of St Cadfan's church, her mantle of silk…
> … Red earth covers her after she became silent,
> It is a sorry thing that hers is the destitution of a
> stone grave in a graveyard.[3]

In the 13th century, times were troubled by dissension between the princes of Gwynedd and those who held the *cantref* of Meirionydd and surrounding areas. In the 1220s Llewelyn ap Maredudd (Llewelyn the Great) built Castell y Bere in an attempt to maintain his authority over the area and also to defend the south-west of Gwynedd. No doubt some of the work on the castle was carried out by men of the area who would also have been involved in supplying the garrison. However, the *cantref* only finally became completely part of Gwynedd in the early 13th century[4].

We know little of the life and events of Tywyn in the 13th century. In the 12th century *Canu Cadfan* had sung of the *claswyr* outside the church ditch and, over the centuries, these people may have provided a nucleus to which others, with no kin connection to the foundation, were drawn. Once a few people moved closer to the church, which probably provided the one public meeting place for the whole area, they would attract others, and bakers, tailors, carpenters and other tradesmen might begin to 'set up shop'. Specialisms such as tanner, smith, cobbler and harness-maker would be more effectively supplied by individual craftsmen in the growing community, which was heavily dependent on agriculture and fishing. The numbers would be small (we would regard it as little more than a village) but the provision for daily life, and the attitudes of the people, would have been those of a small town that had been granted economic privileges by the rulers of Meirionydd[5]. By 1284[6] there was a mill, and, at some stage, a weekly market would have started, providing an opportunity for sale of livestock and other produce[7].

In 1254 the pope ordered a new assessment of clergy property for taxation and the record, known as the *Valuation of Norwich*, shows that the church of Tywyn, at that time, was by far the wealthiest in the area, being valued at 40 shillings – more than double the valuation for any other church in the archdeaconry of Merioneth[8].

TROUBLED TIMES AND CASTELL Y BERE

Llewelyn ap Gruffudd (Llewelyn the Last) spent much of his time as Prince of Gwynedd in attempting to extend his power and influence outside the territory of Gwynedd into areas such as Montgomery which had close English connections. He subsequently failed to fulfil his service due to the English king as his liege lord; he also failed to meet his financial obligations under the Treaty of Montgomery[9]. In 1277 Edward I moved against Llewelyn, forcing him to withdraw to the frontiers of Gwynedd, to accept terms and to pay homage.

None of the above might have affected most of the people of the *cantref* of Meirionydd, but in 1282 Dafydd ap Gruffudd, Llewelyn's brother, attacked Hawarden Castle while other attacks were made on Flint, Rhuddlan and Oswestry[10]. Edward had reached the end of his patience; by the autumn he had gathered forces for the subjugation of Gwynedd, approaching it from the east, the south and from Anglesey. In December Llewelyn died fighting in the March of Wales[11] and Dafydd took over as Prince of Gwynedd.

Castell y Bere now became a bastion of immense importance to the defenders of South Gwynedd. King Edward, expecting determined resistance, planned a large force to take it. On 12 April 1283 700 infantry gathered at Llanbadarn Fawr and three days later they were advancing on Castell y Bere. There they were joined by another 2000 infantry from Montgomery and elsewhere[12].

For a week the castle was besieged and then on 22 April the commander offered the constable of Castell y Bere and those who formed the garrison a sum of 80 silver pounds of the king's money if they delivered the castle within a week. Perhaps the resolve of the defenders had been broken by Llewelyn's death or perhaps by hearing of events in the rest of Gwynedd; three days later, on 25 April, the garrison surrendered[13].

THE TOWN OF TYWYN

Five hundred and seventy of the besieging force set off immediately for Harlech while about 1000 moved along the Dysynni to Tywyn, soon to be joined by many more. Even while the surrender of Castell y Bere was being negotiated, some seventy carpenters, with a hundred foot-soldiers to protect them, constructed a palisade around "the villa of Towyn" to make it defensible. This secured a base which could be victualled and munitioned by sea if necessary. Payments to the force were made at Tywyn until the main body of the army moved to Cymer by 13 May 1283. Tywyn became the base from which groups were sent out north, east and south as far as Pumlumon Fawr (Plynlimon, the mountain to the east of Aberystwyth) to safeguard and secure the countryside and to search for Dafydd ap Gruffudd[14].

With sizeable forces moving through the area it is likely that both crops and property in the *cantref* suffered damage and loss. However, some compensation was paid by the Crown for war damage and disturbance occasioned by houses being occupied by the king and his wardrobe staff whilst visiting Bere and Tywyn[15]. Then, within two months, in August 1283, the king's officers started to make their way through the land compiling the "extents" by which the financial liabilities of the king's free and bond tenants would be established[16]. They reached Meirionydd in 1284, producing a collection of information known as the *Extent of Merioneth*[17]. Although Tywyn was not a town with any formal foundation, the officers were perhaps influenced by the palisade and found it sufficiently urban in character to describe the inhabitants as "bergenses" (burgesses), which implied town status. They also noted that bondmen of the *commote* of Tal-y-bont were allowed to live freely at Tywyn, suggesting that pre-conquest Welsh law allowed residence in a town to confer liberty on those of unfree status[18]. The valuation of the town of Tywyn was £2/6/8d compared to the commotal centre of Pennal which was valued at £4/6/10½d[19]. The church at Tywyn might be well off; the inhabitants were less so.

TRAVELS OF AN ARCHBISHOP[20]

In June and early July 1284 Pecham, the Archbishop of Canterbury, took advantage of the security offered by the presence of the king's officers to conduct a visitation of the Dioceses of St Asaph and Bangor with the intent of investigating clerical standards. Pecham was a highly educated Franciscan committed to reforming the Church throughout the province of Canterbury (which included Wales). Perhaps it is hardly surprising that such a man should be less than happy about what he saw as low standards among the clergy and inadequate ecclesiastical discipline.

While he was staying in Bangor, the archbishop had written to the Bishop of St Asaph about that diocese. Tywyn was his final stop in Bangor diocese and from there he wrote to the Bishop of Bangor about his diocese on 3 July 1284. It is to be hoped that Pecham was not particularly influenced by the time at Tywyn, although his letter may reflect the situation there as elsewhere; like the letter to St Asaph, it was scathing.

Pecham complained about the appearance of parish clergy – long hair, a lack of proper tonsures, brightly coloured cloaks, bare heads and feet – and also about their behaviour, including the keeping of concubines (in Wales, quite possibly many of these were recognised wives) and excessive drinking. Concubines were to be put away within the month on pain of loss of benefice, and proper clerical garb was to be worn. Priests "with a cure of souls" should celebrate canonical hours and ordinary masses "with singing and reverence every day", keep the consecrated host with reverence and be diligent in taking it to the sick with due solemnity.

He declared that he could not recall "ever having seen such illiterate priests and clergy" and was concerned that this, together with poverty, seriously undermined the effectiveness of pastoral care. Writing in Tywyn, which was probably still a portionary church, he proposed that portions should be abolished in churches once the existing portioners died, on the grounds that the portions were inadequate to support resident clergy.

Pecham was aware of the problem caused by non-resident rectors, where a parish's income had been redirected to the support of cathedral chapters, monasteries and individuals. He insisted that these absentee rectors should make adequate financial provision for vicars so that parishioners might receive proper pastoral care. He also issued strict instructions to limit the rights of rural deans and officials to receive procurations from rectors and vicars.

It all paints a rather depressing picture of the church in the Diocese of Bangor and, perhaps also, a picture of the church in Tywyn at the time. However, it appears that Tywyn's income still stayed within the church so perhaps those serving it were better educated and more able to serve their congregations than was the case elsewhere.

Pecham's financial strictures may be seen against the deliberations of the Council of Oxford sixty years earlier, in 1222, which had conceded that the minimum income for perpetual vicarages in England – 5 marks or £3/6/8d per annum – could not be observed in Wales where clergy "are content with a smaller stipend". Pecham decreed that the minimum in Wales was to be half of that in England[21]!

He also decreed that each parish priest should expound a basic programme of instruction to his parishioners four times a year. This should concentrate on the Ten Commandments, the Lord's Prayer, the Twelve Articles of the Creed, the Seven Works of Mercy and the Seven Deadly Sins[22].

CASTELL Y BERE AGAIN

Between March 1284 and October 1285 an isolated expenditure of £31 is recorded at Castell y Bere for a new "upper chamber" which must have been in one of the towers. It is possible that the upper chamber was accommodation for the visit of Edward I in late October

1284 when he spent eight days there[23], perhaps making arrangements for the further changes and improvements which were to take place in 1286-90[24].

With his entourage, Edward then moved along the Dysynni to Tywyn on 8 November for an overnight stay[25]. No doubt they carried tents enough for the whole party but it would be nice to imagine the king staying at the old abbot's house of the *clas* with some of his retinue staying with other *claswyr*. He then crossed the Dyfi southwards to spend 9 November at Llanbadarn Fawr.

On 22 November 1284, while staying at Cardigan, Edward issued a foundation charter for a town at Harlech – and also conferred upon "our township of Bere" (the site of Castell y Bere) the status of free borough and upon its inhabitants the rights of free burgesses! The castle constable was to be mayor, the burgesses were to have commercial privileges and legal immunities, and they might elect two bailiffs from among themselves[26]. Edward had spent some time at the site, so it is hard to understand why he saw it as a suitable place for a town. There is no suggestion that it had ever been a centre of either commercial or administrative activity. In addition the terrain made access difficult; the records of 1284 show that it took seventeen woodsmen to cut a path for the queen's carriage through the heavily wooded landscape between Tywyn and Bere[27].

While concentrating on subduing Gwynedd, Edward was also considering the call of Crusade. In 1288 Pope Nicholas IV granted Edward I one-tenth of the ecclesiastical income of England and Wales to pay for a crusade and a survey was made for this tax. The final document, the *Taxatio Ecclesiastica*, completed in 1292, lists benefices worth more than 6 marks (£4) for most of the country.

Tywyn's entry is particularly interesting as it lists the portioners of the church (the only named individuals in the deanery) and their income as follows:

Gruffudd (the Dean)	-	£13/6/8d
Second Dean (unnamed)	-	£5/0/0d
David ap Llewelyn	-	£6/13/4d
David Crach'	-	£5/0/0d
Adam the Chaplain	-	£5/0/0d

So the portioners of Tywyn between them would have had to pay 70 shillings (£3/10/0d) to the king towards a crusade. The combined income of £35 made it by far the wealthiest church in the whole Archdeaconry of Merioneth, which included Ardudwy, Dyffryn Clwyd, the Abbey of Enlli and Conway. The whole archdeaconry shows a total value of £240/6/8d.

The presence of the "second Dean" may reflect Tywyn's earlier pre-eminence not only over the whole *cantref* of Meirionydd but also, perhaps, into Ardudwy. The reasoning behind this is that the rural dean of Ardudwy is listed separately in the *Taxatio* with a benefice worth £8/6/8d and this, plus £5 from Tywyn, would give him £13/6/8d, the same as Dean Gruffudd[28].

MORE TROUBLE

By 1294 Edward was embroiled in conflict with the French king. To help pay for the conflict, a tax of one-fifteenth of a person's moveable property had been levied in 1291, causing much unhappiness and unrest. Resentment fuelled rebellion from September 1294, with resistance beginning in Gwynedd[29]. As the rebellion spread, Edward (in Portsmouth ready to embark an army for France) heard of it and turned back to Wales. The garrisons of Harlech and Criccieth had been heavily reduced but they were quickly reinforced[30]. The effort to relieve Castell y Bere and secure Merioneth, ordered by the king in autumn 1294, took time to achieve. It was May 1295 by the time Anglesey and Caernarfon had been quelled; Edward advanced south, reaching Dolgellau on 11 May and meeting a second force from Montgomery in the neighbourhood of Tywyn on 16 May[31]. He spent a couple of days there before moving on[32].

Castell y Bere had been relieved but the borough was abandoned since the events of the rebellion had shown the limitations of the site as a strategic centre; neither castle nor borough featured further in the king's plans for the area.

No doubt the people of Tywyn and of the church at Tywyn heaved a sigh of relief.

5. THE 14th AND 15th CENTURIES

In recording his dissatisfaction with the state of the church in the Dioceses of Bangor and St Asaph, Archbishop Pecham pointed the finger of blame at the bishops. Bangor in particular had suffered from lack of direction and this was to get worse. The see had been vacant from 1098 to 1120, 1161 to 1177 and 1190 to 1195. In addition, Bishops Meurig (1140-61) and Richard (1237-67) had spent many years in England[1] having been exiled there by the secular authorities of Gwynedd. Inadequate ecclesiastical oversight remained a problem throughout the 14th century. Over a hundred years after Pecham's time, Bishop Benedict[2] (1409-17) did spend at least part of his time in the diocese but from 1417 to 1541 the bishops were all Englishmen who also held important appointments in England and who were almost entirely absentees[3]. This was at a time when the great majority of people in the diocese spoke only Welsh. Individual parishes were thrown very much on their own resources. Many of them also suffered from absentee rectors who took the income from the church and did not even appoint a vicar or chaplain to lead services and to care for parishioners.

At some time during the 13th or early 14th century, Tywyn Church must have passed from being a *clas* mother church to being the parish church of a single parish, which was still so extensive that chapels had to be maintained at Pennal, Llanfihangel-y-Pennant and Talyllyn. With the conversion from a portionary church to a rectory[4], the incumbency would become more vulnerable to "appropriation" (we would call it misappropriation!) to help finance cathedral canons, monasteries or absent clerics. This had already happened as early as the 12th century in the south-east and south of Wales.

There is no record of appropriation happening to Tywyn – yet – but with the comparative riches of the church it would have been very tempting. There is a possibility that its endowments had already gone to "the nunnery of Barking". Browne-Willis (who surveyed many cathedrals and their sees in great detail in the first half of the 18th century) wrote in an addendum to the second edition of his work on Bangor: "Towyn. This, as I find, belonged to Barking Nunnery in Essex and was Anno 1 Edward 6 given to the See of Lichfield on exchange of Lands."[5] It is difficult to know where he got the information about the exchange as it is not mentioned in the grant given by Edward VI.

THE CHURCH IN THE 14TH CENTURY

What might the church have looked like then? The pillars supporting the tower would have been similar to those still seen in the nave but the four arches, which bore the weight of the tower, were of first pointed work, lower and with a greater expanse of wall above them than at present. By now these and the walls of the nave would probably have been plastered and painted with biblical scenes. A common theme above a tower arch was the Last Judgement.

Instead of the two rectangular windows in the side aisles there would have been small ones similar to those still there. Small 11/12th century windows in the transepts, and probably also at the east and west ends, would have been replaced by larger 14th century ones but the church would still have been much darker than it is now. Lighting was by rush lights (the pith of rushes, soaked in fat or grease). Candles were only for the altar. In the flickering of this limited light the pictures may have appeared to move.

Masses said for the dead had been becoming increasingly common as they were supposed to reduce the time the soul spent in purgatory. Those who could afford it would endow a chantry or an obit[6], by setting up a trust fund which employed one or more priests to sing masses over a stated period of time for the benefit of the departed soul. Altars mainly or specifically for this purpose were called chantry altars and we know that there were at least two, dedicated to Our Lady and to St Cadfan, in the church before the Reformation[7]. Their position is unknown but the transepts are the most likely locations.

With the development of individual parishes in place of a mother church and its dependants, the layman became increasingly aware of, and adherent to, a particular parish. He was obliged to pay tithes to his parish church. For Tywyn this would have included those living in the chapelries of Pennal, Talyllyn and Llanfihangel-y-Pennant. The principal tithes of the area were those of grain, hay, wool and lambs. The churchyard would have been the long-established burial place – with a place inside the church for those of greater means – although probably with separate churchyards at the chapels[8].

Over the 14th and 15th centuries there were two general trends in the life of the church. One was a heightened reverence for the real presence of Christ in the Eucharist. This was reflected in a sharper separation of the clerical space around the altar from the congregation in the nave. The other was an increasing tendency for the crucified Christ to become a focus for devotion alongside the cult of the saints[9]. In some churches like Llanegryn a rood screen was installed but there is no specific record of one in Tywyn. The presence of a rood gallery used for the choir, and therefore presumably a rood screen, between nave and crossing may, however, be surmised from later evidence. In 1734 Lowry David, aged eighty-four, fell down the "gallery" stairs[10] and in 1729 a joiner was paid for altering the "Rooding seats"[11]. In 1839 the church was visited by S. R. Glynne who recorded that there was a gallery at the east end of the nave[12].

THE KING'S TAXES

Meanwhile the town of Tywyn was being expected to produce an increasingly large revenue for the king. From £1/6/8d in 1284 it rose to £6/10/10d in 1302, and £8/0/0d in 1310. While this may have been the result of economic growth, it could also have been due to the Crown Commissioners exploiting all available sources of income[13].

With shorter, wetter summers and long cold winters, a time of great famine arose in 1315-7. Even the Bishop of Bangor bewailed the "bad year" and "the murrain of his beasts"[14]. Food was desperately short for those who lived from one harvest to the next and many people and beasts died. In the old days of the *clas*, stored produce from the endowed lands would have enabled the *claswyr* to help the small community around the church. In a time of new organisation, and with more people in the town, any help the church could give would be far more limited.

Nevertheless, against this background, the amount expected by the king from the town shortly thereafter in 1319 was £9/12/6d.

Perhaps it was as a consequence of both famine and excessive demands for revenue that in 1322/3, Gronw, a chaplain at Pennal, was fined 5 shillings for theft as well as 8d for shedding blood [assault][15].

THE EFFIGIES

Sometime early in the 14th century the church was able to afford a full-size (perhaps oversize) effigy of a priest in full Eucharistic vestments of alb, stole, chasuble, maniple and amice. In time past, it was thought to be the effigy of a woman because, unusually, the amice is drawn over the head as a hood instead of being folded around the neck. The extra decoration on the right side of the figure shows the monument was carved to be put in a niche in the north wall. There is no record of the inscription that must originally have accompanied it, but the effigy must have been of an important member of the church[16].

Not long after this, in the late 1340s, the importance of Tywyn Church was again shown with the installation of a second effigy, this time in full armour, now known as the Crying Knight. By tradition it is ascribed to Gruffydd ap Adda of Dolgoch and Ynysymaengwyn, Raglot[17] of the *commote* in 1331 and 1334. The painted inscription probably only dates back to the 19th century and the shield is so mutilated that it is not possible to see if there was any inscription round the edge. The armour is consistent with these dates[18].

THE BLACK DEATH

In 1349 the Black Death reached the borders of Wales and before long it reached Merioneth. We do not know how it affected Tywyn; people were too concerned with survival to worry about any records. However, as examples, at Caldicot-on-the-Severn thirty-six out of forty tenants died and at Deganwy the manor was totally emptied by the death or flight of its tenants. The plague returned again in 1361-2, 1369 and seven more times before 1420[19]. Throughout Wales much of the land that was left vacant after the plague could only be let as pasture, a situation which heralded a major shift in land usage[20]. Men travelled in search of cheaper, better land and the unfree moved to free tenancies. By early in Henry V's reign (1413) the settlements of the unfree in the *commote* of Ystumanner were completely depopulated. Labour was scarce and therefore expensive so the income from endowment lands fell sharply – and so did the value[21].

ABSENTEE RECTORS

Despite the upheavals due to the plague, the clerical poll tax of 1379 valued the Rectory of Tywyn at 100 marks (£66/13/4d), far more than any other church in the Archdeaconry of Merioneth; even Cymer Abbey was only valued at £20[22]. Perhaps this was the final temptation for clergy officials with greedy eyes for income; had Tywyn's freedom been too good to last? Quite possibly the rectory and its emoluments of Tywyn had been presented to an absentee rector at some time before 1397. The reason for this suggestion is that at that date a vicar, David ap Jevan ap Tuder, rather than a rector was presented to Tywyn[23]. A vicar was "in place of" a rector and was supposed to be provided for by the rector, whether present or absentee, out of the income of the benefice. If Tywyn did now have an absentee rector, the majority of the parish income would be going to him, leaving only a small amount for Tywyn and its chapels.

In 1426 the Dean, Canons and Vicars of the new collegiate church of Our Lady of Leicester petitioned Henry VI to "grant them the advowson of the church of Towyn[24] which is held by the crown" (which they said was worth £40) "and a licence to appropriate it and they will use the income to endow an annual obit for Henry V and distribute the residue amongst the deans, canons and vicars in the same way as the profits from the church of Llanelli are distributed in their aid"[25]. There is no indication of the result of this plea so this may have been the stage at which the endowments of Tywyn Church (rather than its tithe income) went elsewhere. However, if they were asking for the Rectory and all its income from whatever source, their plea must have fallen on deaf ears, as in the same year Reginald Beuchamp (or Bechamp or Beauchamp) became Rector of Tywyn by exchange with Nicholas Harwold, having previously been Rector of Llanfair-juxta-Harlech[26]. Beuchamp may have been resident at Tywyn at least part of the time since, in 1442, he worked with the Rector of Llangelynnin under the direction of the Archbishop of Canterbury on the removal of the incumbent at Llannorin (Llanwrin) "for certain crimes"[27].

Beuchamp's successor, Richard Fowey, was absent for most if not all of his rectorship. At its start he was studying at Oxford, becoming a Bachelor of Canon Law by 1448, and he was subsequently Principal of Solar Hall and then Glasen Hall in Oxford. He also managed to acquire a number of benefices in England[28] and between them all must have been in receipt of a considerable income. However, perhaps he was unhappy with a Welsh rectorship, for in 1451 he exchanged it with John Brugge[29] who was Rector of Lanreythowe, Exeter Diocese[30]. Brugge in his turn must have been unhappy, for in 1461 Owen Lloit (Lloyd), Rector of Hodnet, Shropshire, was presented with Tywyn by exchange with Brugge[31].

Did these absentee rectors appoint vicars to the parish of Towyn? We don't know. Rectors were important people and their names appear in Patent Rolls and elsewhere. Vicars were not important and so seldom appear in the documents which are available from that time.

6. THE BEGINNINGS OF THE REFORMATION

[1]After nearly a century of absentee English bishops, the diocese had for four years Henry Dean, "a bishop of marked power and administrative capacity". Inevitably, he was English. He also held, at the same time, another important post – he was Chancellor of Ireland – but at least he lived within easy reach of the diocese and exercised fairly efficient supervision of it. He was also much involved with rebuilding of the chancel and transepts of Bangor Cathedral and recovering property of the bishopric which had been misappropriated.

When Henry Dean's successor, Thomas Pigot, died, the Archbishop of Canterbury, William Warham (who was concerned about the state of Bangor Diocese), ordered a visitation. The Return in 1504 gives the first list, which still exists, of clergy across the diocese. The names show that, in the main, the clergy were Welsh although English names appear. Among the English names, Pryce specifically mentions "the Dean, the Provosts of the Collegiate Churches of Holyhead and of Clynog, the Archdeacon of Bangor and the important position of Rector of Towyn"[2].

Tywyn still included the chapelries of Talyllyn, Llanfihangel-y-Pennant and Pennal. The positions of Rector of "Twyn" and Provost of Clynnog Fawr were both held by Mathew Pole, who also held the position of Rector of Llangelynnin. We do not know if he was an absentee rector. Llangelynnin parish is adjacent to Tywyn and he could fairly easily have moved between them as well as travelling between Tywyn and Clynnog as necessary. It is, however, possible that he lived elsewhere and simply received the emoluments of these offices. He certainly had assistance in the work at Tywyn as the Return also includes names of a vicar, a curate and three chaplains.

It was not unusual for clergy, especially those associated with the cathedral, to hold more than one parish in the diocese. Many other parishes were appropriated to the monasteries, with the result that a majority of parishes had absentee rectors. Most of these parishes were served by curates, although a few by a vicar, while the endowments intended for the parish went to the absentee rector[3]. Because this money went elsewhere, poverty was widespread among parish clergy in the Welsh Church, with three-quarters of them earning less than £10 per annum and nearly a quarter less than £5 per annum[4].

Ordinary parish priests – the vicars, curates or chaplains appointed by absentee rectors – were usually men of little education and training. The first grammar school in the diocese was not founded until 1550[5] so it was difficult for them to obtain more than an elementary level of education. It was largely because of their ignorance that many were ineffective spiritual leaders[6]. The average priest-to-be learned in the same way as an apprentice: he found a parish priest who, in exchange for some work, would house him and teach him to say the Mass and the Offices as well as how to hear confessions, and conduct marriages, baptisms and funerals. In Wales such an apprenticeship may even have been a son learning from his father[7].

The outward forms of religion, to which they and their people were accustomed, were those which had been practised for generations.

HENRY VIII, PATRON OF TYWYN CHURCH

By 1523 King Henry VIII had become Patron of the Living at Tywyn. This meant that he could "present to the living" (say who should have the post of rector) although in theory it was up to the bishop whether to approve the person so presented. It is clear that Henry VIII made use of his patronage to reward those who served him. It had the advantage for the king that those he presented got the great tithes from the Rectory of Tywyn but it cost the king nothing!

At some stage William Tofte (also Toft, Tost, Toste) became Rector of Tywyn. When Humphrey Thomas was appointed rector in 1523 this was recorded as being because of Tofte's retirement[8] and when John Coole was appointed in 1528 this was recorded as being due to the death of Tofte[9]. Together with John Coole (Cole), Tofte was a priest of the King's Chapel at the Coronation of Henry VIII[10]. They were also (as Sir William Tofte and Sir John Cole) members of the Chapel at the Field of the Cloth of Gold[11]. Tofte also is recorded as being appointed to Meyvot, St Asaph Diocese, in 1510[12], and to the prebend and canonry of the collegiate church of Pontisbury, Hereford Diocese, in 1519[13]. This suggests that being known in court was a good way of getting valuable church appointments. During the time of Tofte's rectorship there is a reference to "John Tona or Touna, clk, late Vicar of Cowen (i.e. Towen), co Merioneth"[14], who had presumably been the one who did the work.

William Tofte resigned from Pontisbury in 1522[15] and from Tywyn in 1523[16] when Humphrey Thomas was presented to the Church of "Towey". Thomas was Master of Battlefield College, Shrewsbury, from about 1524[17]. Perhaps William Tofte somehow regained the emoluments from Thomas which would explain why John Coole MA could be recorded as being presented to the parish church of "Towen Meryoneth" on Tofte's death.

A strange dichotomy appears in 1523. Henry VIII apparently presented the Rectory of Tywyn and its chapels to the Bishop of Coventry and Lichfield[18] and yet the presentation of individuals to the rectory, of which the king was patron, continued throughout his reign. In theory the Bishop of Lichfield was Rector of Tywyn, in practice he was not. This was apparently a promise that had not yet been put into effect.

John Coole resigned from Tywyn in 1529. Perhaps he had fallen out of favour or was less than conventional in his views; this was the time of the Reformation and Martin Luther's writings had reached England about 1519. Ten years after resigning from Tywyn, Coole was examined by the Lord Chancellor, having been indicted for "errors concerning the Sacrament of the Altar in accordance with depositions taken by my Lord of Oxford". Another person detained at the same time, one John Valey, was to be dismissed upon sureties. What happened to Coole is not stated[19].

THE BREAK WITH ROME

Henry VIII had written a defence of the seven sacraments and of the Pope in *Assertio Septem Sacramentorum*. This led, in 1521, to the Pope giving Henry the title *Fidei defensor (Fid Def)* – Defender of the Faith. However, Henry's attachment to the Pope as leader of the Church was weakened by the Pope's refusal to annul his marriage to Catherine of Aragon. He decided to break with Rome and in 1534 the "Reformation Parliament" passed the Act of Supremacy giving him the title of Supreme Governor of the Church of England (which included Wales).

Henry's next step was to find out how much money came in to the churches, cathedrals and religious houses, since they would no longer be sending taxes to Rome. The state would now take the taxation, which had previously gone to the Pope. His commissioners were sent out quickly and in 1535 produced their detailed survey, the *Valor Ecclesiasticus*. This lists thirty-five churches in the county of Merioneth of which Llanfihangel-y-Pennant, Talyllyn and Pennal are specifically said to be chapels of Tywyn. Tywyn was the richest benefice in the county with an annual net income of over £60[20]. We have no details as to the sources of Tywyn Church's income, but in the Deanery of Abergavenny, South Wales (twenty-nine churches) the average proportions were: glebe land 16%, tithe of corn 30%, tithe of hay 9%, lambs and wool 10%, calves 10%, milk and cheese 5%, customary offerings three times a year including Easter 12% and, in addition, there was money from the sale of candles and fees for weddings and funerals. The amounts raised varied across Abergavenny Deanery – from £1/14/9d to £26/16/9d. The average church income there was just over £8 compared to Tywyn's more than £60[21].

In the Diocese of Bangor wedding fees included the right of the parson to an annual payment, known as the "fifth penny", from the married couple. Burials were also associated with a mortuary payment, normally the "dead man's bed or his best cloth or some other thing". Clergy were also sometimes left small sums in wills, often with a request for prayer[22].

Tywyn was still a place of pilgrimage with the holy well of St Cadfan within the churchyard and a separate chapel of St Cadfan[23] containing relics. Offerings from the pilgrims might add £1/6/8d a year to the church's income. This compares with St Winifred's Well at the more accessible and better known Holywell which was bringing in £10 a year[24].

Along with the other lesser monasteries, Cymer Abbey in Dolgellau was dissolved in 1536. Cymer was twenty miles from Tywyn, quite far enough in a time when peasant transport moved at foot pace for Tywyn to be more or less indifferent to its fate. Henry Thomas in his booklet states that "the clas at Tywyn... suffered the fate of all lesser monasteries in 1536"[25], but there seems no evidence for this and it is likely that the clas had disappeared much earlier.

AN ELDERLY RECTOR

In 1529 Coole had been succeeded by John Griffithe who was presented to "the parish church of Towyn, Myryonethe, with the chapels of Taleyllyn, Pennalle and Llanvyhangell"[26]. He may have been quite elderly, for in 1536 the Bishop of Rochester wrote to Thomas Cromwell, Henry's chief minister. The bishop apologised that he had not been able to meet him on account of his "cyatyca" and asked that his chaplain (unnamed) might have the benefice of Tywyn held by the bishop's uncle, Mr Gryffythe, who was dying[27]. This letter would seem to nullify the suggestion made by the Rev. David Pugh, vicar 1906-32, that he was the John Griffithe, Vicar of Wandsworth, who was attaindered for heresy in 1539[28].

A BISHOP'S TASK

Meanwhile, in 1533 a new bishop, John Salcot (or Capon) was enthroned at Bangor[29] and was to "accomplish the diligent setting forth and sincere preaching... Of the royal supremacy"[30]. Apparently he had not thought about the problem of his not speaking Welsh until he arrived at his diocese. A couple of years later he confessed that he was gravely embarrassed by his lack of Welsh although he thought he could use preachers who did speak Welsh to do the job. Another major task was to tighten the discipline of the clergy in the diocese and particularly in the area of clergy "marriages"[31] which were still largely either accepted or winked at in Wales. At that time royal visitors, representatives of the king, were active in the diocese and it must have been as a result of their work that a petition was sent to Thomas Cromwell, the king's chief minister, by a number of clergy of Bangor Diocese. The petition began most submissively but (reading between the lines) went on to say that the clergy couldn't cope by themselves or offer hospitality (important for any clergyman but doubly so in Wales) without the woman of the house; that no "gentleman or substantial honest man would lodge them" so they would have to live in the pub and that they were having difficulty in getting tithes out of people – so could something be done about it[32]? We do not know if the Vicar of Tywyn was among the many signatories as we only know the names of the absentee rectors.

(The reference to those of substance being unwilling to take the clergy into their homes may relate to the Caernarfon Sessions thirty years earlier. Apparently, some priests had been guilty of "ravishing" the daughters of tenants on the Crown estates. There was now a financial crisis as the usual *amobr* or "maidenhead fee" could not be obtained for them as brides. The judgement was that the priest in question had to pay the *amobr* or be imprisoned[33].)

A TROUBLESOME RECTOR

In Henry VIII Letters and Papers of 1538 there is a note "Th. Henage, gentleman of the Privy Chamber. Next presentation to the parish church of St Cadvanus, Towyn Myrioneth, and chapels annexed, Bangor Dioc."[34] but nothing seems to have come of it. It is, however, interesting as it seems to be the first official reference to the name of the church.

The incoming rector would face a whole host of changes in the church and its services if he were resident. In practice the man chosen almost certainly never came near the place. His name was George Woolsell – or Wolfet or Wolflete or Wulflet or Wellifed! – who was the king's chaplain[35], and he seems to have had difficulty in handling the money from his rectorship. Pryce records his installation as probably 1537. In September 1545 John Ponnett was presented to "the rectory of Towen void by reason of the refusal of George 'Wulflet' to pay the first part of the ecclesiastical subsidy"[36]. Two months later, "Wolflete" is recorded as holding a number of benefices and being given "pardon with restoration of his capacity to hold benefices and presentation to" three more benefices[37] and also as having "pardon for all his benefices (except Towen)"[38].

It is to be hoped that George "Wolfet" did appoint a vicar and chaplains to serve Tywyn and its chapels, for the changes would need careful explaining to the people. We do know that there was a vicar there in 1544, as in the will of "William Clark priest" one of the executors is named as "Mr Acrod, parson of Towyn"[39].

CHANGE IN THE CHURCH

The services of the church continued to be in Latin during the reign of Henry VIII; the service therefore remained familiar to the people of Tywyn and its chapels with the responses known. In any church with a conscientious cleric the people would also have at least some idea of what they were hearing and saying.

In 1538 a series of injunctions was issued to the clergy. They must promote bible reading, insist on parishioners learning the Creed and Pater Noster (Lord's Prayer) in English and discourage superstition "as in wandering to pilgrimages, offering of money, candles or tapers to images or relics…". Parish registers of births, marriages and deaths were to be kept and parish chests provided for these registers[40].

In 1539 *The Bible in English* in its first authorised translation was, by royal command, to be placed in all churches, and in 1543 it was decreed that "on every Sunday and holy day throughout the year the curate of the Parish church, after the Te Deum [Matins] and Magnificat

[Evensong] should openly read to the people one chapter of the New Testament without exposition"[41]. These were very worthy and helpful instructions for the inhabitants of England and perhaps the more anglicised parts of Wales, but no help to the parishioners of Tywyn and its chapels who would almost all have been monoglot Welsh speakers.

Some help was to come for the Welsh speakers. In 1546 the earliest known printed Welsh book appeared, *Yny Lhyvyr Hwnn* (In This Book), edited by Sir John Prys; it contained the Lord's Prayer, The Ten Commandments and three verses from the New Testament[42] and it is likely that they had been circulated in manuscript or by word of mouth for some considerable time before publication. The introduction says that it was published to make up for the deficiencies of the clergy in teaching their parishioners.

In 1546 another absentee rector was appointed to Tywyn, John Ponet (also Poynet, Poynte, Ponett). From January 1545 he was a canon of Canterbury Cathedral. He was a chaplain of the king "who granted him at his request a licence to travel with two servants, three horses, twenty pounds in money and other necessaries". He had licence to hold the canon's stall together with his other preferments, "the vicarage of Ashford in Kent, the rectories of St Michael, Crooked Lane, London and of Towen in Merionethshire"[43]. He was consecrated Bishop of Rochester in 1550 and Bishop of Winchester in 1551.

EDWARD VI

In 1547 Henry VIII died and Edward VI came to the throne. Edward (who was only nine years old) and his

Regency Council were immediately petitioned by the Bishop of Lichfield and Coventry "that King Henry by his will, willed that such grant and gifts as he had made given or promised to anyone should be put into effect". A number of gifts are mentioned, among them "all those His Grace's advowson gifts presentations free dispositions and rights of patronages of ye Rectory, Parsonage and church of Towyn Meryon within ye Bishopricke of Bangor and of ye Chappells of Llanvihangell Tolyllin & Pennall within ye same Bishopricke of Bangor...". This was granted, although the Diocesan Year Book for 1778 says that, "according to Brown Willis", Tywyn was made part of the Bishopric of Lichfield and Coventry by forced exchange. There is no indication of exchange in the grant and the almost continuous list of rectors makes it unlikely.

The annual value of Tywyn Parsonage is stated in the grant as £60/13/4d with the bishop paying an annual sum of £6/1/4d to the king and his heirs and successor. Within six months of any of the parsonages becoming "voyd" (vacant) the bishop [of Lichfield] "will nominate and present to the Ordinary one sufficient and able Clerk to be vicar"; within three months of the induction he will be provided with "a convenient Mansion house for his habitation and dwelling" and a yearly pension that for the Vicar of "Towyn Merryon" was a surprisingly generous £20[44] (although not so generous if it was also to cover chaplains at the three chapels).

Of course, getting the money from Tywyn would require organisation. One option would be to put in a steward of some sort to collect the tithe and pass it on. Another option was put in train in 1551 when an indenture was made between the Bishop of Lichfield and Coventry and Francis Everarde, his nephew, a gentleman usher of the king's chamber. Everarde was to have the "mansion house of the parsonage" and the glebe lands for ninety-nine years at a rent of £40 a year but this lease was cancelled "by taking a new lease"[45]. Did someone object to the nepotism, or was he going to pay more – or less?

It is not clear how long John Ponnet's rectorship of Tywyn continued after this grant. As Bishop of Rochester (nominated 1549, consecrated 1550) he was given permission to continue to hold Tywyn among other benefices because there was no Episcopal palace but there is no record of an equivalent permission when he became Bishop of Winchester.

Edward and his Regency Council were strongly in favour of the Reformation. In the year Edward came to the throne a *Book of Homilies* was published, one of which was to be read in church every Sunday. They covered such subjects as justification by faith, the place and time of prayer and the worthy receiving of the Body and Blood of Christ. Later that year an injunction was issued that the Epistle and Gospel at the Mass were to be read in English[46]. Presumably this was expected to happen in Wales as well and four years later, in 1551, William Salesbury brought out the Epistle and Gospel lectionary readings in Welsh for each Sunday and holy day[47]. These would have helped those unable to understand the English readings – provided their church was able to afford a copy.

In 1547, in another attack on the endowments of the church combined with a reforming zeal to abolish masses for the dead, Parliament passed the Chantries Act, taking up a precedent set by Henry VIII. All chantries, free chapels, brotherhoods and guilds were to be abolished and their possessions forfeit to the Crown[48]. The certificate drawn up for Tywyn after this is as follows:

TOWYN
The stipendiary called St Cadfan's chaplain – 70s. in rent of land
The incumbent dead – 70s.
Memorand' there was stock of cattle belonging to this service which is sold by the wardens about 12 months now expired.
Another stipendiary called Our Lady Priest – 40s. of the yearly increase of a stock of cattle now prized at £10/12/4d
Sir John D'd Lloyde – 40s.[49]

The money was all taken, although the custodians of St Cadfan's altar who sold the cattle a year before may have seen how the wind was blowing and managed to spirit some of the money away.

In 1548 came another blow, not financial this time, when four old and well-loved ceremonies were forbidden: blessing of candles at Candlemas, carrying of ashes on Ash Wednesday, blessing palms on Palm Sunday and "creeping to the cross" (approaching it on one's knees and kissing it) on Good Friday. They may have seemed of little consequence but must have caused unhappiness for those who were used to them.

Archbishop Cranmer had been working for years, much of it privately, on a prayer book in English and in 1548 a commission met with Cranmer to complete it. This prayer book was enforced by an Act of Uniformity in 1549 only to be superseded by a second, rather more Protestant, prayer book in 1552 which included instructions to the priest such as saying Morning and Evening Prayer daily in public, wearing a surplice only with no other vestments at Communion and other times and so on. It was again enforced by an Act of Uniformity.

How long would copies of these prayer books have taken to get to Tywyn? And when they did get there, how would clergy and people have managed to use them? In theory they had no option but to obey or face fines or worse. At least people in England could understand the new service. The congregation at St Cadfan's Church had been able to take part in, and respond to, the old Latin services with some degree of understanding. Now they were faced with words they neither knew nor understood – and service books did not exist then, even if the congregation could have read them.

Think of how many older people nowadays still hark back to the old 1662 *Prayer Book* which they knew when young, even though they have individual copies of the newer services in their own language. Then imagine how bewildered and shocked the congregation of St Cadfan's Church would have been.

And then, in 1553, Edward VI died and the Catholic Queen Mary succeeded him.

7. A TIME OF CHANGES

MARY

Mary was a staunch Catholic. One of her first actions as queen was to use the royal prerogative to suspend the second Act of Uniformity and reintroduce the Mass. If the people of Tywyn had tried to start on the new English services, no doubt they would have been thankful to go back to something they at least partially understood rather than the totally incomprehensible English. In October 1553, in the First Statute of Repeal, Parliament began to remove Protestantism from the Church of England. All the religious legislation that had been introduced in the reign of Edward VI was withdrawn and the Church was restored to where it had been in 1547.

The next year further legislation included the outlawing, once more, of clerical marriage, which had been permitted in 1549 to regularise existing relationships. This could have had more impact in Wales than elsewhere, as marriage had been a fairly common practice among the Welsh clergy for centuries, whatever Rome and the bishops might have said. Now, anyone who was married could not take services after the end of 1554. In Bangor Diocese, about fifteen priests lost their living on this issue, including the Parson of Dolgellau, the Archdeacon of Anglesey and one of the cathedral canons[1].

We do not know who was vicar at Tywyn when Mary came to the throne. The only indication is that in 1555 the induction of Arthur ap Hughes occurred on the death of John Kymm. One possibility is that John Kymm was appointed while there was no bishop between the death of Bishop Bulkeley in 1552 (whose last recorded induction was early in 1551) and the appointments by the "Custos of the Spiritualities" from 1554.

Hughes, the new vicar, was highly educated and a bardic patron of repute. His virtues were extolled as a scholar of merit who cherished his Welsh language and had a high level of Latin, Greek and Hebrew. As part of the attempt to provide counter-Reformation literature in Welsh he translated George Marshal's *Compendious treatise*. He was also recorded as being a diligent minister to his parishioners[2].

ELIZABETH

Mary died childless in 1558 and was succeeded by her half-sister. Elizabeth needed support both from Protestants and from those who were most at home with the Catholic faith but were not dogmatic about it. In 1559 her new Act of Supremacy imposed narrower limits of royal authority over the Church than those of her father and brother. The Act of Uniformity passed the same year enforced a Protestant prayer book designed to be more acceptable to the conservative population than the 1552 version; naturally it was in English.

WELSH SERVICES FOR WALES

But what should be done for the Welsh speakers, who were mainly monoglot and illiterate? In Ireland, the new

Protestant services were to be enforced in English. Irish Gaelic was effectively to be suppressed. Representations were made at a high level and the government was persuaded that the Welsh would be more easily turned from the Catholic faith if the new services were in Welsh. In 1563 an Act of Parliament was passed compelling the Welsh bishops to provide a translation of the Bible and the Book of Common Prayer into Welsh and to ensure that a copy of each in both languages should be placed in every church by March 1567. As soon as this was completed the whole of the service in Welsh-speaking areas was to be read in Welsh. In the meantime, the Epistle and Gospel of the day were to be read in Welsh at every communion service and once a week the clergy were to recite to their parishioners the Lord's Prayer, the Articles of the Christian Faith and the Ten Commandments – all in Welsh.

The timescale was very tight. Salesbury had probably been working on his translation of the New Testament while he remained in hiding during Mary's reign. The completion of this translation and that of the Book of Common Prayer, both of which appeared in 1567, were largely the work of Richard Davies and William Salesbury. At last Welsh was the language of public worship. It may have taken some time for the new Welsh service and New Testament to reach Tywyn but we can be sure that Arthur ap Hughes made full use of it as soon as possible.

DIOCESAN REPORTS

In 1563 the Privy Council had called for a diocesan survey. This revealed the problem of absentee hierarchy. For example, "Nicolas Robynson priest, chapplein attenden upon my lord the archbishopp of Canterbury and there remaining to my knowledge, occupiethe the archdiaconrie of Meryonethe"[3]. The survey also gives us information about Tywyn and its chapels. Tywyn Church, with 200 households in the town, had a parson and a curate. The chapels of Pennal, Talyllyn and Llanfihangel-y-Pennant are described as being annexed to Tywyn – Pennal with fifty-six households and a curate, Talyllyn with fifty households and a curate, and Llanfihangel-y-Pennant with thirty-four households and a curate. We do not know how these curates were paid and they do not appear in the lists of appointments by the bishops so their payment may have been made out of the vicar's payment by Lichfield, in which case they would have been very vulnerable to the goodwill of the Vicar of Tywyn. Households would have varied in size, with farms probably having resident farm workers in addition to the family but at an estimate of five per household, Tywyn itself already had a population of 1000[4].

Since Arthur ap Hughes, the vicar, was recorded as being a preacher[5], the situation in Tywyn Church and its chapels was not as dire as that reflected in the report of Bishop Nicholas Robinson of Bangor to the Council of Wales and the Marches in 1567 (a year after he was consecrated) that there were "not six priest that can preach in the diocese"[6]. Robinson also decried what were, in effect, holdovers from Catholicism: "images and altars standing in churches undefaced, lewd and indecent vigils and watches observed, much pilgrimage-going, many candles set up in honour of saints, some relics yet carried about"[7]. Tywyn Church had been a centre of pilgrimage for many generations so quite possibly it is one of those about which he was complaining.

Bishop Richard Davies of the neighbouring St Asaph Diocese reported later of his own see that some priests took on themselves three, four or even five churches; many churches "have not one whole service once a year but upon Sundays and holy days the epistles and gospels only" and that they were served by "a priest that shall come thither galloping from another parish, which for such pains shall have 40 shillings a year or £4 at best"[8].

In 1570 Arthur ap Hughes died, having seen many changes in the church. During his time there appears to have been no adverse reaction to the new religious settlement in the County of Merioneth and he could give his time to ministering to his parishioners as well as to his work of translation.

THE WELSH BIBLE

On 30 November 1570 Gruffith ap Morgan was instituted as vicar; he would serve Tywyn Church for thirty-six years. During his time, he saw the publication, in 1588, of the first complete Welsh Bible including the Apocrypha. This was the work of William Morgan DD, Vicar of Llanrhaiadr-ym-Mochnant (afterwards Bishop first of Llandaff and then of St Asaph). He had received moral, literary and financial support from many others including the Archbishop of Canterbury, under whom Morgan had studied at Cambridge. In the same year that Morgan's translation of the Bible was published, the version of the psalms which it contained was also published separately for use in the daily services, as the versions which had been printed in the Welsh Prayer Book were unpopular.

The 1563 Act of Parliament had stipulated that a copy of the Welsh Bible should be supplied to every parish church in Wales to "remain in such convenient places within the said churches that such as understand them may resort at all convenient times to read and peruse the same". A copy must have been placed in St Cadfan's Church. It is to be hoped that finance was adequate for copies also to be placed in the chapels.

Evidence that standards of clergy education were rising is provided by the appointment of Robert Parry MA as Vicar of Tywyn on the death of Gruffith ap Morgan in 1606.

In 1620 a revised version of the Bible was published, the work of Bishop Parry. It became the Welsh equivalent of the "Authorised Version" and was used well into the 20th century. An even greater step forward for some was the composition of the metrical psalms in Welsh by Edmwnd Prys, Archdeacon of Merioneth. These first appeared in the 1621 version of the Prayer Book and lent themselves to memorisation by the illiterate. Robert Parry may or may not have had access to a copy before his death in 1623 but it would certainly have been of great help to his successor.

A strong Welsh language ethos existed among clergy in Merioneth at the time and with Morgan's translation of the Bible, the Book of Common Prayer in Welsh and the publication of the metrical psalms the county became as receptive as any other to the tenets of the new faith[9].

Parry's successor, Richard Nanney, was an MA of Jesus College, Oxford and had a Faculty Office Grant to be a "preacher of God's word"[10]. Multiple benefices had not disappeared, for Nanney was also Vicar of Llangelynnin[11] as shown by the notice of sequestration on his death in 1633. Meanwhile in 1630 a smaller-size copy of the 1620 bible, the "Beibl Bach", was published at a price of 5 shillings – still a lot of money but now it was possible for better-off households to own their own copy of the Bible.

Tywyn's next vicar, in 1634, was a high-flyer and Tywyn was only a short stop on the way. Robert Price LLB resigned from Tywyn in 1636 to become, in turn, Chancellor of Bangor Cathedral, Bishop of Ferns & Leighlin and Bishop of Bangor[12]. He was succeeded by Richard Jones or Johnes MA ("John Thomas of Dolgelly") who was instituted on 30 November 1636 only to resign and be replaced by John Hughes MA on 20 January 1637. Perhaps this sudden change relates to the Bishop of Bangor's complaint about his diocese to Archbishop Laud in 1638 that "by reason of the poverty of the place all clergymen of hope of worth seek preferment elsewhere". He also said that the weak scholars must be ordained or "some cures must be left altogether unsupplied"[13]. Thankfully the latter statement at least did not apply to Tywyn.

JOHN HUGHES AND THE COMMONWEALTH

John Hughes was to live through eventful times. In 1642 the Civil War broke out between Charles I and Parliament. Reactions in Wales were confused. The majority of the Welsh tended to be royalist but there was support for Parliament in the few parts of the country which were economically better off. Movements of troops took place mainly in the south and in the north-eastern marches, and would have had little impact on the people of Tywyn.

Meanwhile St Cadfan's Church was, as usual, in need of repair and in 1544 Sir Jones (or James) Pryse of Ynysymaengwyn left 20 shillings in his will towards "repairing the church at Towyn" as well as £3 to the poor of the parish[14].

Having effectively won the Civil War, in 1645 Parliament issued an ordinance by which the use of the Prayer Book, in any "public place of worship or in any private place or family" was forbidden – with a penalty of £5 for the first offence, £10 for the second, and "one whole year's imprisonment without bail or mainprize" for the third.

Cromwell finally defeated Charles in 1648 and the next year the Commonwealth came into existence. Parliamentary Puritans used the victory for a series of experiments aimed at planting their interpretation of the gospel in Wales. It was a radical social experiment, which hoped to build a new social order, a "New Wales", on the ruins of a traditional establishment. In 1650 Parliament published "An Act for the better propagation and preaching of the Gospel in Wales", which had been prepared by Englishmen, mainly from the Borders, and Welshmen from the more anglicised parts of Wales. Many clergy were ejected from their livings. A few vacant livings were filled by returning army chaplains and other Puritan clergy but many were still left empty, so itinerant preachers were appointed to preach in such places. They were paid with funds from confiscated tithes and sequestered estates. Some were highly competent, others inexperienced and inadequate. After three years the Act was allowed to lapse and was replaced by "A Commission for the Approbation of Publique Preachers" composed of moderate men who represented different positions within non-conformity. The itinerant system was abolished. Parishes were to be reorganised, with smaller ones united, large ones partially split and suitable ministers found. All this proved harder to do than expected. Scarcity of candidates for the vacant positions led to the appointment of non-Welsh speakers or very young men or men who had received little or no training[15].

The cessation of most of the diocesan records from shortly after the Civil War until 1680 is indicative of the grave dislocation to the life of the church caused by the Civil War and the Commonwealth. Bishops' registers were no longer entered up and most parish ones were left blank. Marriage became a civil contract so that even in the few parishes where registers were still written up there are no entries relating to marriage[16]. In Tywyn the earliest register extant dates from 1662 with the earliest legible record being the baptism of John, son of Lumley Williams and his wife Ann[17]. It is assumed that Tywyn's earlier registers were destroyed during the Commonwealth as happened in the great majority of churches.

At some time during the Commonwealth John Hughes had been ejected from Tywyn as a pluralist[18] perhaps as early as 1650 when the first Act was promulgated. (There is a general supposition that parishes from which clergy were ejected were gravely neglected while the tithes from them went to central funds.)

John Swayne of Pennal, probably curate in charge, was appointed to Tywyn in 1658[19] (there is no record of anyone replacing him at Pennal). It seems likely that this is the same John Swayne who, in 1660, sued Thomas Ellis of Is Cregennan and his companion (both Quakers) for Easter dues and lactuals[20]. The bailiffs took the money from the two of them although Swayne had been "by the Lord struck dead on the highway in a most strange and terrable manner"[21].

How Hughes coped we do not know. He may have been the same John Hughes who was also the incumbent at Llanaber but was not ejected from there, in which case he could just move to Llanaber. If Hughes was ejected from both of his livings he may have stayed with friends or family or taught in a school as many others did. In theory the wife and children of ejected incumbents would receive an allowance of one-fifth of his previous income (paid irregularly) but no allowance was available for the man himself.

8. THE RESTORATION

THE 1662 PRAYER BOOK

1660 saw the restoration of the monarchy under Charles II. He arranged for a conference between twelve bishops and twelve leading Presbyterians to discuss producing an acceptable compromise Prayer Book. However, after three months the bishops found the Presbyterian demands unacceptable and went ahead with the work alone.

In 1661 Parliament passed a new Act of Uniformity which, initially, was to apply to the 1604 Prayer Book. By 1662 a new Book of Common Prayer was ready. This was solely the work of the Convocation of the Church of England (and very similar to the 1559 Prayer Book of Elizabeth). It was neither debated nor amended by Parliament and it received the Royal Assent as part of the Act of Uniformity in May 1662[1]. The Act also provided for the translation of the Prayer Book into Welsh – with the proviso that accuracy of the Welsh version was to be agreed between the four Welsh diocesan bishops and the Bishop of Hereford. The definitive Welsh version was published in 1664. The Book of Common Prayer, both in English and Welsh, remained in use for 300 years (and may still be used legally in both the Church of England and the Church in Wales despite more modern authorised prayer books being produced by each church). At long last ordinary people in Wales, who for the most part were still unable to read, had a service they could learn and take part in and which would not change.

On 20 August 1662 John Hughes was reinstalled as vicar. It is to be hoped that after so many upheavals his congregation welcomed him back and it seems that he laboured on there until 1681, a total (including his expulsion) of forty-five years.

EXTRACTS FROM "AN OLD BOOK"

We know something about the finances of the parish for this period, thanks to some items from "an Old Book" being copied into the "New" (1723) Parish Book[2]. Winding sheets for burials purchased in 1665 and 1666 seemed to have varying prices: in 1665 they were 1/4d and 5/7d; in 1666 they were 3/6d and 6/0d. It is difficult to see the reason for the differences; perhaps the more expensive ones were of wool. That the church should be charged for them also seems unlikely; if they were for paupers surely the cheapest would have been used in each case? During Charles II's reign three Acts of Parliament were made to enforce burial in wool flannel shrouds to encourage the wool industry and in 1678 the churchwardens' book reveals that fines for "not burying in flanen" came to £2/10/0d.

The Parish of Tywyn at that time was divided into a number of townships[3]. In 1665 their portions for repair were Issyrafon 10/0d and Cefnrhos 3/0d, while Vaenol paid £1 towards "repair of the steeple". Repairs of an old church are, as we know, an ongoing problem and some further amounts are recorded:

1668: Issyrafon 10/0d, Kefnrhos 10/0d, Dauddyfryn 5/0d

1669: Dauddyfryn £1/12/0d, Cefnrhos £2, Issyrafon £1/15/0d

In 1677, £4/5/0d is recorded for the purchase of a church bible. Had the old one been stolen or had it just been used so much that it was falling apart?

Whitsun (now more commonly called Pentecost) was one of the days on which all Christians were expected to make their communion, and the copy from the Old Book reveals in 1683 "a quart of wine against Whitsuntide 9d".

DISASTER

Money raised by Vaenol, and the other townships, for the repair of the steeple had not had the required effect and at the top of a page in the church register a stark note appears: "Cloch dy yn Syrthio i Lawr a darn or Eglwys yn y flwyddo hon 1692". This translates as "The bell-house (i.e. tower or steeple) fell down and a part of the church in this year 1692." The whole of this is written in a different hand from that of the register itself. The actual date was later given as 11 September.

According to Titus Lewis, at that time the church "possessed a fine peal of bells which was regarded to be among the best in the country"[4]. One of these will have been the one marked "Mae crie Mari"[5], which may have been the great bell whose sound is said to have been "audible in Cwm Rhwytor beyond the lake of Talyllyn"[6]. If the bells were rung by rope and pulley so that they swung full circle (as some marks on the bell frame seem to suggest) it may explain the fall of the tower, since the method puts a great strain on a structure not designed for it. The collapse was bad enough to damage all but one of the bells irreparably although the bell frame, being of wood and more flexible, remained usable[7].

Looking at the changes in the stonework of the church, it is clear that the tower must have fallen southwards causing major damage to at least the east and south sides of the south transept[8]. The area under the tower would have received some rubble, which may also have extended into transepts, chancel and nave; the south-east pillar of the tower and at least part of the roofs of the south transept and chancel fell in. Much of the church would have been in ruins, open to the sky and with little usable area.

People love to blame such events on others. No doubt some in Tywyn and the surrounding area blamed the fall on perceived shortcomings of William Lewis (who had succeeded John Hughes as vicar in 1681), or on the behaviour of some or all of the people of the town. Some will have travelled to Tywyn to view the ruins, to sympathise or to mock. The Rector of Llangelynnin, Edward Morgan, will surely have ridden over to sympathise with his neighbouring vicar, perhaps bringing his young son Edward to see what had happened.

It was early September. Harvest time. As well as their normal work with the stock, the farmers and their men would have been working from dawn to dusk to harvest, dry and bring in the grain from the fields. Those whose work was in the town were no doubt equally busy, with builders and carpenters trying to complete assignments before the bad weather. Nevertheless it can be conjectured that those who had any spare time might have brought wheelbarrows to start to clear the rubble, and builders would have been asked to make things safer by demolishing dangerous parts of the remaining walls. Looking at the walls today, much of the stone in the south transept can be seen to be somewhat different from the rest of the building, which suggests that some of the old stone may have been carted away for walls or foundations elsewhere. But temporary measures undertaken mainly by volunteer labour could only go so far. Restoring the church to a usable condition would need money – a lot of it.

The task of rebuilding was beyond the finances of the church and its parishioners. An appeal was sent to the Bishop of Coventry and Lichfield as the holder of the rector's emoluments, and disappointment expressed the next year when no reply to the appeal had been forthcoming. John Morgan, probably the bishop's steward, had to return the amount of tithes to the bishop and the account returned in November 1694 has this note at the end: "We are very uneasy... we hear not from your Lordship on ye account of this poor church and hope my Lord of Lichfield... will be a good ... To your Lordship in order to ye rebuilding of it. We are but very poor of ourselves and therefore do wholly depend upon your Lordship's care to further this great and charitable work..."[9]. Did Lichfield help? There is no evidence either way, but if there had been no response for a year it would seem unlikely.

THE ROYAL BRIEF

The only other way to appeal for outside help was by a royal brief. A petition had to be addressed to the quarter sessions of the county by the vicar, churchwardens and parishioners, following which they were issued with a certificate signed by no less than eleven Members of Parliament. With this recommendation, a royal brief was issued to all civil and ecclesiastical officials within Wales and the seven adjoining English counties. It was to be published in every church, and collections taken and sent to named commissioners with donations being recorded in the vestry book[10].

The Letters Patents for the Tywyn brief are unusual in that they bear the Royal Crest with a double crown because they were granted during the reign of William and Mary. Part of the brief reads: "That on Monday the Eleventh day of September last the greatest part of the Parish Church of Towyn aforesaid, (being one of the greatest Churches within the Diocese of Bangor) together with the Steeple and Ring of Bells, (by casualty and great mischance) fell down and Sunk, to the great Grief of the poor disconsolate Parishioners, who are thereby destitute of a suitable and decent Place to meet and celebrate the Worship of Almighty GOD in, according to their Duty and earnest Desire; and not being able to Rebuild the same, without the Assistance and Relief of Pious and Charitable Christians have therefore humbly besought Us to Grant unto them, Our gracious Letters Patents, under our Great Seal of England, to Licence and Authorize them to Ask and Receive the Charitable Benevolence and Contributions of all Our Loving Subjects, in the Counties and Places in these out Letters patents mentioned, towards Rebuilding the said Church"[11].

E. D. Evans[12] queries the date the tower fell; 11 September would have been a Monday in 1693 rather than 1692. He was not aware that the year of the fall was recorded in the old record book. Assuming the book is correct, either the clerk of the court did not have the day of the fall and put in the Monday assuming that it had been in 1693, or someone misremembered or miscopied the date which should have been 12 September.

Royal briefs were a bit of a gamble as the costs, including legal fees, printing and distributing the briefs, and the cost of collection and transmission of the money could exceed the money raised. These figures are not available for the Tywyn brief but as an example, in 1732 Llanddulas circulated 9902 briefs which collected £650 but costs were £433 leaving only £217 for the church.

There was one other possible source of finance for rebuilding and this may have been adopted in view of the urgency of the situation as, left open to the sky, the church fabric would have been deteriorating rapidly. In the 1730s, a number of local people loaned money to the church when it was planned to build a west tower. That money was to be repaid by a tax on all "tenements" for a number of years, to be paid in addition to the tax for the relief of the poor. In the absence of any other source of income, this may be how repair of the church was financed. Unfortunately, those who copied information from the "Old Parish Book" into the 1723 vestry book did not include expenses or income for the Tywyn brief or from elsewhere. Perhaps the figures were too depressing. Sadly, we have no record of how and when the repair work was completed and the church made usable.

William Lewis continued as Vicar of Tywyn until his death on 6 March 1716. There is a monument on the south wall of the chancel which says he and his wife were buried "underneath"; if so, their remains were probably disturbed during the 1880-4 restoration. His successor, appointed on 5 April 1717, was Edward Morgan, the son of the Edward Morgan who had been rector at Llangelynnin[13] when the

The church with no tower (computer simulation)

tower of St Cadfan's Church fell. The new vicar had studied at Jesus College Oxford, receiving his BA in 1708[14] and subsequently his MA. He was to be supported throughout his time as vicar by Ann Owen; she was daughter and sole heiress of Vincent Corbet of Ynysymaengwyn, the largest landowner in the area, and wife of Athelstan Owen of Rhiwsaeson in Montgomeryshire. Her monument in the church records that she was "a lady of exquisite sense, great piety, charity and other fine endowments", "in whose benevolence and sincerity her friends and particularly the poor have had an inexpressible loss".

9. CHURCHWARDENS AND THEIR ACCOUNTS

The office of churchwarden dates back to the 14th century when, as now, their duties were purely ecclesiastical. Over time these came to include maintenance of the church building and its furnishings, upkeep of the churchyard, provision of bread and wine for communion, custody of any animals belonging to the church, maintenance of order and due reverence in church, and enforcement of church attendance when it was compulsory. There were no separate parish treasurers, so churchwardens had to look after the church finances – and be able to account for every penny. Later governments, particularly from the days of the Tudors, added civil supervisory duties including oversight of the poor and road maintenance[1].

By the 18th century, the vestry of a parish had the double purpose of caring for the church and its people, and of acting as the equivalent of a town council with the incumbent of the parish as chairman.

THE CHURCHWARDENS' ACCOUNTS BOOK

When major work started at St Cadfan's Church in 1880 an old wooden box (originally ordered for documents in the time of Henry VIII) was found. It contained, among other items, two books of churchwardens' accounts, one covering the period 1723 to 1743 and the other starting in 1767[2]. Extracts, compiled by R. Prys Jones (Robyn Frych), were printed by the *Cambrian News* between December 1880 and May 1881.

In the 1930s the vicar, the Rev. Henry Thomas, could find only the earlier book in the safe and, on enquiring of the sexton what had become of the later book, was told that his father (the sexton before him) had said it had been lent to the author of *Cantref Meirionydd*[3]. To prevent the 1723 book disappearing in the same way, Henry Thomas took it to the National Library of Wales to be photostatted and then returned it to the safe. It was subsequently transferred to the Merioneth Records Office in Dolgellau.

The book is written from both ends, the back being upside down compared to the front. Despite the fact that church services were all in Welsh and many of the townspeople would be monolingual Welsh speakers, the majority of it is written in English with only two portions in Welsh.

The front has an impressive first page as may be seen in the picture overleaf. The interpretation is "The Account book of Tywyn Church bought for 2 shillings in the year 1723. Edward Morgan Vicar John Hughes of Dyffryngwyn and Humphrey David of Benorvern Wardens. Written by Edward Hughes." This is followed by a quotation from St Matthew's Gospel chapter 7 verse 12.

The book shows the interaction of church and town, with the vestry laying down the rate for the relief of the poor and, in most cases, also a rate for the repair of the church. Details are given of those poor entitled to relief and the amounts given to them as well as amounts spent on the repair of the church building. The front of the book chiefly relates to the duties of the wardens acting as "overseers of the poor". Most of the vestry records are signed by Ann Owen as well as by the vicar, Edward Morgan.

Front page of the Churchwardens' Accounts Book

The back of the book contains information about collections at the church, mainly for named persons needing assistance, and the amounts paid out to these and to others. It is difficult to compare in detail the individuals helped both via the poor rate and by the church. In general, however, it seems that the church collections very frequently went to those who were ill and temporarily in need of help as opposed to the long-term poor who were helped via the poor rate.

Both ends of the book contain other items in a rather haphazard way including some information copied from an even older book, like that quoted in Chapter 8. One is the "List of Church Wardens of Towyn as far as they can be traced by ye old book". This list, which starts in 1693, shows that the two wardens almost invariably changed every year and that it was most unusual for a warden to be re-elected at a later date. When one considers the obligations of a churchwarden it is hardly surprising that no-one wanted to carry it out more than once. The list starts from 1693, the year after the tower fell; perhaps the church register had been protected by that "wooden box" but the account books had not been kept in it and they were lost.

Britain was still working on the Gregorian calendar with the year ending on Lady Day (25 March). This means that items dated January, February or most of March 1692 referred to what we now call 1693. Where specific dates are quoted here, they are shown as in the account book.

POOR RELIEF

For 1724 there is a list of twenty people "entitled to funds". The amounts (which were to cover the whole year) range from D. Humphrey's boy who received 6d to Vincent John who got £2/12/0d, though he was exceptional, the next highest figure being 15/-. Most received less than 6/0d[4].

Immediately thereafter is the record of the vestry meeting of 28 May 1724: "It was agreed by ye major part of the Parish then present y^t ye sum of twenty pounds is to be alowd for ye poor and ten pounds more for and towards ye repair of ye church to be payd severally and now on for and towards ye above in Confirmation whereof we have hereunto sett our hands ye day and year above written." First and boldest of the signatories is A: [Ann] Owen followed by the two churchwardens, the vicar and four others including Edward Hughes who wrote the first page of the 1723-43 churchwardens' accounts. It does not say how the money is to be divided between the various parish residents although that may have been dealt with in an earlier book.

This is an indication of much of what occurs in the first half of the book. Most years there is a note of a vestry at which the retiring wardens handed over the amounts still in their care. In May 1725 Humphrey Price and Hugh Rees Thomas handed over 20/0d and 43/0d respectively. John Tybotts and John Pughe are then recorded as "appoynted" for the year 1725. There is no further comment about the amount to be raised for the poor until, in 1729, a note says that the tax is to be the same as before.

In the back of the book, undated but 1728/9 by comparison with an entry in the 1729 wardens' accounts, is a list of the "tenements" (apparently a mixture of estate, farms, dwellings and land – plus wool and lambs!) and "The rent of each tenement as charged by the Land Tax"; this had been set in 1692 as the rent of the land. One hundred and twelve names are listed together with "A meadow in Hugh Bevans" and "Wooll and lambs of whole Parish". The total rent on which tax was charged was £710 with the valuations ranging from Ynysymaengwyn (£80) to Perth y pobty (10 shillings). In 1730 the amount of tax had been specified at "six pence in ye pound" (and "£6 of ye said sum to be reserved towards ye use of ye church &c"), which suggests that it was at this stage that the method of sharing the tax was formalised in Tywyn. Sixpence in the pound was 2.5% so the tax would have raised nearly £18.

Over thirty years earlier, in 1697, Parliament had passed a Poor Law that all people in receipt of parish relief were to wear a badge on their right shoulder – a badge with a letter P and the initial of the parish – presumably to reduce misuse of the Poor Law and to deter the able-bodied from becoming "Paupers"[5]. This may or may not have been applied in Tywyn at the time, but in 1727 there is a note that it was agreed at a vestry that the poor should wear a "Bag" (presumably a badge) at the charge of the parish. At a vestry in 1729, after a list of the poor, it was recorded that "ye above poor shall wear badge upon right shoulder upon their upper garment visibly or forfeit their allowance". There are no entries showing the sums of money awarded to those to be badged, but later the same year a list is given with amounts varying from 2 shillings to £2/2/0d. At a time when a craftsman/builder would earn 2 shillings in a day they must surely have been desperate to allow themselves to be badged for such small annual amounts.

Sometimes the parish found itself completely responsible for individuals, perhaps the very old. In January 1732 a vestry agreed "the following Poor were settled with

Humphrey David of Tu Mawr namely Jonett Edwards, Elin Humphrey and Jonett William at 3-4d a week for all the three together for diott and nursing".

If it was possible to show that someone was not originally of the parish, and to move them elsewhere, this would help to keep the poor rate down. In 1727 Jenkin Jones needed proof of his residency; a copy of his certificate reads "we... Being churchwardens and overseers of the poor in ye Parish of To in ye C of M do hereby certify own and acknowledge y^t Jenkin Jones shoemaker with his wife and children are parishioners legally settled in ye parish of Towyn aforesaid as witness out hands ye 11 day of July 1727".

Moving those who, it was thought, had no claim on the parish was a lengthy business. Catherine Griffith had, or was expecting, an illegitimate child, and warden Thomas David first took her under warrant to Llanbrynmair which, presumably, would not accept her. He then had to take her to Dolgellau before a Justice of the Peace at a total cost of 10/0d to obtain an order for her removal. The next year, in 1732, warden David Evans had to go to Hencwrt for an order to move Catherine Griffith. He then had to go on to Llanbrynmair where he spent two days to find the supposed father of the bastard child. Finally, he had to take the child to Llanbrynmair. All this, which cost a total of 9/0d, had to be met out of the poor rate.

The poor rate increased over time. In 1741 it was ninepence in the pound, in 1777[6] it was one shilling in the pound and in 1778 one shilling and sixpence. This increase must have been anticipated, for a vestry on 30 May 1777 resolved "whereas the Poor's Rate within these few years very much advanced to the great Grievance of this Parish in general & poor Tenants in particular the Inhabitants of this Parish have consented and agreed that a Workhouse be erected with all convenient speed for Lodging, maintaining and setting to work the poor of the said parish…".

THE CHURCH RATE

For most vestries where the poor rate was set, a rate for "the repair of the church" – or just "for the church" – was included. In the early part of the vestry book there is no record of how this money was spent. However, perhaps as a result of parishioners wanting to know where their money was going, church and other expenses also appear in the accounts for 1729, though it is not possible to determine which were met by the church rate and which by the poor rate.

There seem to be two sets of churchwardens' accounts in some years, each including the amounts to the poor and expenses. It would seem that each warden dealt with part of the parish (so different paupers) and where "a moety of…" appears – the gate, the spade, communion wine and so on – the expenses were shared between the two parts.

In 1729, for the first warden (whose name is illegible) the list of expenses, apart from money paid to the poor, is:

p^d for writting ye Church miz & bill	00/02/00
p^d ye moety for a gate	00/05/00
p^d ye moety of Wine for Sacrament	01/03/03
ye moety of Communion bread	00/01/00
p^d at ye Collection for Oath & Charges	00/01/08
p^d for Hinges for ye Reeding and for mending	
ye Bell Clapper ye smith finding iron	00/03/01
For washing ye surpluss	00/02/06

for writing ye Register Roll	00/02/06
for drink at ye Vestry	00/01/06
for ye moety of a spade	00/01/03
pd ye glazier	00/06/05
Treating ye…, swearing ye Poor's…	
To ye Clerk then attending	00/02/09
pd for making wardens accounts	00/02/00
for notices to poor	00/02/00
for handscribing ye church wardens names	
in this book of both parts of the parish for	
39 years past	00/01/00
for writing all ye tenement names in…	
with their Poor Act rents as Charged by	
ye Land Tax	00/01/00
pd David Griffithe ye slater	00/12/00
pd him more for a load of slates & nails	00/00/10
pd to ye Joynor for altering ye Rooding	
seats and Vestry	00/04/00
pd at ye delivering up of my…	00/00/10
for one bier	00/04/00

The expenses of John Edwards of Caithley (Caethle), the second warden, has duplicate amounts for all items with "a moety" as well as for the slater and "joyner" and some other items. He also made payments of 2/6d and 2/4d for two shrouds and payments of 2/6d each for killing polecats. Payments for killing other birds and beasts of prey included 4d for a raven, 5/0d for a fox and 1/3d for a "kitlin" (perhaps a young polecat). It is hard to see why the church should have been responsible for such payments, which presumably were made on behalf of the parish as a whole.

In 1730 the accounts include payments to David Griffith, slater 12/0d, for lime 2/3d and for the carriage of the lime 1/10½d, while in 1731 there are several costs for bringing various individuals before a Justice of the Peace.

Work on the roof and the windows must have been ongoing, for in 1732 there is another total of £1/4/0d for the slater (he also got an extra 10/0d for stopping pigeons coming into the church) and 16/0d for the "glacier"; the bell clapper had to be mended again "with iron".

The churchwardens' accounts book was also the repository for information which the wardens, vicar or town clerk wanted recorded. The church is a high one and (as current churchwardens know) the only way to remove cobwebs is with a brush on a very long pole, but once, when the pole was needed, it could not be found. This is recorded:

Memorandum. I was informed Apr 27 1733 that one or other of ye owners of Towyn Boat took the long pole bought for a brussing pole for ye use of ye church and converted it into a hook pole for their last fishing season at Dovey without leave and the pole is missing ever since. Enquire about it at next Vestry as an uncommon pitch of impudence.

Did it come back? Unfortunately the subsequent accounts are rather skimpy, but a replacement does not seem to appear anywhere.

Rather later, in 1742, another misuse of church property is recorded at a vestry. "It was agreed that whoever burnt lime in Towyn church yard kiln shd give for every tun of stone there burnt a quarter of unslacked lime hot from the Kiln to the use of the said church and that either Clerk send or take care to demand, receive and keep the same for the forsaid use." Why was there a churchyard kiln in the first place? That the church used lime frequently is clear from the accounts; it would have been used for lime mortar, for lime plaster and for limewash as necessary, and the kiln may have been left following the building of the west tower in 1735-8. Limestone is not local and the carriage (shown in 1730 accounts) was nearly as much as the stone itself so perhaps the vestry was concerned to penalise the use of church property without permission.

SERVICES AND COLLECTIONS

Apart from Easter and Christmas, the sacrament (Communion or Holy Eucharist) was celebrated only once or twice a month. At that service it was usual to have a collection for a named purpose, most commonly for individuals in need for some reason. Only some of these individuals were also receiving poor relief. Sometimes the collection was large enough to be shared with several of those in need.

To take some examples from 1725:

May 16 For Mary Richard Bryn y cryg 4/0d
For Mary Bach Tal y rhian 3/10d
June 13 For Susan's daughter a cripple to go to Holy well 5/0d
July 18 For an old fellow from Caernarfon a cos. of Mr Perris 2/0d
July For Elizabeth Humphrey 2/0d
but gave out of it to Mary Meredydd 2/-d Margt... 2/0d
August 3 For Mary Bach Tal y rhian 1/0d
but gave out of it to Elizabeth Humphrey 2/0d

This pattern continues, mainly for named individuals:

1725: To a blind woman from Llanaber 6/6d,
For Richard James, Penal, that lost all by fire 10/6d
For Hum. H.Owen's wife 2/6d
1727: For Howel's wife and son-in-law being both
sick two months upwards 6/3d

There are also entries about bequests. In 1729 Humphrey Owen left 40 shillings, and Jenkin John of Vainol, Ursula Hugh and David Humphrey all bequeathed 20 shillings to the poor of Tywyn "making a whole five pounds". This was handed over and paid by the executors on 12 December to the churchwarden for the Poor of the Parish. Another bequest of £3 is recorded in 1731, this time followed by a list of sums paid out.

In some years, in addition to the amount collected at a service, the number of communicants is recorded. In 1732 the record of communicant numbers starts in May:

May 7 – 23; June 25 – 50; July 5 – 70; Aug 3 – 86;
Sept 5 – 67; Oct 3 – 51; Nov 2 – 49; Dec – 47

The next year the stark statement appears "No collections at Easter 1733 because no sacrament because the wardens refused to provide bread and wine." What was going on? Was the Easter collection a customary offering to the vicar and were vicar and wardens at odds? Were the churchwardens, David Evans and Rowland Rees, inimical to discussions about reinstating the tower (which must have taken place during this year) and blamed the vicar? The sacrament – and the collections – were back in place the next year.

At the sacrament on 20 January 1734, a collection was made "for Lowry David aged 84 who wounded herself very much with falling down the church Gallery stairs Xmas Day last 5/0d". Why was she up in the gallery at her age? Perhaps she had been in the choir most of her life and had taken her place there at the Plygain in the early hours of Christmas Day. As she came down what would have been steep and winding stairs with nothing but a rushlight for illumination it would be only too easy for her to miss her footing.

Among the other sources of revenue mentioned there is an unusual item. In 1740 "July 15. By Mr Vaughan for permission to open Cadvan's grave, 2/6d." This presumed grave is marked by four short stone posts about 30 yards to the west of the church, on the centre line of the nave. It may at some time have supported the Cadfan Stone to enable the writing on three of the four sides to be read[7]. Tradition says that no traces of human remains nor indications of any burials were found there, which is not surprising if Cadfan did move to Bardsey Island to found a community and was subsequently buried there.

10. TYWYN CHURCH IN THE 1700s

At the beginning of the 18th century the people of Wales were almost all members of the Church of England, and perhaps 5% were Protestant dissenters (Baptists, Congregationalists, Presbyterians and Quakers), these latter being mainly found in the English-speaking border counties[1]. However, by the middle of the century it was said in a letter (possibly with some exaggeration) that Anglesey was "now full of Methodists, Independents and Presbyterians"[2].

EDWARD MORGAN

Edward Morgan had taken over as Vicar of Tywyn in 1717. Pluralism[3] was still quite widespread in the diocese and nine years later, while remaining Vicar of Tywyn, he was appointed Rector of Llanaber, just north of Barmouth, presumably to increase his income. We do not know how, or if, he shared his time between them. The two churches are thirty miles apart – a good hour's drive even nowadays – so he may have been based at one parish and visited the other occasionally. Where he lived may have depended on whether there was church accommodation at either of them. A copy of the *Rights of the Vicars of Towyn* written in 1750[4] indicates that, although there was a vicarage, the Bishop of Lichfield and Coventry had still not built the dwelling house promised in the Edward VI Letters Patent. If Morgan remained based at Tywyn, the most obvious solution would have been for him to appoint, and pay for, a vicar at Llanaber (or he could have lived there and put a curate at Tywyn – although no doubt Ann Owen would have had something to say about that!).

THE WEST TOWER

The people of Tywyn may have been regretting for years the loss of the central tower or steeple that had fallen in 1692. Perhaps it was the lack of true bell ringing which concerned some of them – and from the amounts spent on bell repair it sounds as if the remaining bell was unsatisfactory. To rebuild the central tower would have required more funds than the church had available and there may have been informal discussions about it. The central tower had fallen because of a weak pillar and the subsequent repairs had done nothing to address this problem. Major structural support work would have been needed to rebuild the tower – and would have rendered the church unusable for a considerable time. A tower at the west end would do as well and be less costly.

A decision was made "At a Vestry Lawfully Called and Requested by Mr Lewis Vaughan ye first Day of November 1733 we the persons undernamed have agreed to advance the tax 6d in the pound towards the Rebuilding of ye Church of Towy ye said 6d in ye Pound is to be paid over and above the yearly tax of ye Church and Poor as Witness our hands ye day and year above written." There are thirteen signatories starting with An: Owen and the vicar, Edd: Morgan, although three are marks with the name written alongside. They were making decisions which would affect many people in Tywyn but, as the rate was paid by the occupier and they were the major occupiers in the area, the chances are that they themselves would pay much of it.

Costs started to arise quickly – and faculties (permission to carry out alterations to a church) are not a modern annoyance:

To Mr Hughes when he went to treat about
the steeple   2/6
[this was to Aberystwyth]
For carrying the steeple petition to Bangor   5/0d
For the proclamation there of the following:

Proclam fee	5/0d
To register for the proclamation	6/8d
Stamps	1/6d
Seal and wax	6d
For carrying ye proclamation there	5/0d
For fetching ye faculty	5/0d
For ye faculty	13/4d
For a decree for the same	10/0d
Fee & Act	1/4d
Informing ye judge	13/4d

They had spent £3/9/2d and that was just to get permission to build.

With the faculty approved, a vestry was summoned and recorded in detail:

Merioneth shire Parish of Towyn
At a Vestry summoned and kept on ye 13 of Jly 1734
for ye Parish, it is agreed by ye inhabitants of ye sd

Parish & by ym directed yt a steeple or stone Tower be made and raised at ye west, and within ye west end of ye Parish chch of ye sd Parish, and yt ye present chchwardens of ye sd Parish shall set out ye same to be made and raisd to workmen Tradesmen and Artificers in such manner & form as to ym shall seem most proper & reasonable; the sd inhabitants agreeing yt ye sd Vestry to stand to ratifie and confirme any agree– as shall be so made with all every or any person or persons.

That dealt with the actual building, then came how to pay for it. The decision to levy a rate of 6d in the pound over and above all other rates and taxes every year for as long as necessary had to be formally passed by the vestry. A proviso that no-one should have to pay more than 6d in the pound in any one year was also passed.

The builder of the tower was Owen Humphrey who marked on the tower O Humphrey Fecit 1736. He received stage payments of £40 in 1735 and 1737 with a final payment of £50 in April 1738, a total cost of £130. In addition the carpenter, Thomas Griffith, received £52 in 1738 on the completion of his work (this entry is in Welsh and uses the word "*Clochdy*" rather than tower or steeple). The same year there is also a note, "Due to Mr Griffith Owen Glazier for glazing the great west window of the steeple the sum of 01-05-00". At that stage the wardens had only paid him in part 12 shillings and there does not seem to be any record of his final payment.

Leaving aside any minor extras that may not have been recorded, the west tower/steeple/*clochdy* cost just under £193. In the accounts book from 1735 onwards there are repeated notes of amounts raised by the steeple tax (it was eventually set at 3d in the pound each year and does not seem to have exceeded this level, which would only have brought in about £9 a year), gifts, payments, loans and repayments. How long the steeple tax itself continued we cannot tell. The last entry in the book is for 1741, which agrees that "towards church and poor" a rate of 9d in the pound shall be raised.

Edward Morgan was one of those who had agreed to advance money towards the building of the *clochdy* when it was first mooted[5], which suggests that he had more than just his tithes and dues to depend on (these would have included the money from Lichfield and the Llanaber Rectorial). He may have inherited land from his father, the former Rector of Llangelynnin, for in 1739 Edward Morgan set up what was effectively a trust with Thomas Parry of Aberystwyth[6]. The trust involved transferring to Parry two holdings, Brin y porrodd and Tyddyn y Mirio Bychan, "in the Township of Bodgadfan in the Parish of Llanglynin" in exchange for 5 shillings. Out of the income from these properties, Parry and his heirs forever were to pay 40 shillings a year to Llanaber Parish and 20 shillings a year each to Tywyn and Llanymawddwy with the remainder of the income going to Llangelynnin. In each parish, half was to go to the elderly poor and half to poor children who, in both cases, could repeat and say by heart the Church Catechism on Easter Monday including always the Lord's Prayer, the Apostles' Creed and the Ten Commandments. A note on the outside of the vellum confirms that this tradition was maintained by David Pugh, vicar from 1906 to 1932. Michael Edwards, churchwarden from 2002 to 2010, remembers going on Easter Monday in the 1950s to get the money before the Easter fair.

In 1749 Edward Morgan died, being remembered as "a pious and charitable man"[7]. His successor was William Lloyd BA. He only stayed for four and a half years after which he may have retired to Penyrallt near Pennal[8] or may have been made Vicar of Bangor[9].

JEREMIAH GRIFFITH

In 1753 Lloyd was replaced by Jeremiah Griffith MA. Titus Lewis records him as "a most estimable man, marks of whose goodness and piety are noticeable even to the present day. During the 30 years he resided at Tywyn he did a vast amount of work and maintained order and discipline to a remarkable degree"[10]. In 1774, perhaps to celebrate twenty-one years of his ministry in Tywyn, he paid for the renovation of the silver goblet used for Holy Communion.

Early in his ministry, Griffith would have become aware of the shortcomings of the bell to call people to services. The church had its west tower or steeple, but it was a *clochdy* or bell tower with no bells (except, perhaps, that one which had needed repeated repairs some twenty years before). In 1759 three new bells were cast for the church by Abel Rudhall, a very celebrated bell-founder in his day, possibly using some of the metal from the broken bells. These bells are still in use today. Their details are as follows:

Bell	Inscription	Diameter (inches)
Treble	MAY THE CHURCH FLOURISH 1759	26
2	CAST IN GLOUCESTER BY ABEL RUDHALL 1759	26¼
Tenor	PROSPERITY TO THIS PARISH AR 1759	28¼

The bell frame itself had survived the collapse of the tower (the form of the frame suggests a 17th century origin). It is very weathered, so may have stood outside, perhaps holding that unsatisfactory bell, until the new tower was built[11].

In 1761, or shortly before then, a Dr Taylor arranged for the Cadfan Stone to be removed from its place "as a gatepost" and erected as a pillar in the churchyard. In 1761 he made three engravings of the markings on the stone as he saw them[12].

In 1773[13], flagstones were laid in the north and south aisles and also "the alley leading from the great door to the opposite wall" at a cost of 1/6d per yard. A new communion table was purchased, part of the south aisle roofed and a new gate placed "leading eastward to the churchyard". The October vestry recorded "whereas the main timber work in the roof of the body of the said church is, to all appearance, in a ruinous and tottering condition, it is hereby further ordered that the said timber-work be secured at as small an expence (sic) as possible".

Also in 1773, there was a proposal for an addition to the church: a gallery. The inhabitants of Tywyn were not happy about the idea, possibly because of the amount already spent on the church that year, and the faculty application started by "moving for a proclamation against the Inhabitants of Towyn to show cause why a Faculty should not be granted". Eventually, after two months, the decree for the faculty was issued. The total cost of getting to this stage was £2/1/10d[14]. There is no record anywhere of the design of the gallery nor where it was situated, although a description of the church as it was in 1839 does mention a gallery at the east end of the nave[15].

Three years later, in 1776, a more radical activity was envisaged. The "gentlemen free holders" and others had subscribed for a clock for the church tower, but putting it into the tower was not as easy as had at first appeared. A vestry on 12 April agreed that the bell loft in the steeple should be raised by means of screws and wedges. Another loft would then be set beneath the bell loft, which would hold the clock together with its frame, case and weights. This was to be done "at the expense of the parish"[16].

It may have been about this time that the ancient prayer sundial, or mass clock, was moved to become a milestone, since the writing which now can be seen on it, "from Towyn 1 mile", is said to be in an 18th century hand[17].

A BISHOP'S VISITATION

In 1776, there was a bishop's visitation which included, as nowadays, a questionnaire on the church and its activities[18]. This reveals that all services were in Welsh (11am and 3pm on Sundays) and that, as shown in the churchwardens' accounts, the Lord's Supper was held monthly and on Good

Friday, Easter Eve and Christmas Day. Unlike the modern communion service with its central sermon, preaching was every Sunday **except** sacrament Sundays. There were about 60-100 communicants each month and "near Easter 600 as usual", rather more than were shown earlier in the century. It would seem that, unlike Anglesey, Tywyn had not been affected by the Methodist movement as "there are no dissenters of any denomination in my parish to the best of my knowledge".

Children were instructed in the catechism either by the vicar or the schoolmaster "of whom we generally have two or more in the Parish". There was "no Free School" in Tywyn but, for twenty-one children of parishioners, there was a charity school at which both boys and girls were taught to read English. The schoolmaster was paid the interest at 3½% on £200 plus £4 but the school was "now vacant because the master died some months ago".

The churchwardens were nominated yearly on Easter Monday, one by the vicar and the other by the "Heir of Caethle", so there was no input from the parishioners for either post. Offertory money was handled by the vicar and churchwardens for the poor of the parish.

The vicar lived in the vicarage but "the Bishop of Lichfield and Coventry was enjoined to build a competent dwelling house" which was "very much needed".

THE TERRIER

The existence of a terrier (inventory) of the church for 1776[19] may be partly explained by the bishop's question as to whether they had one! It includes not just the contents of the church but also details of the church itself: "The length of the Church and Bell Tower within 36 yards 1 foot" with widths of nave and side "Eyles"; the "Cross Eyles" were each 7 yards 2 feet long and 6 yards 2 feet wide. The outward circumference of the "Church Yard Fence" of limestone was 326 yards. The furniture of the church included a reading desk and pulpit, communion table and font and a chest for linen and plate. The plate was a silver base (presumably a paten) given in 1773 by Dafydd Jones and a silver chalice given by Jeremiah Griffith in 1774. In addition, there were two pewter flagons and a pewter platter (all still in the church safe), two surplices, tablecloths and towels.

There is then a description of the vicarage that certainly does not sound as bad as the visitation answer suggests. Built of stone and slated it had a cellar, hall, parlour, closet and two butteries, three lodging rooms (presumably bedrooms) and four garrets, a brewhouse with a store room over it, a stable cum cowhouse with three bays, a coach or drag house and a small stable. There was also "an Eyle of four bays divided into a Turf house, and an house of office[20] and a coal house".

GRIFFITH'S SUCCESSORS

Following Griffith's death in 1784, John Pierce was presented to the benefice but stayed only six months before moving to Llanhychan. He was succeeded by Pryse Maurice, brother of Mr Corbet of Ynysymaengwyn, which was by far the largest estate in the area. Corbet solved the problem of the vicarage by presenting the parish with suitable land and assisting financially with its building. This new vicarage remained in use, although with some updating, until the 1990s. In many ways it still fitted the description in the 1776 terrier: a cellar, a hall and two living rooms with kitchen behind, bedrooms on the first floor and more rooms on the second floor (though these cannot really be described as garrets!).

Pryse Maurice died in 1803 after eighteen years in the parish. He is remembered on the monument which commemorates his mother Anne, who was herself the daughter of the Ann Owen of Edward Morgan's time.

A LINK WITH JOHN MILTON

One unlikely inhabitant of Tywyn about this time, and almost certainly a member of St Cadfan's congregation, was Louis de Saumaise who is remembered on a plaque in the north transept. He was descended from the Comtes de Saumaise of Burgundy, a Catholic family. Claude de Saumaise[21], Louis's "several greats" grandfather, was born in 1588 of a Catholic father and Protestant mother but became a Protestant against his father's wishes. He left France some time around 1629 and had a distinguished academic career in Heidelberg before settling in Leiden. Claude was considered one of the foremost Protestant scholars of his day with a Europe-wide reputation. Charles II commissioned him to refute John Milton's attack on Charles I. Claude's descendants remained in Holland and by the late 1700s there was only one lineal descendant – the father of Louis – and his three elder brothers and a sister. The three brothers were in the Dutch army (two were generals and one a colonel) and his sister married a Russian nobleman who was a Prussian general. Yet somehow, by some strange chance, Louis had ended up in Tywyn and married the daughter and only child of William Anwyl of Bodtalog.

11. TITHES, TYWYN AND MY LORDS OF LICHFIELD (1690-1900)

GREAT AND SMALL TITHES

In England, tithe law defined tithes as one-tenth of the yearly profit from crops, stock and "personal industry" such as manual occupations, trades, fisheries etc. – in other words, anything which yielded an annual increase. These were divided into the "great tithes" of corn, peas and beans, hay and wood and the "small tithes" covering everything else. Where there was a vicar as well as a rector, the great tithe went to the rector and the small tithe to the vicar.

In England, where large quantities of corn and hay were grown, the great tithes were generally worth very much more than the small tithes. However, in Wales this was not the case and the tithes were divided differently. This was especially true in areas such as Tywyn with limited flat land suitable for growing crops. Much of the correspondence between Tywyn and Lichfield related to tithes and especially what the vicar should have (as opposed to what he had been getting). This seems to have been finally resolved by 1751 and then recorded by the vicar, Edward Morgan[1]. His statement was included in the terrier for 1776[2], which spelled out those tithes which were the right of the vicar:

1   A sixth part of the tythe wool and lambs throughout the parish and when summing up the whole and subtracting the vicar's dividend the Farmer of the

Tythes gives him his choice of payments as far as his share goes.

2 All the Tythe of corn, Geese, Pigs, Eggs and honey in the Township of Dauddyffryn [roughly from the old Toll House, Tywyn, to Rhowniar and up Happy Valley].

3 Lactuals of the whole Parish viz for every Milch cow three half pence, every heifer one penny every mare and colt one penny every 20 ewes one half pence.

4 A Gift in Lieu of Tythe Herring.

TITHES OF ABSENTEE RECTORS

Where there was a non-resident rector (for example, the Bishop of Lichfield and Coventry), there were effectively only two ways to collect the tithe money. One was to employ a steward or bailiff to collect and account for the money in detail. The other was to farm out, or lease, the tithes to a leaseholder who was known as the impropriator or the "farmer" even though he might not have been involved in any sort of agriculture himself. We still use the expression "to farm out work" where we pay someone to do something on our behalf. The tithe farmer would pay the bishop for the lease. Details of how much was to be paid yearly to the rector (in this case the Bishop of Lichfield and Coventry) and others would be specified in the lease. Once the farmer had made these payments, he retained the rest of the tithe income as his payment (although, as tithe was frequently paid in kind, it could be that his 'payment' was standing in the field and still needed to be collected – or even reaped).

After the 1547 grant of the rectory to the Bishop of Lichfield and Coventry and, in 1551, a lease to his nephew (subsequently cancelled) we do not know anything about the value of the tithes, or the relationships between the Church of Tywyn and the Bishop of Lichfield and Coventry, until the late 17th century.

In January 1692 (1693 in modern dating), four months after the central tower had fallen, John Morgan, perhaps the bishop's agent in Tywyn, made a return to the Bishop of Lichfield and Coventry. This showed that the value (in income from tithes) of the Rectory of Tywyn was £300, Llanfihangel-y-Pennant £35, Talyllyn £50 and Pennal £60. Outgoings of £100 were recorded as "rent to all" and may reflect the sums shown rather later of £40 to the Vicar of Tywyn and £20 each to the curates of the chapels. A total of £345 was leaving Tywyn to be paid to the bishop. The record only contains extracts from the accounts and does not mention the fall of the tower[3] but it seems likely that it was about this time that John Morgan wrote to the bishop asking for help. We do know that, with the following year's returns, he expressed disappointment that no help had been forthcoming. Two years later the value of Tywyn was £312/12/0d, with the three chapelries at £50 each, mention being made of wool, lamb, hay, water fishing and tithe herring (with the tithe of wool and lamb being valued at £40).

THE GILBERT FAMILY AS LESSEES

Late in the 17th century, John Gilbert had taken the lease on the Tywyn tithe from the "Rectory of Tywyn". The lease included a requirement for him to pay £40 a year to the vicar and "three score pounds" (£60) to be shared between the curates of the three chapels. The vicar should also have been receiving the small tithes but there was disagreement as to what, exactly, they should be. In 1693 John Gilbert wrote to the Bishop of Lichfield and Coventry[4] complaining about claims by the Vicar of Tywyn, particularly about tithe on the herring fisheries. An agreement was brokered between the vicar and Thomas Gilbert (John's son) by one W. Pughe (who seems to have been pressurised into the job of bishop's representative) whereby the vicar should have the tithe herring and pay Gilbert a rent of 40 shillings a year for it.

John Gilbert died within a couple of years and in 1696[5] his widow, Elizabeth Gilbert, renewed the lease for twenty-one years. She was not at all happy about the tithe herring agreement and Pughe wrote to the bishop outlining the situation and what had been agreed. Mrs Gilbert was outraged and wrote three times to the bishop in 1698 saying that, as she had not been party to the agreement, it should not be binding on her. Her second letter, in August, was an impassioned plea on the subject of the "Tyth-herring" in which she complained of being "shamefully abused by the vicar Mr Lewis" and maintaining that "all Lawyers whom I have consulted do say it is as much my right as ye rest of ye Tyths". On the back of the third letter is a detailed note, presumably written by the bishop's secretary, outlining what he was to include in his reply to her: "If she will not hold to the agreement and allow the vicar to have his tithe herring for a rent of 40 shillings then the vicar should not contest it. However, if she wants to renew the lease she must expect to reimburse the vicar his costs and damages, with interest, for her refusal and she would also be compelled to stand to the agreement." This warning was obviously sufficient for her to yield as she sent no more letters on the subject.

William Price, the Curate of Pennal since 1686, wrote a number of times to the Bishop of Lichfield and Coventry – the first one in 1708. Most of them concerned Mrs Gilbert, the impropriator, and tithes or other sources of money. In August 1718 he wrote of having at last been able to see the 1696 lease and having discovered that he and his brother clergy at Talyllyn and Llanfihangel-y-Pennant had been deprived of their rightful money. They had only received £10 per year each instead of £20, on top of which Mrs Gilbert had claimed the Easter offerings which, for Pennal, were "upwards of £4". He calculated that, on the Easter offerings alone, he had lost £88 over twenty-two years. He asked His Lordship to intervene, as life was very difficult with nine children, one of whom might become a minister if he could afford to support him. Unfortunately, because of his handwriting, his subsequent letters are mainly indecipherable so it is not possible to determine what happened!

A DISAGREEMENT BETWEEN BISHOPS

At some stage, a disagreement must have been fermenting between the Bishop of Bangor and the Bishop of Lichfield and Coventry as to which had the right of patronage of the Vicarage of Tywyn – in other words who should select the vicar. For some reason this matter was so contentious that eventually, in 1747, the facts (as seen by each side) were put on paper for the opinion of a Dr Andrews, perhaps a king's counsel or other senior member of the Bar. After studying the submissions, which included a copy of the original grant of the rectory from Edward VI and also copies of the Bishop of Bangor's registers as far as they were available, he gave the opinion that the patronage of the Vicarage of Tywyn belonged to the Bishop of Bangor. This seems mainly to have related to whether the appointments recorded were by "collation" or "institution" (the first means the bishop is patron, the second means someone else is patron)[6]. One does wonder what Dr Andrews thought about such an argument coming up after nearly 200 years! Perhaps the Vicar of Tywyn, Edward Morgan, had been trying to get Lichfield to exert more control over the way that their lease-holders treated the curates of the chapelries and Lichfield wanted to appoint more amenable vicars in future.

THE EDWARDS FAMILY AS LESSEES

About this time the leaseholder must have been a James Phillips, for in 1752 Lewis Edwards purchased from him the existing lease for the remainder of the twenty-one years it had to run[7]. He split the lease equally between his two sons, John Edwards of Machynlleth and Dr Edwards of Jesus College, Oxford. The two brothers are named (as the Rev. Edward Edwards of Jesus College and John Edwards of Machynlleth) in the earliest extant leases[8] in 1763, 1770 and 1777. These and subsequent leases were all for twenty-one years and are worded similarly. They relate to "All that the Rectory and Parsonage of Towin, Merionethshire and all those chappels of Llanvihangell Tal y Llyn and Pennall under the said rectory and parsonage annexed... also all the glebe lands, water fishing, Tythe rights, fruit…". An annual rent of £40 was to be paid in portions on the feast day of the Nativity of St John and on the Nativity of Our Lord in the cathedral between 9am and 11am, also £60 in the south porch of the church of "Towin" in parts on the quarter days for the use of the curates of Llanfihangel-y-Pennant, Talyllyn and Pennal.

New leases to the two Edwards brothers were taken out in 1770 and 1777. Then in 1784 the 1770 and 1777 leases were surrendered by "John Edwards legatee and sole executor of Edward Edwards" and a new lease made to John Edwards alone. Nearly all the leases were surrendered and renewed at less than twenty-one-year intervals and all referred to a "sum in hand" (to Lichfield) of an unspecified amount. Apart from one lease in 1791 to "Humphrey Jones, David Davis and Turner Edwards", every single one of them after 1784 was to John Edwards. At the turn of the century, strangely, the lease was surrendered and a fine paid and, at the same time, another lease was taken out on the same terms, a sum in hand, almost every year for several years. It certainly looks as if something odd was going on.

THE VALUE OF THE TITHES

In 1787, the Bishop of Lichfield and Coventry sent an agent, Richard Owen of Wem, to look into the value of the Tywyn tithes[9]. Owen found it difficult and, in his letter of 9 August, wrote that he had "not met with that success which he hoped for, owing in great part to Mr Edwards's private method of collecting them, and his ease apparently to conceal their value". Having discussed the case with "substantial inhabitants", he was sure that the amount for the four parishes was not less than £800 per annum with some saying £1000 and some even more. He also commented that "the Tythes of wool and lamb, which make a principal part of your Lordship's property in those Parishes can not so easily be ascertained as those of corn or any of the general Produce of Parishes in England, on account of the Extensiveness of the sheep walks and the consequent difficulty, especially to strangers, of obtaining a tolerable knowledge of the Number of Sheep and Lambs kept thereon". He was seeking further advice from a friend of a friend, the former agent of "Some Gentlemen" in the parish, and hoped to get a more accurate valuation.

The next letter, sent less than a month later, is from Robert Pugh, also of Wem[10], who had consulted with three or four Welsh friends and was expecting even more information. He had also heard that the tithes of the four parishes were worth £800 to £1000 and had been told that the father or grandfather of John Edwards was the first lessee and that Mr Edwards "makes upwards of £400 a year clear of payments to the bishop, vicar and curates". "The churches of Penall, Llanvihangell and Tall y Llyn are now considered as Parish Churches wherein every kind of parochial duty is performed. The four Parishes are very extensive and abound with fine fruitful valleys and high hills." "It is generally allowed that Mr Edwards hath a great bargain in it and that Mr Corbet of Ynysymaengwyn and other gentlemen would gladly give much more for it." It was clear that a survey of the area might be carried out and Pugh says that this had been done on several estates in Merionethshire belonging to Sir Watkin Williams Wynne and others without trouble, so a surveyor should be safe. He also comments that "Mr E.

himself is generally considered to be a gentleman of great and increasing property" and is able to give a handsome fortune to each of his four or five daughters.

What effect these reports had on financial arrangements in subsequent leases it is not possible to determine, as the leases in the National Library of Wales are all in similar terms to the earlier ones and continue to refer to "a sum in hand". One imagines that the sum in hand to Lichfield increased considerably after the reports from Richard Owen and Robert Pugh.

In 1789, John Edwards died (his brother having died earlier, with his share of the lease going to John) and his will divided the lease between his two sons, John Edwards and Henry Arthur Edwards, with John succeeding to the whole of the lease when his brother died in 1797[11].

MONEY PAYMENTS

Over the years, money payments were increasingly substituted for payment in kind. One purpose of the Enclosures Acts (1773 onwards) had been to get rid of the obligation to pay increased tithes on improved land. This was done either by allotting land to the church or by a money payment that might be fixed or might vary with the price of corn. By 1836, tithes were still payable in the majority of parishes and the Tithe Act 1836 substituted corn rents (i.e. money payments linked to the price of corn) for the payment of tithes in kind. Almost every piece of land across the whole of England and Wales had to be surveyed, its owner and the current value of the tithe determined, and agreement reached as to the appropriate corn rent. This led to the production of the tithe maps that tell us so much about the countryside in the 19th century.

A return to Parliament for 1847-8[12] shows for Tywyn:

To bishop of Lichfield or their lessees: £793/10/0d
To the vicar £180
To the parish clerk £6/10/0d.
The returns for Pennal, Talyllyn and Llanfihangel-y-Pennant show: To bishop of Lichfield: £223, £250 and £190 respectively. (This was money which originally came for "Tywyn and its chapels".)
To the incumbent: nothing
To Pennal Parish Clerk: £2

The money to the Vicar of Tywyn would presumably have come from the tithes due to him as detailed in the 1776 terrier, probably stretching across all four parishes. (Money due to vicar and curates from Lichfield or the lessees under the charter is not included.) Of the total tithes of the area, originally intended to support the clergy of the area and to provide relief for the poor, £1456 (88%) was going out of the area and only £188/10/0d remaining. One wonders how much the lessees had paid for the lease.

THE ECCLESIASTICAL COMMISSIONERS

In 1840 the Ecclesiastical Commissioners had been set up, initially to report on "The State of the Established Church" particularly episcopal dioceses, revenues and patronage. One purpose was to look at how much money was coming in to each bishopric and to use some of it to make provision for clergy in areas where there was insufficient money or no churches[13]. In their 1856 report to Parliament[14] the commissioners' main recommendation, to which the Bishop of Lichfield and Coventry had agreed, was that "a number of Estates belonging to his See" should be transferred to the commissioners in exchange for an annual payment to the bishop of £884 (any income above this amount would go to the commissioners to fund other clergy and churches).

The biggest section in the list of estates to be transferred is: "All that the Rectory of Towyn Meirion and the chapels of Lanvyhangel, Tallyllyn and Pennal with all the appurtenances belonging". The lessees were Lord Adolphus Vane Tempest and John Edwards – and they must have anticipated the change for they had a lease for twenty-one years from 25 March 1854. This was "subject to annual reservations amounting to £123/3/6d in aggregate" – perhaps the amounts due to the vicar and the curates of the "chapels".

The lease of the tithes came to an end on 25 March 1875[15]. The vicar, Titus Lewis, must have written to the Ecclesiastical Commissioners at once, or even in advance of that date. He was seeking financial support from the money that would have previously gone to the lessee, both for himself and for a curate for a "proposed Chapel of Ease" in Bryncrug. In June the commissioners replied. They stated that the tithe rent charges[16] held by the commissioners amounted to £793/10/d[17]. They would make over to the Vicarage of Tywyn enough of the money to raise the vicar's income to £300. This was to be done by adding particular portions of the tithe rent charge to the benefice. If the chapel at Bryncrug was built and approved then a grant of £120 per annum would be made "conditionally upon the appointment of a duly licensed assistant curate". A copy of the *London Gazette* of 26 February 1876 contained the conveyance to the incumbent of the Vicarage of Tywyn of the tithe commutation rent charges of a number of lands with a total rent charge of £200/1/9d (which was expected to bring in £150 net). It was to have and to hold "to the use of the said Incumbent and his successors for ever". Presumably the vicar himself, rather than representatives of the Ecclesiastical Commissioners, would have been responsible for collecting the tithes from these sources.

In 1880 the Ecclesiastical Commissioners decided to make an ecclesiastical district for Abergynolwyn by taking parts of the parishes of Tywyn, Llanegryn, Talyllyn and Pennal[18]. It was proposed that the whole of the balance of the Tywyn tithes remaining in their hands should be made over to the church in Abergynolwyn. Titus Lewis wrote requesting them to reconsider the matter and suggesting that the tithes should be divided between Abergynolwyn and "a proposed church in Happy Valley". The vicar of Llanfihangel-y-Pennant had suggested to the commissioners that Llanfihangel-y-Pennant and Abergynolwyn combined would be better served by one vicar and a curate rather than by two independent incumbents, while Titus Lewis reported that he would be content with the endowment of a curacy for Happy Valley. Perhaps surprisingly, this met with a positive response from the commissioners who decided not to assign a separate ecclesiastical district of Abergynolwyn. Instead, provided the parts of Tywyn and Talyllyn parishes that were to have been assigned to Abergynolwyn were instead assigned to Llanfihangel-y-Pennant, they would take steps to assure an income to that vicar of £300. If the Happy

Valley church was built then they would arrange a grant of £120 per annum for a curate there. After over 350 years at least a quarter of Tywyn's tithes were coming home

The church in Happy Valley was never built but in 1882, on hearing that the new church at Bryncrug was to be consecrated that September, the commissioners confirmed that the promised grant of £120 a year would be paid from the date of the appointment of the curate (or from the date of consecration if this was later). Grants for curates were not in the form of permanent transfer of rent charges; they could be given or withheld at any time at the discretion of the commissioners.

This was a happy outcome for the churches of the area, but the whole principle of tithes was increasingly opposed by many of the people of Wales. This opposition was one manifestation of the non-conformist feeling that had been growing for a couple of centuries. It was calculated that by 1850 only one quarter of those who worshipped in any church or chapel in Wales went to an Anglican (Church of England) church. The logic was clear. Why should tithes, which solely benefited Anglicans, have to be paid by Anglican and non-conformist alike? After all, the non-conformists had to fund their own buildings and ministers from their own resources.

THE TITHE WARS

The agricultural depression of the late 1870s and early 1880s turned an irritant into an economic hardship. The "Tithe Wars" developed. If a farmer could not, or would not, pay the tithe rent then the Church had to send in bailiffs and auctioneers to secure payment – a lengthy and costly procedure. The bailiffs might also meet with violent resistance from the farmer, his friends and those who were opposed to the charge.

In Tywyn anti-tithe meetings were held, with protestors arguing for a 20% reduction in the amount of tithe to be paid. Collections were made at the meetings to help with the expenses of those who refused to pay. A petition gained 132 signatures and a committee was empowered to meet the receiver (who worked both on behalf of both the Ecclesiastical Commission and the vicars) to argue the case for a 20% reduction[19]. While the Ecclesiastical Commissioners remained adamant that they could not reduce the amount, the Vicars of Tywyn and Aberdyfi offered a 10% reduction in the small proportion of the tithes which came to them. A meeting of many of the farmers involved decided unanimously not to pay except by distraint unless the commission also made a reduction of 10%[20].

Matters came to a head in June when the tithe officers started to move from farm to farm, asking each farmer to pay his tithe money or else goods would be confiscated and auctioned to pay it. On the first day they were escorted by eight police constables and there was some trouble, especially on their return to town when they "were escorted through the town by a few farmers and some 150 boys with large sticks, which they brandished about in an alarming manner". The next day the escort was just one man, Inspector Hughes, "a native of the district, speaks Welsh like a parson, and is liked and respected wherever he is known". The farms visited paid up and although there was some barracking by a small crowd, the day passed off peacefully[21].

[22]Ten days later the tithe officers were back again, having only managed to visit a limited number of farms the first time. Again Inspector Hughes was their only escort and his peaceful mediation proved invaluable. However, all did not proceed smoothly. The group went by Talyllyn Railway to Dolgoch from where they walked to Ty Mawr Farm. On arrival they discovered that the indispensable maps had been left on the train and a messenger had to be sent to Abergynolwyn to recover them. The two-hour delay gave time for a group of protesters to gather, but among them were the chairman and some members of the Anti-Tithe League who helped to maintain order. At farm after farm, the tenants agreed to pay, apart from the costs of the visit, and this was accepted by the tithe officers.

However, there were those who continued to resist payment. At Penybontfawr, Mrs Pugh, the tenant, declined to pay and the animal left for distraint was a great pig. The mob protested vigorously at the "intentions vile upon the pig", and the sale did not proceed – at least at that time. At Bryncastell, the tenant handed over the amount of tithe less 6d, which he said he would not pay, as "we never pay coppers in Wales". One of the tithe officers then paid the 6d out of his own pocket. And so it went on; the total collected was about £200 but forty had still not paid.

An account in the *Cambrian News*, in December 1889[23], of a visit of agents who were selecting items to be seized for sale to pay the tithe suggests that a newspaper reporter went round with the tithe officers and had difficulty in finding anything exciting or interesting on which to comment, unlike many areas of Wales.

His descriptive comments include the following:

… one after another the hill tops became visible, though Cader Idris' head continued throughout the day wrapped up in what a poet has been pleased to call folds of areophane…

… the farm houses in the district are remarkably well built and comfortable. In fact some of them are mansions in comparison with some of the hovels used in Cardiganshire for farm houses…

… the land in the valley is well cultivated, pure bred cattle of the Welsh breed pasture in the meadows instead of the mongrels too usually met with south of the Dovey, and there were many indications of home comforts altogether absent in the rural districts of the Cardi where flower beds and carpeted floors are as rare as pianos on the higher slopes of Cader Idris.

At one farm the tithe officers were met by a farmer who declared he would not speak to the children of hell – "*plant uffern*" – but as he spoke in Welsh, which the visitors could not understand, "they were like the jackdaw of Rheims and not one penny the worse for the compliment". They were looking for something on which to distrain when the man said, "Look here I will show you something to seize" and, taking them to the garden, pointed out several hives of bees.

They were also told that "tithe collection had caused a remarkable cure in the neighbourhood. A young woman belonging to the district came home from London, as it was thought to die of consumption. When the officers visited the place last year she made a deafening noise with a tin can which she beat, and wrought herself up into a white heat of excitement. From that time, it is said, she gradually recovered, and is now as well as ever."

All delightful to read, but rather disappointing for a newspaper reporter hoping for excitement and riot.

Over the next couple of years there were more meetings of the Anti-Tithe League, more protests to the Ecclesiastical Commission and to the Vicars of Tywyn and Aberdyfi. Increasingly there was hope that Parliament would legislate, either for abolition of tithes or for the disestablishment of the Church in Wales, and that tithes would be distributed more equitably among the denominations of Wales.

Many landowners, sympathising with the financial load of tithes on their tenants, made reductions in their rent charges[24]. In the Tywyn area these included Mr John Corbett[25] of Ynysymaengwyn estate with a 20% reduction and Mr John McInnes of Caethle estate, 15%.

As the likelihood of disestablishment became ever clearer, the protests petered out and peace returned.

12. FROM 1770 TO 1870

THE TOWN IN THE EARLY 19TH CENTURY

Visiting Tywyn about the turn of the 19th century, the Rev. J. Evans described it as having respectable appearance, finely situated with a fine and sandy beach, and frequented during the summer by numerous genteel families for the purposes of sea bathing[1]. Perhaps he only saw that part of Tywyn which fringed the sea because it was described by others as a "secluded and poor place", possessing few resources except a market to which only part of the local produce was brought for sale[2]. "As for streets, it has none... merely lanes adorned with wide and dirty ditches meandering placidly along their centres. It contains half a dozen good houses, and a church with no great pretensions to elegance."[3] However, "poor as it is, it possesses a blessing, at least in the estimation of the natives, in a Well which like the pool of Bethesda cures, or is supposed to cure, the maladies of all who bathe in its waters... The number of patients, all however of the lower order, who resort to it is astonishing."[4] A little later, Paterson reported that "during the bathing season, many respectable families frequent this place in preference to Aberystwyth" and that "a machine [presumably a bathing machine] is stationed on the beach but seldom used"[5].

Change was coming, at least to the extensive marshes that had, over the centuries, gradually formed over much of the Dysynni estuary as the river silted up. Edward Corbet succeeded to Ynysymaengwyn in 1782, an estate of 600 acres including 261 acres of turbary (land used almost solely for cutting turf for fuel). Between 1788 and 1794 he drained this land. He kept the cost down by inviting the poor of the area to cut turf for fuel without payment – provided that they cut to a specified depth in specified places and that they left the surface completely smooth[6]. This apparent generosity saved him the wages of the men he would otherwise have had to employ. It also meant that the poor were transforming the area, which they had used for generations for fuel, into one where they would no longer be able to go. Corbet improved the land with copious quantities of lime at a cost of £820/6/3d. By 1794 this improved land produced about 500 tons of hay a year giving an increased profit on it of £440/6/9d – an annual return on capital of more than 50%[7]!

Fenton walked the area in 1804 and recorded that reclaimed land stretched "from the former old Embankment of Towyn Demesne to the Beach about two Miles, and in breadth about a Mile". He also saw the well "lying on the edge of the Marsh. There I saw two Boys and an old Woman bathing. The Water was foul and turbid, but is esteemed uncommonly efficacious in various complaints, particularly of the Rheumatick kind, though Mr Corbet has told me he finds great relief from it in fresh contracted Coughs, but then he follows the Water up to the Eye [presumably the source], just at the back of the Cemetery to the N. West. It certainly has some degree of sulphur and sea salt in its composition. Pity it is not well analyzed."[8]

THE CURATES OF TYWYN'S CHAPELS

Robert Pugh, in 1787, had written that the churches of Pennal, Llanfihangel-y-Pennant and Talyllyn were now considered as parish churches, and it was just before that date that clergy began to be appointed to these churches by the bishop (before that they had been curates of Tywyn and appointed by the vicar there). Vincent Humphreys was appointed to Llanfihangel-y-Pennant in 1769, Maurice Anwyl to Pennal as curate in 1780 and Evan Pugh MA as permanent curate to Talyllyn in 1787. However, the three churches were not always kept separate; in 1795 William Pugh BA was appointed curate both for Llanfihangel-y-Pennant and Talyllyn[9]. There is then a continuous list of appointments into the 20th century.

The case of Maurice Anwyl is interesting. He was appointed as curate to Pennal in 1780, and there was a subsequent appointment of Edward Hughes in 1799. A letter to the Bishop of Bangor dated 7 June 1800 referred to Maurice Anwyl, curate of **Tywyn**. The letter said that Anwyl would have liked to keep the curacy of Pennal, but it did not carry enough salary to maintain his five children and so he had had to go to Tywyn. He still lived in Pennal and the eighteen-mile round trip to Tywyn was "inconvenient particularly in Winter". His current salary was £30 and if the salary in Pennal were to be increased it would be "more agreeable to serve that church"[10]. This suggests that the income for Pennal, and presumably for the other two ex-chapels, was still only the £20 per year from the lease-holder. It would seem that Anwyl's plea was not met, as in 1802 he is recorded, in the list of benefices in the diocese[11], as being aged forty-seven, a non-resident curate at Tywyn "licensed 11 October 1802" on a stipend of £35. Pennal, with an income of £20 plus fees, is recorded as being a perpetual curacy with Thomas

Evans as current curate. He was, presumably, soon to be moving, as Edward Hughes, though not yet resident, had been licensed to the parish on 1 May 1801.

The same record includes the premature death in 1803 of vicar Pryse Maurice aged forty-nine and the collation of his successor Robert Davies MA, aged fifty, Rector of Mallwyd[12]. In 1827, Robert Davies died and was succeeded by John Maurice Edwards BA.

The Tabernacle, the first chapel in Aberdyfi, was registered in April 1829[13] and for some time there had been hopes of a church there as well. It was during John Maurice Edwards' time as Vicar of Tywyn that St Peter's Church was built there in 1837. Aberdyfi was still part of the parish of Tywyn, being only a district chapelry in 1844[14]. In 1861 it was made an ecclesiastical district within Tywyn Parish and an annual sum of £23 was paid to the perpetual curate of Aberdyfi Church[15]. Benjamin Morgan was appointed at the end of 1846 as the first incumbent[16].

THE CHURCH IN 1839

Meanwhile the interior of St Cadfan's Church itself remained much as it had been from the mid-18th century. It was described in detail by S. R. Glynne, who wrote notes on numerous Welsh churches over a period of fifty years[17]. He was in Tywyn in August 1839 and saw "a cruciform church, larger and more interesting in its architecture than usual". The tower at the west end was "low, modern and plain". He noted that the nave was "divided from each aisle by three very rude semicircular arches on low round pillars of Norman character" and added that the clerestory

The church in the 19th century

windows were "Norman but all closed internally". Had they been filled in to reduce draughts? It must have made the church much darker!

It sounds as if he considered the crossing to be part of the chancel: "the chancel opens to the nave by a plain pointed arch". There was a perpendicular east window of three lights but other windows were "mostly mutilated or modern". The nave had "crowded pews and a gallery over the eastern portion" but the western extremity was cut off and free from pews. There were monumental remains in the chancel with pointed arches (much as they are today) and the knight's arch had "a fine crocheted ogee canopy". The altar was "thrown out of its proper place by vile pews", a situation which would be remarked on later.

An account of the life of Griffith Evans, who was born in 1835 in a farm near Bryncrug, the son of Evan Evans, one of the biggest local farmers,[18] gives us some idea of life and the church then. When vicar Edwards died, Griffith and his sisters were dressed in their best clothes and taken to view his body, a mark of respect by both adults and children. Their nursemaid told them that they must be sure to take hold of the vicar's big toe so that they would never see his ghost. She also told them that when the vicar died the effigy of Gruffydd ap Adda in the church had been seen to weep real tears. Young Griffith's father laughed when he heard that and on a wet day took the boy to church to see moisture in the eye, and explained it was the result of condensation in humid weather.

Griffith also remembered lanterns swinging in the stable yard when guests arrived at the farm for the feast of St Cadfan or for Christmas. He was of a practical turn of mind and looked at Tywyn marshes and wondered why, in summer, so many mosquitoes danced down there while on the moors there were few. The old people who lived on the marshland complained of the ague and said it came from the mosquitoes.

Although Griffith's father, Evan Evans, liked to maintain good relations with St Cadfan's Church, the church of the gentry, his sympathy was with the non-conformists. He often provided hospitality for travelling evangelists and after the service would invite his farm workers and maids to meet the preacher around the kitchen fire. One old shepherd was a lay preacher who had once denounced Evan Evans in his sermon in chapel because washing had been left on the line on the Lord's Day, so it had not been kept holy.

Tywyn Charity School[19], largely supported by Lady Moyer's Trust, was in existence but it had strong connections with the church as she had specified attendance of the charity pupils at church twice on Sunday. As a non-conformist, Evan Evans may not have wanted his children to attend what he saw as the church school. Griffith and his sisters were educated by a governess, to whom Griffith ascribed his clear script, dexterity with figures, lucid biblical English and love of reading. However, in 1846 a British (i.e. non-denominational) school opened in the nearby hamlet of Bryncrug and Griffith was one of the first pupils. A couple of years later he moved to Pennal school, lodging in the village during the week to continue his education.

TYWYN IN THE LATE 1840S

The anonymous writer of 'Tywyn Past and Present' in the *Aberystwyth Observer* described the town and the church at this time: "Everybody did as they liked, all the pigs roamed at large through the streets and acted the part of street scavengers." "I looked into the church and saw only one individual downstairs, the clergyman and a quaint looking clerk. I could hear there were a few persons boxed up in the gallery."[20] At another time[21], hearing the bell for a funeral, he went into the church: "The clergyman appeared to read the service very impressively and he afterwards proceeded to the altar and stood upright facing the congregation. People marched up the aisle to the clergyman and tendered him some coin. The total amount of the offering was declared." After the corpse was put into the grave then "the sexton, who also acted as clerk, handed round a spade to all who stood by, some dropping shillings and some sixpences on it". The sexton then declared the amount and filled in and tidied the grave. There was a place "beneath the belfry" (i.e. the west tower) "where bones that had been dug up were formerly laid" although it was then in use as a storeroom.

The writer also found two gravestones with interesting inscriptions, which seem now to have disappeared. One was of a celebrated harper who had drowned crossing the Dysynni:

Ye nymphs of the flood were missing, plague rot 'em,
With the genius of music when he went to the bottom –
Their care and attention else would have supported
The child of the harp whom the muses all courted.[22]

The other was for a servant who had worked at Ynysymaengwyn for fifty years:

If honest labour, industry and truth
Can claim from heaven a just reward,
Learn, learn ye Welshmen all, both age and youth,
How patient merit claims regard;
Here lies a man who never swerved at all,
His honest worth was only known to few, –
His daily labour furnished means but small
His worth too little known, his name JOHN PUGH.[23]

OWEN JONES

Owen Jones had succeeded John Maurice Edwards in March 1841, and it may have been soon after that the

Cadfan Stone was returned to the church since it is said to have been done under the will of Edward Scott of Bodtalog who died in that year[24].

In July 1844 Jones applied to the Ecclesiastical Commissioners for financial assistance, which may have been towards repair of the vicarage; the request was recorded as having been "postponed for lack of funds"[25].

Owen Jones seems to have thought of himself as very busy. In the return to Parliament of the numbers of services in the last quarter of 1848[26] he stated that, as the incumbent, he was resident in Tywyn and took two Welsh services in Tywyn and two Welsh services in Aberdyfi; also that he was non-resident incumbent for Llanfihangel-y-Pennant and for Talyllyn with two Welsh services between them. He also said that he was performing the services himself. These claims were made despite the existence of permanent curates in Aberdyfi, Llanfihangel-y-Pennant and Talyllyn as shown in the diocesan records.

It would also seem that Jones was not unduly concerned with the details of ecclesiastical rules for he, and presumably the churchwardens, allowed a Mr John Vaughan to erect a very elaborate monument to Lewis Vaughan on the wall of the chancel without any faculty. There must have been objections because, in 1852, the Honorable Adolphus Frederick Charles William Vane and James Edwards Esq. (who between them held the lease of the great tithes from the Bishop of Coventry and Lichfield) applied for a decree to cause John Vaughan to remove the monument and make good or restore the wall[27]. The decree must have been refused since the monument is still on the south wall of the sanctuary. It is indeed an elaborate one and includes an oversize figure of a woman with folded hands wearing a robe and looking piously up to heaven.

Like much of Wales, Tywyn now had a large proportion of non-conformists. They were unhappy with the church rate, an increasingly unpopular tax. This fell heavily on non-conformists who were expected to pay it even though they had to raise money themselves for their own ministers and buildings. Parliament sought evidence of the amounts raised from Easter 1853 to Easter 1854 including whether any objection had been made to the demand. The return[28] shows that in Tywyn the church rate raised £80/10/0d and that £88/17/2d was expended including £12/13/7½d to build a hearse house and £20/3/0½d for repair of the church.

When Aberdyfi Church was built the arrangement had been that the church rates should continue to go to Tywyn as before for twenty-one years. There was a plaintive note[29] in the parliamentary report that the expenses of maintaining the building in repair had fallen on the officiating clergyman, although no amounts were given (surely, in less than twenty years there cannot have been too many repairs required). In neither case had rates ever been refused.

An Act for the Abolition of Compulsory Church Rates was eventually passed in 1868[30].

Owen Jones must have been getting increasingly incompetent or old and ill or possibly affected by his alcohol consumption following the death of his wife[31] for, in January 1861, a Commission of Enquiry was set up by the Bishop of Bangor to investigate the performance of his ecclesiastical duties. The commissioners were the Rector of Machynlleth, the Perpetual Curate of Aberdyfi and the

Incumbent of Llanegryn as well as the Archdeacon of Merioneth and a commissioner nominated by Owen Jones. They met on 29 January in the Corbett Arms Hotel. Owen Jones was made aware, if he did not already know, of his own shortcomings and on the outside of the subsequent report is a statement by him admitting that "in consequence of the state of my health… The duties… for some time past and are still inadequate." The statement requested the licensing of a curate with stipend to assist him in the performance of duties "which would be allowed if I were non-resident"[32]. There were no pensions in those days and clerics normally remained in post until they died. Depriving Jones of his living would have very serious consequences for him and his family; on the other hand the welfare of the parishioners had to be considered and later in 1861 Titus Lewis was appointed as Curate of Tywyn.

THE COMING OF THE KETTLE FAMILY

There was a long history of summer visitors in Tywyn, and an increasing number of families with money and time to spend on holidays were taking houses for the season in the area. The Kettle family was one that would have connections with Tywyn and with the church for several generations.

Initially, road transport was the only way to travel to Tywyn. In his first visit to Tywyn in 1862 since his youth, Rupert Kettle and his six-year-old son travelled by pony carriage from Wolverhampton, taking three days for the journey. They stayed at the newly furnished Neptune Hall and paid a total of 14 shillings for eight days' full board.

Only two years later a railway reached from Machynlleth through Borth to Ynyslas and another existed between Aberdyfi and Tywyn. The whole Kettle family, including six children under eleven, travelled by train from Wolverhampton to Ynyslas, then crossed the Dyfi by ferry steamboat before completing the journey by train[33]. Once the railway line from Machynlleth to Aberdyfi was completed it was possible to travel the whole way by train and the number of English visitors increased. Many of these would have worshipped at the English service in St Cadfan's Church on Sunday afternoons, services that may have been started under the influence of Titus Lewis at a time when the chapels retained a Welsh-only tradition[34].

OWEN JONES IN DEBT

Sadly, by 1868 Owen Jones had for some reason got into debt to one Catherine Jones to the extent of £130/2/10d, so she took a case against him. On 11 March the court found in her favour and directed that the amount should be recovered from Owen Jones's goods and chattels. As he was a vicar living in a vicarage and had (or said he had) no goods or chattels which could be used, the Sheriff of Merionethshire formally issued a writ to the bishop: "we command you that you enter into the same vicarage and Parish Church of Towyn and take… into your possession… The rents, tithes, oblations, fruits, issues and profits thereof and other ecclesiastical goods in your diocese and belonging to the said vicarage and Parish Church and to the said Reverend Owen Jones to be rendered to the said Catherine Jones."

The bishop gave authority on 27 July 1868 to William Griffith of Dolgellau to act as sequestrator and to receive the

> ... rents tithes tithe-rent charges oblations obventions fruits issues and profits and all other Ecclesiastical goods dues or Emoluments belonging to the said vicarage and Parish Church and to the said Reverend Owen Jones Clerk as vicar thereof Subject nevertheless to the payment thereout in the first place of such stipends or salary as we shall from time to time lawfully assign unto the Spiritual Person or Persons for the time being authorised by us or our successors to have the Cure of the said vicarage and Parish Church and of all other charges of duly serving the said Cure and maintaining in a proper and sufficient state of repair the Parsonage or Glebe House and all other buildings (if any) belonging to the said Benefice or vicarage and also of all lawful and usual costs and charges of and incidental to this our Sequestration.

Accounts were to be rendered annually. This was to continue until revoked by the bishop, presumably when the sum necessary had been paid. There was an addendum that the stipend or salary to the Spiritual Person or Persons was to be £150 a year paid quarterly until otherwise directed [35]. As the tithes coming to the incumbent were only £180 a year and the rent from glebe lands about £1 a year, it would have taken a long time to pay off the debt which, with expenses, would probably have grown considerably. Meanwhile any future incumbent would have his annual income reduced by £30 and so would be suffering financially because of the debts of his predecessor. There is no record of what, if anything, was taken from the church towards the payment of this debt.

Owen Jones did not long survive the shame of this judgement, dying in 1869. He was an alcoholic and in the last stages of delirium tremens. Griffith Evans, who sat with him for three nights until he died, said "I felt a deep pity for him knowing that it was loneliness after his wife's death which had started him drinking."[36]

13. TITUS LEWIS

Titus Lewis[1] was born at Danygarth near Lampeter in 1826 and grew up there until his family moved to London ten years later. After returning to Wales for a while, Lewis went to America with his uncle and worked there for some years before returning to his native parish. It was then that he decided to prepare for Holy Orders and studied at Lampeter Grammar School before entering St David's College, Lampeter, in 1854 for theological training. He was ordained deacon in 1857 and priest in 1858, serving as curate at Llanelli from 1857 to 1859 and then at Llandovery under the Rev. Joshua Hughes, who was later to become Bishop of St Asaph.

In 1861, the Bishop of Bangor offered Lewis the curacy in charge of Tywyn, which he accepted. He was vicar in all but name for eight years. During this time he also studied for his degree of Bachelor of Divinity, which was awarded in 1869. After Owen Jones's death in 1869 Titus Lewis succeeded him as vicar. In 1876 he married Elizabeth Carnegie, a widow with one daughter, Mary[2].

THE CHURCH IN THE 1860S

An account of the church at this period, by an older member of the Kettle family[3], is worth quoting in full[4].

It is very interesting to remember what the church at Towyn was like in 1864 when we first knew it. It was a church for the Welsh then. The English service, an extra, was always held in the afternoon in the summer months, in winter there was no English service, except perhaps a celebration once a month at 9 am.

But it is not easy to distinguish fact from imagination and sentiment, associated as it all is with childhood's affection and uncritical observation. The exterior has changed but little[5]. There was a dark wood altar rail, three sides of the square around the altar. This would be of Jacobean date. There was a high square pew on each side of the altar. There were several high square pews in the church, one of which was allotted to the family. Pews with doors were throughout the church. Our pew was lined and cushioned with red baize, worn, faded and moth-eaten. A bat once fell during the sermon from the roof into the pew. Once a white goat walked up the nave and was led out by the horns. There was a gallery across the nave where was a harmonium and a mixed choir; notably conspicuous therein were the figures of Rowley Price and the old vicar in shiny black broadcloth. But he no longer officiated, Titus Lewis was practically the vicar and he became so actually when the older man died.

The three bells rang, as now, ding-dong-dell, and then singly. The verger was Roberts, the shoemaker. He could talk English a little. He did not always know the time. He came (when it was already 9.15 am.) to ask the Misses Kettle what time it was one Sunday morning!

The floor was of slabs of slate, very uneven, the pulpit was a three-decker, but nothing could detract from the ancient dignity of St. Cadvan's. St. Cadvan's Pillar stood upon a mound to the right of the south door. There was not yet a porch. Red curtains inside blew wide when the heavy door was opened.

The ancient rite of Plugen was still continued early on Christmas Day, but it was not until many years after that we were there at Christmas; by that time the original form of the service had been somewhat modified by Titus Lewis, the vicar. It was quite primitive enough to be very striking and impressive. The service began very early, long before daylight. The church was lit up and thickly decorated with evergreens, and the Welsh folk sang hymns and part-songs according to their ancient custom. To come out of church into the early daylight of a winter morning, with the weird music just ceasing was an unique experience.

During his first few years as vicar, Lewis introduced a surpliced choir and the wearing of permitted vestments. Morning and evening prayer were read in church every day as instructed in the prayer book rubric. Candles and flowers on the altar[6], a three-hour service on Good Friday and several communion services on Easter Day were seen by some as definite signs that he was introducing Popery[7]. These changes at first caused offence to some church-goers, as changes always do, but over time they came to be appreciated. After one letter attacking him appeared in the *Cambrian News* a reply was published rebutting much of what had been written, recording the flourishing state of the church and adding that the "congregation before the appointment of the present hard-working priest, could be carried on a wheelbarrow"[8]!

THE CLOSURE OF THE CHURCHYARD

One of Titus Lewis's early actions after becoming vicar must have been to deal with a letter from Whitehall[9]. Under an Act of Parliament it directed that "for the Protection of Public Health, no new Burial Ground shall be opened in the Parish of Towyn without previous permission" of the Secretaries of State and that "Burials be limited in the Parish Churchyard of Towyn after the 31st May 1870 to the Parishioners of Towyn excluding the Ecclesiastical District of Aberdovey, except for the interment of the Widowers Widows Parents Brothers and Sisters of those already interred in that Churchyard." Apart from the fact that there was no other graveyard in Tywyn at the time, and that St Peter's Church had only a small graveyard, the people of Aberdyfi had "always" been buried in St Cadfan's churchyard. Their ancestors were there, they still had strong links with Tywyn Church and they still wanted to be buried there.

There is no record of the correspondence that must have gone to and fro, nor of the meetings that must have taken place in Aberdyfi, but five years later, in August 1874, another letter was received from Whitehall[10]. The letter made reference to "a Memorial from the ratepayers of Aberdovey praying that the Order in Council closing Towyn Churchyard may be cancelled" which had been forwarded by Lewis in June. The order was not to be cancelled but a recommendation was made that the words "excluding the Ecclesiastical District of Aberdovey" be deleted from the order. It was not until 1887 that the plan for a proposed new cemetery for Tywyn was produced[11] and, in practice, burials in the churchyard continued with decreasing frequency until the early 1950s.

PREPARING FOR RESTORATION

During his eight years as curate, Titus Lewis had become increasingly aware that repair and restoration work was urgently needed. He had developed a vision for the improvement of the church and for a restoration to its former glory. In the autumn of 1870, helped by several others, he started on the work of improving the inside. They knocked down "those high and unbecoming pews" which had filled every space between the altar and the pulpit, so that now the altar could be clearly seen. Two high reading desks from which the priest used to "pray over the people" were demolished and the three-decker pulpit lowered and moved[12]. By December the gallery had been demolished, which altered the appearance of the church appreciably – and the vicar passed the old timbers to local people for firewood. The choir was moved to temporary seating in the chancel and the harmonium was replaced by a small organ[13].

Lewis listed work that was needed on the building; he must also have started approaching people who might donate funds. Possible sources of money were not only the owners of local estates, such as Ynysymaengwyn and Peniarth and their guests, but also those who were regular visitors to the area.

THE CHANCEL INSPECTION

In taking over the income from rectorial tithes, the Ecclesiastical Commissioners had also taken responsibility for repairing the chancels of the ancient churches involved. In 1875 there was an inspection of the chancel of St Cadfan's

Church, probably prompted by a request from the vicar in search of funds for his rebuilding project. The surveyor, Ewan Christian of 8 Whitechapel Place, London, reported to the commissioners[14] on 31 May that:

This Chancel is a rude but interesting building of the 13th Century. The walls are built of rough local stone that on the south side is much bulged and with the east Gable requires rebuilding, the coping of the latter is very defective. An ancient single light window remains in the north Wall but it has been closed internally by the insertion of a Monument which should be removed. The east and south Windows are formed in cement[15] on the remains of decayed masonry. These will require entire renewal as will also the stonework of the doorway. There are two very interesting monumental effigies in arched recesses on the north side.

The roof was constructed in the 17th Century part of oak and part deal the trusses of which are of oak and tolerably sound, but the rafters and the slating are very defective. It would be desirable to put an entirely new roof of a higher pitch. All the plaster is rough and defective and that on the north side damp. The boarded floors are fairly sound but the other portion which is of stone and tiles mixed is very defective. The Chancel is at present seated with moveable benches and the organ is placed on the south side.

The Church is in a somewhat better state of repair; it is proposed to restore the Transepts and east end of Nave, rebuilding the central Tower which fell in 1692. The vicar is desirous of beginning these works as early as possible.

I estimate that the repairs such as could be charged to the Lessee would cost about £150.

The further cost of an entirely new roof, new east and south windows and improved floor of tiles would be about £395.

New seats and Rail of oak about £56.

This gave a total of £609.

Surprisingly quickly, only eight days later, on 8 June 1876, a letter was sent to the vicar from the commissioners enclosing a copy of the report and saying that, provided the "late lessee" (i.e. the Bishop of Lichfield and Coventry) would pay for the repairs (£150) and that the restoration of the nave was done simultaneously by the parishioners, the commissioners would be prepared to fund the whole of the work recommended by their surveyor. By 1876 Miss Davies of Penmaendovey had promised a gift of £1000 provided it was matched by other fundraising[16].

A letter from the Ecclesiastical Commissioners in December 1876 said the work on the chancel would be carried out under the superintendence of the architect of their board. A letter in February 1877 said the architect had been instructed to obtain tenders for the work on the chancel. Then, eighteen months later in October 1878, a letter reminded the vicar that the work on the chancel was conditional on the central tower being rebuilt "at the cost of the parishioners or other parties".

A PLAN FOR RESTORATION

For the next two years, letters flew to and from Bangor about the restoration, although unfortunately we have only those that were retained at Bangor[17]. Although the architect's plans are no longer in existence, the specifications from February 1878, as modified in January 1879, have survived, as well as the builder's contract figures and some notes by Titus Lewis[18]. Then as now it must have been common for major building projects to run over budget. The final total after completion came to £4031/18/2d compared to the initial contract sum of £2027/7/0d (of which £609 was to be paid by the Ecclesiastical Commissioners). The specification does refer to the possibility that more work may be required and it would seem that this was indeed the case – although perhaps some of it was cosmetic. For example, there is no description of work on the arches of the crossing in the specification (although it may have been shown on the plans). In his description of the church before the restoration[19] Lewis refers to the west and north arches of the crossing as having the same rude treatment as the arcades and being thought to be of very early first pointed work; yet now all four arches match. He also mentions a "modern window" located over a mutilated Tudor doorway in the south wall of the chancel. The doorway is mentioned in the specifications and costings, but in the end a decision must have been made not to reinstate it when the chancel wall was rebuilt.

From the information available it is possible to reconstruct a picture of the events of these momentous years.

A restoration committee was formed, possibly as early as 1877, with John Prichard, Diocesan Architect of Llandaff, appointed as its professional adviser[20]. He produced drawings and specifications for the repair and restoration of the church, which were accepted by the committee. In addition to the work on the chancel specified by the Ecclesiastical Commissioners and the replacement of the west tower by a central tower, the plans originally included the reinstatement of the fourth bay at the west end of the nave. This had been lost when the west tower was built in 1736. Hope was high that work might be able to start early in the spring of 1877 but this was put back and it was not until spring 1878 that four tenders ranging from £3460 to £4993 were received. In the event the committee decided to award the contract to the second lowest tender of £3964 from Mr Henry Jones of Tywyn who was the only local tenderer. The vicar must have assumed that the granting of the faculty would be a formality and take place quickly, but there were many troubles still in store.

DISSENSION AND ITS SOLUTION

At a vestry meeting held on 18 July 1878, to recommend that the application for faculty should proceed, the first problem arose. A resolution was proposed by Thomas Edwards and seconded by Mr Roberts "that it is not desirable that a faculty should be applied for to carry out the alterations to the church as proposed and shown in the plans and specifications, as they would unnecessarily interfere with the graves of parishioners"[21]. No doubt Titus Lewis had been aware of some discontent at his plans, but this formal opposition may have been a shock. After discussion with the churchwardens, the application for faculty was sent on 2 August quoting what had happened at the vestry, saying that over £3000 had been raised or was promised and asking that, despite the decision of the meeting, a faculty be granted[22].

Thomas Edwards was just as quick off the mark. His solicitors, Lois and Edwards of Ruthin, sent a caveat (a formal notice requesting the postponement of proceedings until their client had been heard) to the diocesan registrar. No doubt Edwards was also rallying support in Tywyn and its environs, where a petition against the work was circulating[23]. In September Lewis wrote to the bishop that the architect might modify the plans in such a way as to conciliate the "aggrieved parishioners".

The content of the petition, with its 303 signatures, is interesting. The petitioners say that, while they "would gladly contribute towards the fitting and proper restoration of their Parish Church, they are extremely adverse to the proposed extension of a building which is already too large for the average congregation, which during the summer months when the services are carried on in English does not exceed 500 and during the rest of the year not more in the morning Welsh service than 30 to 40 and in the evening Welsh service including the choir from 50 to 60". Objections include unnecessary expenditure, doubtful taste and needless harrowing of the feelings of the living by the disturbance of the graves of their departed relatives. It is also maintained that, with proper utilisation of the area, the existing church could hold "not less than 900"!

There could, however, have been a more important reason to modify the plans than the caveat from Thomas Edwards and the petition from some parishioners. Earlier in the year Miss Davies of Penmaendovey had placed the promised £1000 in the hands of her solicitor. When she saw the plans that autumn (perhaps at that vestry meeting), she expressed her disapproval and instructed her solicitor to withdraw the £1000. The architect modified the plans by removing the proposed rebuilding of the fourth bay of the nave. The modified plans were approved by a vestry meeting on 16 January, following which Miss Davies expressed her approval. No doubt influenced by the vestry meeting, Thomas Edwards's solicitors sent off another caveat, although it was later withdrawn.

On 11 January 1879, Lewis wrote again to the bishop, requesting the grant of a faculty. With the letter, he sent the modified plans and specifications, the petition against the work and some financial information. Probably because of the doubt over Miss Davies's gift he had revised the amount available to "upwards of £2000 excluding money promised by the Ecclesiastical Commissioners" and said that he was ready to become responsible for the remainder if necessary. He added that Mr Corbet had promised £200 but had now died and so it was not expected. One wonders if Lewis was afraid that, for some reason, Miss Davies's money would not materialise. Shortly thereafter the plans were handed to Henry Jones, the builder[24].

A delightful letter to the *Aberystwyth Observer* at this time[25], purporting to come from the tenor bell, includes "I will not attempt to describe the fearful sufferings we have endured from the inclemency of the weather in our exposed situation this long winter. One Saturday night a severe frost set in after a heavy rain and wind. The following morning, when the sexton commenced to pull my rope, he was greatly alarmed to hear a crash on to the belfry floor. It was the fall of icicles which had collected during that terrible night on every inch of my shivering frame. We can scarcely hear the vicar on Sundays for the coughing of the congregation, occasioned by the wind whistling down through the belfry door and broken windows of the old church upon their defenceless heads, and the parson has nearly lost his voice in his efforts to make himself heard."

Over the next four months there were increasingly urgent letters from David Howell, solicitor for Miss Davies, to the diocesan registrar asking for a copy of the draft faculty and contract, and pointing out that the church was in danger of losing the £1000 if he did not see it. The matter was eventually solved in mid-May when the bishop himself instructed the registrar to send the draft faculty and contract. Within ten days Howell wrote to say that they were acceptable.

COVERING THE COST

Meanwhile, the chancellor of the diocese was insisting that a bond must be given to cover the whole cost involved. Titus Lewis hoped that David Howell would join him in giving the security required by the chancellor "as Miss Davies's £1000 is in his bank in his name and mine" but both he and Howell wanted to see a draft of the bond.

On 20 August the Church Restoration Committee resolved to carry out the work "provided faculty be granted".

In early September an outline of the application for faculty was sent to the diocesan chancellor, A. J. Stephens, at his chambers in London. At first he believed that the faculty was still contested and said he must go to Bangor to hear it. His misapprehension was corrected but he refused to sign the proposed citation until the plans and specification had been deposited in the registry and the bond and other security had been given for the payment. He also specified that these facts must be entered in the citation.

It would seem that there was then some difficulty over who was prepared to sign the bond for it was not until 5 December that Titus Lewis returned the draft bond to Bangor asking that it be engrossed for signature as soon as possible and saying that David Howell's name should be replaced by that of David Edward Kirkby. The bond had not been returned to Tywyn by 10 January 1880 so an urgent letter went to Bangor requesting that the bond be returned before a restoration committee meeting on 22 January when it would be signed. The letter also asked that the faculty be ready for completion as soon as Bangor received the signed bond. A subsequent letter said "All who were hitherto opposed to the work appear now to be anxious for it to begin at once. It is therefore very important even on that account to avoid, if possible, any delay lest something fresh starts up and they again fall back into the old rut."

The bond, which was for £4000[26], was signed by Titus Lewis, William Parry, one of the churchwardens, and David Edward Kirkby JP of Llanfendigaid. It was returned to Bangor on 24 January accompanied by a letter saying that the contract was ready for execution as soon as the faculty was issued.

Only a week later, the vicar sent another letter to Bangor asking urgently for the faculty, as the contractor was keeping a number of men ready to start the work and it would be a sad disappointment to many if the work could not start some time that week. He may have been optimistic in expecting the faculty to be signed so quickly but it is clear from the wording of the faculty itself that part of the hold-up must have been the death of the chancellor and the time taken to appoint a new one. It was, in fact, not signed until 12 March and even then it was not sent to the vicar, although he received a letter saying it had been signed.

Titus Lewis's letter in reply makes it clear that he had, in fact, allowed the work to start before the faculty was issued, although he had been increasingly anxious as to whether this had been a wise thing to do (pulling down of the church had begun on 11 February)[27].

THE WORK IN PROGRESS

During construction work on the north-east pier of the tower, a vault was opened which revealed a coffin in good condition covered with velvet. The inscription on the coffin was "Edward Corbet, Esq. Died Dec.2[nd,] 1820, Aged 79 years."[28] It is not known whether this vault was subsequently filled in, nor whether any other vaults were found as might have been expected[29]. The ground beneath the church floor was everywhere to be excavated to a depth of 2 feet (60cm), so if there were any other vaults they must have been beneath this level.

The start of the work was not the end of the vicar's worries. Although good progress was reported in mid-1880[30], by April 1881 a long standstill was reported with a mention of plans "not being returned by the architect"[31]. This suggests that problems had arisen which required rethinking of part of the work. It was not until the end of that year that recommencement of the work was reported[32]. By February 1882 the tower was up, "a veritable

The church from the south-east in the late 1880s

The church from the south-west in the late 1880s

Interior 1885 facing east

Interior 1885 facing west

pillar of strength in appearance which with its bold embattlements has a very imposing effect"[33], but there was apparently then another hold-up with "the works, in all the nakedness of their incompletion having been exposed to the inclemency and storms of several winters"[34]. It was only in September 1882 that it was reported that the long lull in the work was about to be broken[35]. Apparently work then went ahead rapidly with new east and west windows being installed at the end of 1883. The reopening service, at which the Lord Bishop of Bangor preached, took place on Easter Tuesday, 15 April 1884[36]. By then gifts towards the refurnishing of the church had included an altar service, the oak lectern, altar cloths and an altar cross, as well as the east and west windows. More was donated in subsequent years.

Throughout the time the church was closed, the large schoolroom of the National School was pressed into service in its place, generally with great success, although sometimes when there were many visitors in the town it was not large enough to accommodate all those wishing to attend. Titus Lewis recorded that "services have been carried on through the greater part of the work".

Other activities impinging on Tywyn were also in train in 1880.

St David's Church in Abergynolwyn had been consecrated in that year and it was proposed that it should be given a separate ecclesiastical district (effectively the basis for a new parish). Abergynolwyn village overlapped the parishes of Llanfihangel-y-Pennant, Talyllyn, Pennal and Tywyn. Part of the argument put forward to support the formation of a new area was that "the Mother Church is 'down' for restoration and Aberdovey is 11 miles off". One wonders why they carefully refrained from mentioning the much closer churches of Llanfihangel-y-Pennant and Talyllyn! In the event, part of the parishes of Tywyn and Talyllyn were transferred to Llanfihangel-y-Pennant, which took over responsibility for Abergynolwyn.

ST MATTHEW'S CHURCH, BRYNCRUG

In the mid-1870s, possibly with the encouragement of Titus Lewis who had been thinking about it since at least 1875[37], Mr W. W. E. Wynne of Peniarth had expressed an interest in building a church in the growing village of Bryncrug, which was on the Peniarth estate but within the Parish of Tywyn. Bryncrug is two miles from St Cadfan's Church and this made it difficult for older people and children to get to the church – although there had been two chapels in the village for many years. By 1876 fundraising was already taking place and in August the following year there was a grand bazaar "under the distinguished patronage of the Marchioness of Londonderry, Lady Williams Wynne and Lady Harlech". It took place over three days in the (old) Market Hall in front of which a pavilion had been erected. There were all the usual stalls and refreshments which are still so well known and nearly £200 was raised.

Mr W. W. E. Wynne had promised a site for the church. On his recommendation, Edmond Ferrey of London, who had worked on the 1876 restoration of Llanegryn Church, had been appointed architect and the plans had been approved before Wynne's death early in 1880. It was resolved that the proposed church be erected as the Wynne Memorial Chapel. The promised site was given by his son and additional funds were donated by family and friends. The foundation stone was laid on 26 September 1881 and the Church of St Matthew was consecrated on Tuesday 12 September 1882 at a total cost of £1584/12/2d including gifts[38]. All this was taking place in addition to the work being undertaken at St Cadfan's Church!

So now the Vicar of Tywyn had two churches to look after – though the Ecclesiastical Commissioners' earlier promise of a grant for a curate enabled one to be appointed. The bishop's returns for 1884[39] show that Tywyn Church had services at 11am and 6pm with Holy Communion held weekly (possibly after the morning service, as was customary at that time), the total number in the congregation varying from 100 to 200 and the total number of communicants as forty-seven (an average of ten a week). Bryncrug services were at 10am and 6pm but no other details are given except that there were only four communicants (perhaps the story that travelling to Tywyn was too difficult had been only an excuse). For comparison, attendances at the other churches were Pennal eighty-seven, Talyllyn forty, Aberdyfi English service 100, Welsh service 120, Llanfihangel y Pennant fifteen and Abergynolwyn sixty-five.

Plygain remained a unifying service for the community. "At the bidding of those ancient bells, ere the glimmerings of the dawn appear over the mountain tops… people sink their differences and flock to St Cadfan's Church, the same as their fathers and ancestors did for untold generations."[40] And "the old church was filled by all sorts of people who in ordinary religious matters differ most widely. All meet this one day, for this one purpose, the Conformist and the Non-Conformist, the sceptic and the devout were there together and there appeared on earth peace, goodwill to all men"[41].

A NEW ORGAN

The small organ on the south wall of the chancel had had, of necessity, to be moved while that wall was rebuilt and had been resited under the south arch of the crossing. Even though it was now closer to the congregation it was clearly inadequate either for range of notes or for volume. The vicar's wife and stepdaughter made themselves responsible for raising £365 for a new double manual organ which was placed under the arch leading to the north transept[42]. The organ was still pumped by hand[43] as was usual at that time. It was built by Messrs Ingram & Co to specifications approved by the organist of Bangor Cathedral. The organ was "opened" on 20 October 1897 at the morning harvest thanksgiving service, which was followed in the afternoon by a recital by the organist of Bangor Cathedral.

In 1901 the curate, Richard Davies, left to become vicar of Llanerchymedd on Anglesey and the bishop appointed David Pugh as stipendiary curate in his place.

14. THE TOWYN-ON-SEA AND MERIONETH COUNTY TIMES

In the late 1890s the *Towyn-on-Sea and Merioneth County Times* came into existence[1]. Its remit widened over the ten years it was published and events related to the church appeared in it regularly, as did reports of the meetings of the Tywyn and Aberdyfi Urban District Council, local events and lists of those spending all or part of the summer in Tywyn.

The effect of summer holidays on church attendance is noted; for example on 9 August 1897, "the English services at St Cadfan's Church are most popular. The attendance on Sunday morning was exceptionally large, the church being uncomfortably full, several being unable to obtain admission. Benches were conveyed from the Assembly Rooms and never before was the church so well filled."[2] However, the comments were not always so kindly. In August 1899 the church was "full to overflowing" with the comment that the wardens should secure additional seating in advance and fill up the transepts first – "it would also be the proper thing if some prayer books were ordered and handed to the visitors for their use during the service". In August 1901, "the parish church was overcrowded with many people failing to obtain sitting accommodation. The question of adequate religious provision for visitors without encroaching on the rights of parishioners is a delicate one which grows more acute each year."[3]

Plygain continued to be celebrated, although sometimes just referred to as the early, or 6am, service; the report on

20 December 1897 even included a list of carols and who sang each of them. However, in 1898, Christmas Day fell on a Sunday and as a result there was no Plygain. "In the evening service several carols were sung. Instead of a sermon the vicar catechised the children on the incidents in connection with the birth of Christ. The church was tastefully decorated."

One concern of the Tywyn and Aberdyfi Urban District Council was the narrowness of College Green, especially in the area from the Market Hall to Corbett Square where it was not much more than an old narrow track going past the churchyard wall. In February 1898[4] the surveyor reported to the council that the vicar would consent to the churchyard wall being pulled down and set back, provided the council would obtain a faculty for the purpose and defray costs. On no condition, however, could soil be removed from the churchyard. This desire to widen the road, and the need to obtain a faculty, would be ongoing for many years, with a faculty finally being obtained and the work carried out in 1908.

The restoration work of 1880-4 had concentrated on the chancel, transepts and tower. Titus Lewis must have been only too aware of the gusts of cold air entering the church every time the door was opened, whether or not they were ameliorated by the red curtain across the doorway remembered by some parishioners. In 1899 he expressed an intention to erect a porch[5], presumably to help with this problem, and this intention was repeated eighteen months later. However, nothing came of it at the time; Lewis was now in his mid-seventies and may not have felt up to the strain of raising money, negotiating with an architect and seeking a faculty.

A bathing fatality in August 1899[6] gave rise to a leader in the paper commenting that "There was a time when bodies were laid awaiting inquest inside the tower of the old Parish Church but the erection of the centre tower did away with this." Old pictures of the church seem to show that the main entrance then was by a west door under the tower; what must it have been like if there was a body laid there?

Related to bathing, a letter was received by the council in summer 1900 from "a family man" saying that he would not have booked to come to Tywyn if he had realised that mixed bathing was prohibited. The council hastily put up notices on the beach allowing mixed bathing for families. This, however, was not deemed to be satisfactory as it was pointed out that ladies who were not with a family might prefer men to be close at hand when they were bathing, in case they got into difficulties. Eventually it was decided to allow mixed bathing for all in certain areas of the beach and the clerk was instructed to amend the by-laws accordingly[7].

Little by little the services in the church were being adjusted to encourage wider participation. Lessons were occasionally read by a layman – "a timely assistance to the vicar"[8] – and in May[9] "the bishop decided to take the confirmation service in Welsh and English, a most satisfactory arrangement in parishes where both languages are spoken".

Music in any church is heavily dependent on the organist/choirmaster. In October 1899 it was reported that Mr Owen, head of the National School, would also be organist and choir trainer of the parish church. In November it was said that, since his advent, the rendering of sacred music had greatly improved[10]. Despite those words of praise, there was a complaint in April 1900[11] that "there was no choral celebration at Easter" and that "the congregation are kept in ignorance of the existence of musical productions which are superior to 9/10ths of the so-called popular productions of the day". This criticism may have been taken to heart, for later that year[12] it was reported that "Mr Tookey, the new schoolmaster, has already succeeded in improving the music at the church. Church people have been complaining, and not without cause, that the services are not so hearty as they used to be. It is to be hoped that the unremitting attention which Mr Tookey promises to give the choir will bear good fruit."

Titus Lewis's wife died on 30 August 1900. On the day of her funeral the mourners attended Holy Communion at 8am. The funeral itself was attended by almost all the townspeople. The bishop read the lesson and the bearers were the churchwardens of St Cadfan's Church, sidesmen of St Matthew's Church and "male communicants of the church"[13]. Her daughter, Mary, had died earlier so Titus Lewis, at the age of seventy-four, was once more alone.

During this time new choir stalls of solid oak for the chancel were made by a local firm, Messrs Jones, Hughes and Edwards[14]. Then, in May 1902, the firm made twenty-two new pitch pine pews for the nave to match existing pews in the transepts, the work being paid for by a generous donor. There were no further reports of complaints about a lack of seating for summer services, although the next year[15] there was a letter complaining that "some officers and men of the various Welsh battalions" attended St Cadfan's on Sunday night for the Welsh service and "no-one stirred from their places" and there was no offer of hymn or prayer books and no welcome!

The vicar himself was no stranger to controversy, perhaps because of his increasing age and also because, after his wife's death, he had nobody at home with whom he could talk things through. In April 1900[16] he was reported to have preached against football, especially the behaviour of onlookers, and also against playing in Lent. Two years later, at a meeting to discuss a children's tea party as part of the celebrations for the coronation of King Edward VII, "the Rev. Titus Lewis gave utterance to the statement that 'all non-conformist children were the children of the wicked one' and, rather than withdraw the remark or offer an apology to the non-conformist ladies present, he left the room"[17]. This was the subject of the first leader in the paper that week. It referred to "a spirit of intolerance of the narrowest and most bigoted kind" and that the use of "such language as that ascribed to Mr Lewis is contemptible". Nothing further on the subject appeared and the remarks do not seem to have worried the non-conformists unduly, for the Plygain at the end of the year was well attended.

The following year[18] the editorial reported that the vicar had made known that he regarded the refusal of a licence to allow the railway refreshment room to serve alcoholic liquor was placing the town under a disadvantage. The editor agreed with him, saying that Tywyn people could not expect the assistance of the Railway Company in developing the town unless it was given proper and reasonable facilities for providing for the comfort of travellers. But the Plygain that year was poorly attended, with non-conformist singers being notable by their absence. Clearly the vicar's support for the sale of alcohol was considered more offensive than his comments about non-conformist children the previous year!

"An Ecclesiastical Strike"[19] – such was the headline to a report in the paper in early 1904. "On Quinquagesima Sunday the usual English morning service at St Cadfan's Church had to be conducted minus the organ. The ghost had not run away with the organist but with the blowers. Two boys were generally engaged to do the work of forcing air into the bellows, the work being too hard for one, but recently the pneumatic part of the organ had been put in a better order and eased, so that one boy can now do the work of two. Hence the strike, not one could be persuaded on this particular Sunday to blow." The accounts for 1906-7 show that, at that time, the organ blower received £2 a year, or just over 9d (3.5p) a week. Was the strike because the one boy pumping was only receiving his old rate and not the double rate he expected for doing two boys' work?

In 1904 the Welsh revival began seeking to kindle non-denominational, non-sectarian spirituality in South Wales. It was widely reported in the *Western Mail* and the *South Wales Daily News*, and the revival spread into North Wales about the turn of the year. The effects were also felt in Tywyn. For "we understand that last Sunday week over 20 young people who had been brought under the influence of the revival voluntarily attended the Established Church Sunday school and asked the vicar to hold special services in the church. A service was held on Wednesday evening conducted by the vicar and curate. The Litany was said and appropriate hymns were sung; also a suitable and practicable address was given by the vicar which was much appreciated by those present."[20]

It was in the final few editions of the paper that the resignation of Titus Lewis as Vicar of Tywyn was announced with an account (not entirely accurate) given of his work. Details were given of a meeting to discuss a presentation to him. When it was decided to make a presentation, the vicar had suggested that this might be in the form of a new communion table and perhaps a reredos for St Cadfan's Church. Finally, the paper ran a brief account of the last morning and evening services at which he "preached his farewell sermon as vicar of St Cadfan's Church which he has served for upwards of 44 years"[21].

15. DAVID PUGH

The Rev. David Pugh, curate at St Cadfan's Church since 1901, was appointed as vicar in 1906. Titus Lewis's time had been one of expansion and renewal. David Pugh's was to be one of enhancement, defence and retrenchment.

NEIGHBOUR PROBLEMS

David Pugh's incumbency began in a most unusual way[1]. On Gwalia Road, adjacent to the north boundary of the churchyard, stands the Cadvan Arms. This is now just a house but at that time it was a public house owned by the City Brewery Company of Lichfield. The churchyard boundary on that side was of unmortared stone in a bad state of repair. It ran alongside the house, about 6 feet from the then house wall, and for the length of its garden. At some time, an existing pigsty behind the Cadvan Arms had been extended along the side between the building and the churchyard boundary. In one place the pigsty even encroached on to the churchyard. The relatives of some of those buried in graves close to the sty had complained for some time and had even approached the ecclesiastical authorities on the matter.

David Pugh wrote to the brewery proposing to rebuild the wall in mortared stone on the churchyard side of the boundary so it would go through the site of the sty. He offered to have a new sty built on the opposite side of the

Cadvan Arms garden to the same measurements and style as the existing one. He had checked that the local authorities would approve.

At first all seemed to be well, with agreement by the directors of the brewery, but there were objections from the owner of the house to the north of the Cadvan Arms, who did not want the pigsty built adjacent to his garden. It was then proposed to rebuild the wall and site the pigsty near it but not between the house and the churchyard. It would seem the work had not started[2] when, in June 1907, builders started to lay foundations for an extension to the Cadvan Arms actually within the churchyard boundary. An urgent letter went to the brewery from the vicar stating what was happening and saying that "As custodian for the time being of this churchyard it is my imperative duty to safeguard the boundary of God's Acre." The work was put on hold while discussions took place. Unfortunately, there are no further letters to explain what happened. It must have been agreed that the wall built by the brewery as part of an extension to the Cadvan Arms was also to act as the churchyard wall, with the churchyard coming right up to it, while the church was to rebuild the rest of the wall and build a new pigsty. The saga does not finally seem to have come to an end until late 1908 when no doubt everyone breathed a sigh of relief – including the pig.

PAROCHIALIA

Meanwhile, during his first year, the vicar completed a new terrier (inventory) covering all physical and financial aspects of both church and vicarage. He was also required to complete "preliminary questions" for the Royal Commission on Religious Bodies in Wales and Monmouthshire, which required current attendance figures and finances together with details of voluntary contributions for different purposes as far back as 1873. Notes show that Pugh had difficulty in getting the necessary information from his predecessor, who probably thought he would be free of the responsibility for providing such detail now he was retired!

Perhaps it was this difficulty that encouraged Pugh to produce a yearly printed Parochialia[3] from 1907. Each year's Parochialia began with the names of clergy and other officials of the church, a report from the vicar and a list of gifts given during the year. It contained statements of account for the church and the Sunday school, and increasingly for other activities. Where a special appeal had been made (such as one in 1906-7 for new cassocks and surplices for the choir) there was a list of subscribers and the amount each had given. At that particular time there were two curates: one paid by the grant from the Ecclesiastical Commissioners, the other from parish funds. In some years subscriptions to a clergy fund are recorded: 1907 – £30/5/6d, 1908 – £19/14/6d, 1910 – £174/16/3d (thanks to one donation of £80 from W. Kettle).

Over time, the Parochialia reflected many aspects of church activity, and its problems, some of which are still relevant today:

- The state of the churchyard? 1907-8 shows "Cutting hay and labour in churchyard £1/15/6d" and "Received for hay on churchyard £1/10/0d". Future years also dealt with the need for "better keeping of the Churchyard".

- Children in church? 1908-9 appeals for every boy and girl under fifteen to attend the 10am Sunday children's service.
- Money? 1909-10 "My wardens and I reiterate the appeal of previous years for more liberal offerings on the part of habitual worshippers..."
- Work needed on the church? 1908-9 mentions the need for better ventilation, lighting and heating (a heating, ventilating and lighting fund was set up). Better drainage from the foundations of the church walls was also needed (was the drainage installed in 1880-4 inadequate or had the ditches between walls and grounds been filled in?).

WIDENING THE ROAD

The continuing saga of the widening of College Green (referred to by the vicar as "the main street of the town"[4]) came to its conclusion with the granting of a faculty to the Urban District Council of Tywyn (UDC) in September 1908[5]. The council agreed to bear the cost of removing all bodies in the affected area and reburying them in another portion of the churchyard. They also agreed to rebuild the section of wall affected and to give £10 to the church towards the erection of a new lychgate. The land was, however, to remain the property of the church and would revert to it if, at any time, it should fall into disuse.

There is an interesting letter from the chancellor of the diocese to the registrar[6] on the subject:

You are most correct and provident to keep as clear of the parties as possible in this case and I venture to advise, or even to enjoin, you to maintain that attitude with the utmost care. Let us remember nothing officially, except that you are registrar and I am judge in this matter. It would almost amuse me, but for the subject matter, to notice the casual way in which the UDC tell of bearing the expense of the removal of bodies for, as to the exhumation, of course difficulties and conflicts of jurisdiction are extremely likely to arise. However let us by all means wait until they do.

It would, however, seem that the work proceeded smoothly. The lychgate was replaced by one designed by the architect Harold Hughes and a dilapidated bier house alongside the old lychgate was demolished[7]. At the same time, the church repaired the remaining walls as necessary. The £10 given by the UDC towards the new lychgate only covered a small part of the cost. The clergy collected subscriptions of £127/7/8d; another £16/8/8d was raised by a concert organised by Miss Cave-Browne-Cave and £8/12/1d was left over from the choir supper fund! Although the cost of the lychgate had been covered and collections were up by £24, there was still a deficit of £31/19/1d at the end of the year.

LIGHTING AND HEATING

The church was lit by gas flame, taller and wider than a candle flame. This was better than candlelight but still not very strong. It was possible to get a much better light by converting the gas outlet to take an incandescent mantle. In 1907 two incandescent lights were given for the chancel by "Messers Davies and Sons", possibly a local firm. They may even have been given as samples, in hopes that the church would want to install them everywhere. Certainly a great improvement was noted in the chancel and, over the years, money was raised for further incandescent lights. The work was completed by 1910-11. The improved efficiency is clearly shown by the reduction in the gas bill – from £9/2/8d in 1906 down to £7/0/6d in 1913.

Heating the church[8] would have been a greater problem than lighting it and architect Harold Hughes was employed once more. A "heating chamber" (boiler room) was built in the corner between the north transept and north aisle with a coal boiler and plenty of room to store coal. Radiators were installed in the nave, side aisles and transepts, although apparently not in the chancel. There was some concern that warm air standing in the church might lead to rot so ventilation shafts were put under the transept and west windows and through the roof of the crossing to the bell chamber. To reduce draughts, new red curtains were hung inside the main door. By 1912, the church must have felt much warmer, although it would still have been cold by 21st century standards. The funds for this improvement had been the particular care of the ladies of the congregation who had solicited donations, run a "Forest of Trees" which raised a net sum of £50 (out of the £200 gross) and organised other activities. Over the years there were frequent thanks to the ladies for the amounts they raised.

CHURCH IMPROVEMENTS

As successor to Titus Lewis, and having been his curate for five years, David Pugh would have been very aware of the historical importance of the church. He had a desire to see it furnished as it should be. One of Titus Lewis's wishes had been that a reredos should replace the curtain that hung behind the altar under the east window. The money for one was donated in 1908. Subsequently, panels were extended to the sides of the church, then to the altar rails and finally down each side of the chancel. Each stage was funded by a donation, often from a family in memory of a deceased relative.

Although the organ had only been installed in 1897, it was moved in 1911 to the south transept where it was rebuilt and upgraded with a new case[9] all of which was paid for by William Kettle, second son of Rupert Kettle. His younger brother, Alfred, was a missionary in South Africa where he died in 1900 and it is said that the organ was a memorial to him, although there is no record of this. The "hydraulics" of the new organ meant that the church now had to pay an annual water rate in the region of £4.

While he was involved with all this development work and the proper running of the parish and its two churches, the vicar also had other worries. The enquiries for the Royal Commission at the start of his incumbency were just a preliminary to the disestablishment of the Church in Wales (see next chapter). In addition, there were major difficulties regarding the church school (see Appendix D).

The Rev. Titus Lewis had died on 27 June 1912 and was to have been buried in the grave holding his wife and stepdaughter. The parishioners, however, wanted a suitable memorial to the man who had done so much for the church for more than forty years. They proposed that he be buried where the paths from the lychgate and the side gate met, opposite the main door of the church. A faculty was sought to move the coffins of his wife and stepdaughter to this new site so that the three bodies would be together. Lewis's executrix opposed this but eventually she withdrew her objection and the faculty was granted in March 1914.

WAR, DEATH AND REMEMBRANCE

In the summer of 1914 tension was rising in Europe. Although a resurgence of imperialism on the part of some nations was an underlying factor, the immediate trigger was the assassination, at the end of June, of Archduke Franz Ferdinand, the heir to the throne of Austro-Hungary. As the church financial year ran to the end of March, it is possible that the Parochialia had not even been prepared by the time war broke out. If it had, then all copies were lost and it did not reappear until 1926. As the young men went to war as volunteers or conscripts, the workload increasingly fell on the women and the older men who remained. Tywyn Parish was still heavily dependent on agriculture and there soon was little time, or money, or heart, for producing church paperwork, as families lost sons, brothers, fathers, or they returned crippled by wounds.

In November 1918 an appeal went out to the parishioners of Tywyn suggesting that a porch to the western entrance[10] of the church be erected as a memorial to those who had died. A public meeting was held shortly after the Declaration of Peace to consider this and other suggestions. The vicar must have approached Harold Hughes immediately after the armistice for, by February 1919, he had produced plans and specifications for the porch and by May the faculty had been granted[11]. Hughes approached three companies, one in Birmingham and two in London, to quote for the marble slabs for the inscriptions, and clearly thought that one of them should be chosen. Perhaps rather late in the day an approach was made to a local firm, Roberts & Jones of Tywyn, who quoted £62/10/0d for four black marble slabs with two white slabs inlaid into each. Fixing and cutting the letters would be extra (letters 5/0d per dozen) while R. R. Davies of the Idris Monumental Works, Tywyn, quoted £250 for the porch itself.

In the event, the building and the marble tablets with their inscriptions were all undertaken by R. R. Davies as contractor, while he and two fellow workers – ex-servicemen – chiselled the inscriptions "for many succeeding generations". The amount required was collected from 435 individuals, couples and families, with the gifts varying from 3d to £25, most being for less than 10 shillings. There were also contributions from St Cadfan's Women's Guild for the porch lantern, which showed some of the tools of war. The total cost of the work was £394/8/6d and the porch was dedicated on 17 October 1920.

In addition to the porch, the town of Tywyn also built the Memorial Hospital as a practical remembrance of those who had died.

THE COST OF A CURATE

In 1914 it would seem that the parish was having difficulty in paying for a curate, even though £153 had been collected for the clergy fund in the previous year. David Pugh had written to the bishop in June asking if it would be possible for a lay reader to take the services at St Matthew's Church, Bryncrug. The reply that it was only allowable if the church had not been consecrated (which, of course, it had been in 1882) did not solve the problem. Pugh also wrote to the Ecclesiastical Commissioners about the terms of the grant for a curate, which had been promised in 1883 – when Titus Lewis had requested it in anticipation of the opening of St Matthew's. The commissioners replied that the grant had been made to Tywyn Parish and not to, or on account of, Bryncrug. This meant the grant was still valid even if the church had only the one curate who did not concentrate solely on Bryncrug.

In 1920, the Church in Wales was disestablished and the financial situation of both the central organisation and the parishes changed.

In 1924 the vicar and churchwardens were shocked to receive a schedule from the Bangor Diocesan Board of Finance informing them that the curate's grant to Tywyn was to be reduced to £66/13/4d from £120 – a near halving of the grant.

An urgent letter was sent from the churchwardens to the secretary of the Representative Body (RB) appealing against this action. The letter pointed out that the grant of £120 had been given in 1883[12], that the capital sum to provide it had been transferred to the RB after disestablishment and that the RB had continued to pay £120 annually to Tywyn with the proviso that the church found an extra £80 a year to make the curate's stipend £200 in total. Although it had been difficult, the church had managed to raise the extra £80 each year. If the cut in grant was not reversed, the church would be forced to dismiss the curate and close St Matthew's

Church as it would not be possible to raise the additional money needed. The vicar wrote in similar terms to the Diocesan Board of Finance. The RB's response was that, following disestablishment, all grants from the Ecclesiastical Commissioners had stopped. The RB had allocated a number of portions of £66/13/4d for curates to each diocese and it was for each diocese to decide how to distribute the money. The Diocesan Board of Finance was slightly more helpful, offering an extra £54 from the Church Extension Committee to make up the difference.

However, in 1927 it would seem that this extra £54 grant was withdrawn despite the vicar's vociferous objections. The Bishop of Bangor himself wrote twice to the vicar agreeing with Tywyn's original argument but reiterating the changes which had occurred following disestablishment – and pointing out that money passed to the RB from the Ecclesiastical Commissioners was not ring-fenced. Money from the Church Extension Committee was intended for poor and working class parishes. They would make a grant of £40 for 1927-8 but there would be further reductions in future. The Parochialias show that the curate, Daniel Evans Davies, was maintained until early 1930 when he became incumbent at Bryncoedifor. Thereafter, there was usually no curate at Tywyn, as the vicar had predicted in the 1928-9 Parochialia.

CHURCH FINANCES

It was not until 1924 that printed lists of the church finances reappeared with the balance sheet and list of subscribers for the year 1922-3. A note at the beginning stated that: "An appeal was issued last February for a minimum contribution of 5 shillings from each individual member of the congregation to meet the expenses obligatory under the new Constitution of the Church in Wales." The note explained that the parish was required to send £84 a year to the Diocesan Board of Finance, towards paying the vicar's stipend. In addition the parish needed to raise £80 a year to make up the curate's stipend. It ended by saying, "The Towyn Finance Committee are responsible and take this opportunity of repeating their appeal to each member of the congregation of a contribution of the minimum Five Shillings." This contribution was known as the "Freewill Offering" and was needed in addition to the usual church collections, which were used for the running and maintenance of the church.

The list of subscribers shows that, while five people gave only 2/6d, thirty-three gave 5 shillings, twenty-seven gave 10 shillings (but often this was between a husband and wife) and there were increasing amounts up to one contribution of £7. The whole, however, raised only £110/7/0d, to which was added just over £16 from a whist drive, well short of the £164 required to meet the financial commitments.

By 1926, in response to a request by the PCC, the Parochialia had reappeared. An envelope scheme had been introduced for the freewill offering, with the amount given listed by envelope number rather than by name. The total received was £159/10/9d including a £15 contribution from St Matthew's, Bryncrug. There was an additional donation from the Women's Guild. The only outgoings from the freewill offering account were the quota, the curate's stipend and printing costs.

Separate from the information in the freewill account was a receipts and payments account for the church which showed the amounts from collections in church and from donations. Outgoings from this account included insurance, the organist's salary (still £52 as in 1908), repairs, heating etc. There were also separate accounts for the Sunday school and the Band of Hope and for the "Church House Improvements Fund". In 1913 the National School had been closed and was made available for the use of the church; it was now called Church House.

Over the next few years the amounts given to the freewill offering fund via the numbered envelope scheme fell from £159/10/9d to £128 and then down to £116. In 1927, thirty-seven people who had promised to contribute through the scheme gave nothing at all. A further fifty-three who had promised £37 between them only actually gave £4/15/7d. The Women's Guild came to the rescue once more with a donation of £30, in addition to which they raised £70 towards repairs to Church House. It is clear from the accounts and the vicar's comments that many "modern" problems blamed by some on "people not coming to church/not giving etc" have repeatedly occurred in the church's past.

THE VICAR'S HISTORICAL RESEARCH

In April 1920 David Pugh received a letter[13] from the secretary of the Royal Commission on Ancient Monuments in Wales and Monmouthshire to inform him that certain members of the commission proposed to visit the church to examine the "Cadfan Stone". David Pugh was encouraged by his wife to gather together everything that he knew about the stone before they arrived. On studying the stone, he became convinced that, among the larger letters, he could see some of the words of the Lord's Prayer in a form of Welsh. He offered this information to the commissioners on their arrival but it was not included as a possible reading when their report was published. Pugh wrote three articles for *Welsh Outlook* on the subject. Subsequently he put his thoughts into writing and included them, together with drawings of the stone and its inscriptions, as he saw them, in a clearly illustrated notebook. He included cuttings of his articles and letters he had received on the subject. Some gave limited support but others queried his interpretation of the inscriptions. It is clear from his notebook, written mainly in 1921-2 that Pugh was not happy about the lack of support for his reading of the stone.

In January 1923 a professional photographer from Birmingham was specially commissioned to take photographs of the stone on 12 inch x 10 inch plates. Details of what was taken, and copies of the prints obtained, are included at the end of the notebook. Pugh hypothesised that the carvings on the stone included heads of figures and also words but he was clearly disappointed with the responses he received. When he left the parish in 1931 he gave the notebook to Mr H. H. Shuker whose son gave it to the church in 1987.

Pugh's research into the stone sparked within him an interest in the wider history of the church and its previous incumbents. He also asked parishioners to provide him with any information they might have about the church in the past[14].

There was one local tradition that Pugh heard from the church clerk, Mr Hugh Roberts, and many others. It was said that, before Aberdyfi Church was built, worshippers would walk to Tywyn Church on Sundays and on reaching Bryn y Paderau would fall to their knees and say the Lord's Prayer. In 1924 the story was reiterated by the Aberdyfi blacksmith, Mr Edward Jones, whose father (who died in 1876) had been clerk to Tywyn Church for thirty years. Towards the end of his time as clerk, he lived in Aberdyfi and walked to church with his son. Edward was often told how the "old people" used to kneel on that hill and how carriages would stop to allow their occupants to dismount and kneel. This was said to be because the summit of the rise gave the first view of the church. (Pugh never met anyone who could recall this actually happening even a generation or so earlier. It is possible that the tradition recalls the days, hundreds of years before, when pilgrims to Tywyn knelt as they first saw St Cadfan's Church.)

The blacksmith also showed the vicar and his companions what he called a "Bass Viol" which his father used to play regularly at services. It had been made at Llanfaircaereinion and Pugh described it as being like a small violoncello. It is now on display in the church. The blacksmith also had a flute played, he believed, by a Thomas Edwards[15] and this, with the viol, were the only instruments he himself remembered being played in the church.

In 1921, A. I. Pryce, Bangor diocesan registrar, published *The Diocese of Bangor in the Sixteenth Century* based on the old bishop's registers plus the return made to Archbishop Warham in 1504. From this, many incumbents in the diocese, including Pugh, started to compile a list of their predecessors.

Although not mentioned in Pryce's book, Pugh found that John Griffith was presented to the parish church of Tywyn on 3 April 1529[16]. Either he then found mention of a

John Griffith, Vicar of Wandsworth, or he was approached by the Parish of Wandsworth where, apparently, there was a tradition about a link to Tywyn. The Griffith of Wandsworth was attaindered by Henry VIII and subsequently hung, drawn and quartered. Pugh was keen to identify them both as the same person but was discouraged by A. I. Pryce. When Pryce published his second book, *The Diocese of Bangor During Three Centuries*, in 1929, Pugh used it to complete his list of Tywyn incumbents (adding that Griffith was executed). This list was lettered by Ywain G. ap Griffith in May of that year and is on display in the church.

Through all of this, the vicar did not neglect the physical state and furnishings of the two churches in his care. In 1927 a sanctuary chair for the use of the bishop at confirmation services[17] was presented to St Cadfan's Church and additional lighting was provided for the chancel. Over that year and the next, various repairs were carried out in both churches so that the architect, Harold Hughes, could certify to the diocese that repairs were complete and "the buildings now came under the Dilapidations Scheme of the Church in Wales". As reported in the 1929 Parochialia, this work included cleaning the walls of St Cadfan's Church and rewhitening them with "Duresco", "so that its description in the thirteenth century as the white-washed church of Towyn is partly true today"[18]. A churchyard fund was started with a gift of £100, the interest on which was to be used for churchyard maintenance. In addition the organ was completely overhauled – dismantled, cleaned and refurbished as necessary, the work being paid for by the original donor, William Kettle.

Meanwhile a "heating apparatus" (a stove) was installed in St Matthew's Church. The chancellor duly signed the faculty although he thought that the heater would be "unsightly".

For some reason there was no Parochialia in 1930. In the 1931 edition the envelope scheme report provides names (rather than envelope numbers) and amount given. It also names those who had envelopes but gave nothing. This may have been done in an attempt to encourage more generous giving, especially from those whose promises were greater than their gifts. If so, it was counter-productive, for the amount given dropped dramatically the next year, although it subsequently recovered to some extent. But times were hard. Wages and salaries were being reduced and many parishioners were earning far less than the vicar.

In April of that year the councils of the Sunday schools of churches and chapels in the parish organised a pageant to celebrate the 200th anniversary of the founding of circulating schools by the Rev. Griffith Jones (these schools later developed into the Sunday school movement). As might be expected, the church Sunday school was asked to portray the arrival of Cadfan and his monks. The children showed them erecting a stone on a hill which Cadfan blessed and renamed "The Hill of the Lord's Prayer" or "Bryn Paderau".

Towards the end of 1931, David Pugh moved to become Incumbent of Penstrowed, a small parish between Newtown and Caersws, where he had a lighter workload and so could be, effectively, semi-retired.

16. DISESTABLISHMENT[1] (1689-1950)

CHURCH AND CHAPEL

At the beginning of the 18th century the people of Wales were overwhelmingly members of the Church of England. Only 5% of them were Protestant dissenters, mainly living in the English-speaking border areas, while Roman Catholics were even fewer in number. During that century increasing numbers were drawn to non-conformity and no doubt there were some in the Tywyn area at that time – despite Jeremiah Griffith's declaration to the bishop in 1776[2] in his visitation answers. Eglwys Maethlon, a non-conformist chapel in Cwm Maethlon (Happy Valley), opened in 1785. There may have been a chapel in Y Cwrt area of Abergynolwyn towards the end of the 18th century for it was to the Sunday school there that Mary Jones walked from Llanfihangel-y-Pennant each week to learn to read the Bible for herself. (She later saved up for a bible and walked to Bala to buy one. Her actions were one of the triggers for the formation of the Bible Society.)

Under the Toleration Act of 1689, Protestant dissenters were permitted to worship in public provided that their premises were licensed by registration with either quarter sessions or the church authorities. Bangor diocesan records of this licensing start in 1809. The earliest records name meeting houses which were already in use in 1809, while later records cover meeting houses or chapels which had recently opened.

It is possible that Tywyn had a comparatively strong established church tradition. Whereas the village of Llwyngwril[3] (near Llangelynnin) had five non-conformist registrations[4] (for Wesleyans, Independents, Methodist and two Calvinistic Methodists), there are only three registrations for Tywyn itself. In March 1816 there was "a house or schoolroom in the occupation of Vincent Davies" for the "Wesleyans or Methodists", a "new chapel called Bethesda" for Protestant Dissenters (May 1820) and the Independent Saron Chapel (October 1837). In Bryncrug there was a Wesleyan chapel (April 1809) and also "a house in possession of Mr David Davies shopkeeper" for the Protestants (December 1827).

The great Calvinistic Methodist Tabernacle at Aberdyfi pre-dates St Peter's Church, having been registered in April 1829. Its opening may have been an incentive to erect an Anglican church in the rapidly growing coastal community.

The need for registration was modified over time. It was finally discontinued in 1852, so there are no registrations for later chapels in Tywyn. Bethel Chapel displays the date 1871, although its original building was earlier. There is no indication as to when Ebenezer Chapel was built. All these non-conformist chapels were Welsh speaking and, unlike St Cadfan's Church, there seems to have been no provision for English-speaking non-conformists such as the servants of the increasing number of summer visitors. However, in 1893 the Tabernacle in Aberdyfi funded the building of the English Presbyterian Church there, specifically for such people. In Tywyn, Bethany, the English Presbyterian Church, had opened in 1871 and the Baptist Church, which seems to have been mainly English speaking from the start, was built in 1900. Almost all these churches or chapels were built or rebuilt with a large "school-room" or "vestry" attached which provided space for meetings and Sunday school away from the area used for worship – an advantage not available to St Cadfan's Church.

A religious census in 1851 showed that nearly 80% of worshippers in Wales attended non-conformist chapels and that less than 20% attended the Church of England in Wales (but half the population did not attend a place of worship at all). By 1882, out of a total Welsh population of 1½ million, there were 390,000 members of non-conformist chapels with over 460,000 scholars in their Sunday schools. It was also a time of Welsh cultural nationalism and there was a widely held view that the church of a small minority should not be the established church with all the attendant privileges (its clergy entitled to receive tithes from all and its bishops having seats in the House of Lords). The Church of England also tended to be more English in outlook than most of the other denominations and this added to its unpopularity. It was fast becoming a question of when, not whether, disestablishment would occur, but that was a matter for Parliament. A parliamentary motion in 1870 and bills in the 1890s all came to nothing. The matter was raised again in 1906 when the religious revival of 1904-5 had sharpened the enmity between Church and Chapel.

A ROYAL COMMISSION

A Royal Commission[5] was set up to obtain full information on the state of religion in Wales and Monmouthshire over the course of 1906-10. The commission looked at changes which occurred over a period of time. Statistics covering population, number of churches, parsonage houses, resident incumbents and curates, and numbers of Sunday services were collected for 1831 and 1906. Numbers of communicants, baptisms and numbers at Sunday schools and day schools were also elicited. Inquiries were made as to what the money raised by voluntary contributions was spent on. For example, in 1906 St Cadfan's Church spent £120 on clergy (the curate), £69/18/2d on church expenses, £12/5/5d on church societies and home & foreign missions, £5/9/8d on support of the poor and the hospital, £70 on the "Day and Sunday School" building – a total of £277/13/4d (and nothing had been spent that year on maintenance).

The vicar, David Pugh, made notes against the tithe rent charges due to him to show the church or chapel connections of those involved. The results were:

Church/chapel connection	Number paying	Total sum
Church	12	£261/0/6d
Nonconformist	26	£107/15/3d
Other (e.g. Railway)	3	£11/6/0d

In addition to showing that the non-conformists outnumbered church members by more than two to one, this also revealed that the church people, in general, held more land, on average paying nearly £22 each, while the non-conformists paid just over £4 each. Pugh's submission to the commission also showed that, within Tywyn Parish, there were a total of ten non-conformist chapels including three in Bryncrug and one each in Abertrinant and Cwm Maethlon (Happy Valley). Between them they had a total of six resident salaried ministers.

DISESTABLISHMENT AND DISENDOWMENT

After Parliament had considered the commission's report, a disestablishment bill was published. It had its first reading in the House of Commons in 1912 and was eventually passed, receiving the Royal Assent in September 1914. The Welsh Church Act 1914 provided not only for disestablishment with all that implied, it also brought disendowment. Perhaps like Henry VIII, Parliament had seen money – and wanted it; not for themselves, of course, but for the good of the community. Unfortunately, in an age when everything was recorded, it was not possible to 'spirit away' money as had happened for St Cadfan's chantry in 1547[6]. Endowments to the Welsh churches and dioceses that had been made before the Act of Uniformity in 1662 (when, it was considered, they had been made to the national church of the whole population of Wales) were to be expropriated, except for such items as church plate. The expropriated endowments and also all existing tithes of the new Welsh Church were to be divided between the Welsh local authorities and the University of Wales.

With the advent of the Great War the Welsh Church Act was suspended and the church had some opportunity to reduce the financial loss that would have been caused by the expropriations. An Amending Act in 1919 preserved some of the endowments and the Treasury made a grant of £1 million to the Welsh Church Commissioners as a partial re-endowment. Nevertheless, when the Church in Wales became a disestablished church on 31 March 1920 it was estimated that its income had been reduced by £48,000 a year (roughly the amount needed to pay 150 vicars when they no longer had income from tithe rent charges or glebe land). This was despite the fact that the Welsh Church had always been much poorer (proportionally) than the English Church. Of the money from disendowment about £2½ million went to the county and county borough councils and almost £1 million to the University of Wales[7].

This disendowment took place despite protests by members of the Welsh Church in 1912 as well as by many Welsh non-conformists.

Towards the end of 1912, the Vicar of Tywyn and two other clergy collected 488 signatures against disestablishment from church people (out of a total population, including children, of 2211). In 1914, they collected signatures from twenty-six non-conformists and four Roman Catholics objecting to the disendowment. Copies of both lists of signatures were placed in a sealed envelope in the vestry safe.

The vicar appended some observations to a copy of the church people's list as follows:

The age of every person who signed was 15 years and upwards. ALL the signatures were collected by the three clergy of the parish – Rev D R Pugh, Rev R R Roberts and Rev R Parker Jones – who vouch for their correctness.

Many sympathetic nonconformists were unable to subscribe their names because they had been informed that this petition would be 'scrutinised' by the local Member of Parliament – H Haydn Jones Esq – and feared that their business connections would be adversely affected. A few deacons of nonconformist chapels admitted to me that this was the case.

I wish to preserve this record of Parishioners favourable to the Establishment and the continuation of the Endowments of the church and acknowledge its incompleteness. In the midst of the usual Parish duties and with a time limit to obtain the signatures it was impossible to reach even all of our strongest church people.

I consign these papers to the 'safe' in the church vestry, hoping that they will not be disturbed by anybody inimical to the interests of the Church Catholic, for the instruction of generations to come of the state and condition of Towyn Church as it is today.

This 'copy' of the signatures has been made by the Rev R Parker Jones, Rev R R Roberts and Mrs Vaughan the landlady of the Rev R Parker Jones.

These observations signed by D R Pugh vicar Christmas 1912.

Forms for a protest against disendowment by non-conformists, which was to be submitted to the Prime Minister, were circulated in early 1914. They were headed:

A PROTEST
To be signed only by Nonconformists, men and women, over 21 years of age.

We, as Nonconformists resident in the Diocese of Bangor, desire to express our conscientious opposition to proposals to deprive the Church in Wales of her unclosed antient (sic) churchyards and to take away for secular purposes £157,000 of her antient endowments.

The forms for the protest had been accompanied by a letter emphasising that the protest must be signed willingly and that no pressure should be put on anyone to do so. The vicar's note at the end of the copy of this reads:

> 30 Nonconformists including 4 Roman Catholics. No Nonconformists were found willing to ask for signatures to this protest – and Churchmen in most cases were more than reluctant to ask them – vide letter attached from churchwarden – one of our most faithful churchmen.
>
> Many nonconformists strongly object to this measure of Disendowment – but political pressure makes them afraid to sign. D R Pugh, vicar, April 1 1914.

How would disendowment have affected Tywyn? The vicar's income had been made up to £300 per annum by assigning tithe rent charges to the incumbent of the parish on top of the amount received from the vicar's tithes (as recorded in the 1776 terrier) and glebe land (only just over an acre on Tywyn Marsh meadow[8] which brought £3/10/0d rent). All £300 was taken away. Other parishes would have been similarly affected.

With the loss of endowment money, and with so many incumbents losing their income from tithe rent charges, the Church authorities had to find money. An appeal was made across Wales to raise £1 million to provide an income to match that of the lost endowments. However, the difficult conditions of the post-war years meant that, by 1923, it had produced less than two-thirds of the target. Most of the Church's income went to pay clerical stipends, which were now on a standard scale (except for those who had already been in their current post in 1914). Much of the money had to come from an annual contribution from each parish, the dreaded "quota". Small parishes were grouped under one incumbent to save on clerical salaries. Unfortunately, over the course of years the value of the stipend was reduced by inflation. Many clergy, concerned for the well-being of their families, moved to England for better stipends.

17. THE MID-20TH CENTURY[1]

CANON HENRY THOMAS

Canon Henry Thomas came to Tywyn early in 1932, having previously been Incumbent of Llanfihangel Ysgeifiog. A man in his fifties, he came to a parish rather set in its ways after effectively having had only two vicars in sixty-five years. Thomas revived regular Welsh services in the church, being helped in this by a gift of Welsh prayer books and hymn books. One of his earliest actions was to approach the Representative Body about a grant for a curate. The RB agreed to pay 50% of the annual cost, enabling a new curate to start in September 1933, but the parish needed to find £100 a year towards his stipend.

Although the freewill offering fund had been in credit in 1932, the coming of the curate left it in arrears the next year. Thomas followed his predecessor in appealing for more generous giving. He pointed out that the combination of quota and curate's stipend contribution needed an average of 16/- per head per year from those on the electoral roll. Despite this, the churchwardens' account (church collections etc.) found the money to carry out restoration work on St Matthew's Church at a cost of over £50.

BUILDINGS AND FABRIC MAINTENANCE

The "long-lasting" Duresco paint applied to the church walls in 1928-9 cannot have lived up to its name, as in late 1932 a sum of £33/10/- was spent on whitewashing the interior of the church. It was also necessary to improve the drainage and carry out other repairs. Work was done on the fabric and grounds of Church House; in addition its lighting was improved and a piano purchased, both through voluntary efforts. Church House became the venue for a new literary class, which ran for a number of years with such activities as lectures, lantern slides and competitive meetings.

Since the early 19th century the Cadfan Stone had been lying in the north aisle of the church, despite a suggestion in 1903[2] that it should be erected inside the church. It was at last erected there in 1934 "in remembrance of long association with Towyn" by grandchildren of Rupert Kettle.

At the same time, it was reported that considerable work was needed on the tower[3] (which was probably letting in the damp). This included repointing the south and west faces of the tower and all four faces of the battlements, repairing decayed stonework of the tower windows and rendering the inside of the belfry. An important modification to keep the tower dry was the fitting of louvre windows to the belfry. Although the belfry floor was lead-lined, the totally unprotected openings were a major source of damp when the rain blew in.

An appeal for £300 for this work raised £347 over two years, enabling extra work to be done on the fabric of the building. This included work on the south-east corner of the vestry where it joins the chancel (an area still giving problems), fitting a lightning conductor, refurbishing the weather vane, repairing some cracks in the nave, and plugging between the oak rafters and the walls of the nave.

Meanwhile the amenities in Church House had been enhanced by the installation of an inside lavatory and

"Cloke room", the enlargement of the kitchen and by making the roof waterproof, all of which was funded by the Women's Guild. At the same time electric light was installed in the vicarage.

The next year saw electric light in Church House "thanks to the generosity of Mrs Kettle" and the Parochial Church Council approved its installation in the church. The work was completed in 1937-8, the actual cost being £217, of which £20 had been given by the Women's Guild. They were also staunch supporters of the freewill offering fund, giving sums of between £20 and £60 most years from 1925 to 1959.

Before every annual bishop's visitation a series of questions had to be answered by the incumbent. Answers in early 1939 showed that the church was in good repair but that water was entering the tower, which was "now being repaired" (was this a continuation of the 1935 work or were there new problems?). The church was insured for £20,500 (but not for third party risks) and money for church expenses was raised by the church collections. There were just over 200 on the electoral roll for St Cadfan's Church and another forty for St Matthew's, Bryncrug.

THE SECOND WORLD WAR

Troubled times lay ahead with the outbreak of the Second World War but, at first, work on the church continued as usual. In 1939-40, repairs were carried out to the tower and roof at a cost of £31/16/4d and granite slabs were laid either side of the path from the lychgate to the porch. It was also necessary to spend £31 to provide blackout. The curate left in late 1939 and it was six months before his replacement was appointed. This delay in curacy cover did have the advantage, however, of leaving the freewill offering fund in the black, since nothing was needed towards the curate's stipend for that period. Sincere thanks were proffered in the Parochialia to the licensed lay reader, Mr H. H. Thompson, who had conducted the evening services at Bryncrug throughout the time that there was no curate.

The following year saw Church House requisitioned for war purposes – perhaps that indoor lavatory had been a mistake! This meant that the Women's Guild could no longer function in its accustomed way and it had to hire the Tywyn Institute for meetings. Church House became an annexe to the hospital and the rent of £104, in theory paid quarterly, had to cover the cost to church funds of the lighting, cleaning and repairing of Church House while it was being leased out.

In the church itself, solid oak panelling was installed on the walls of the baptistry. The vicar's letter in the Parochialia mentioned once more the need for regular giving to the freewill offering fund in addition to collections in church. He congratulated St Matthew's Church for raising 50% more than their expected amount towards this fund. Their contributions were to remain at this high level for several years to come.

In 1941-2, with the wartime shortage of labour and materials, it was only possible to undertake urgent repairs to the buildings. Nevertheless, work carried out on the organ was little less than a revolution. The hydraulic engine which provided the air to the organ had required someone pumping by hand the whole time to keep the bellows full. Now it was replaced by a new electric blower – and so a source of pocket money for one or more boys of the parish disappeared.

Mr Thompson, the lay reader, had been assisting in various ways throughout this period. With the departure of the curate to be curate-in-charge of Tyddyn Gwyn, Ffestiniog, Thompson helped to ensure that services continued at both churches.

The 1942 bishop's visitation is very interesting. At the time, people were enjoined not to say or discuss anything which might be of value to enemy agents – "Walls have ears" and "Be like Dad – keep mum". It seems that anyone really interested in troop movements would only have to look at some visitation returns. Under notes on the effects of the war the vicar wrote, "There is an aerodrome situated in the parish with about 400-450 men in training. No spiritual provision seems to have been made for these men. A few of them attend the services of the Church more especially Evensong on Sundays. There is an anti-aircraft Training Camp in the parish. A military service conducted by a Military Chaplain is held in the parish church at 9.30 am."

At the beginning of 1944 the quota was raised by 25% throughout the Church in Wales. This meant that Tywyn (with Bryncrug) now had to find £125 instead of £100. The increase was to enable the province to raise the stipends of clergy in the smaller livings and to provide bonuses for clergy with children under eighteen years of age. This was very important, as many Church in Wales clergy had moved to England where the stipends were noticeably higher. Most young people went straight into work at fourteen, the school-leaving age. The bonus for children up to the age of eighteen recognised that clergy intended that their children would have more than an elementary education.

Towards the end of the war, tax law was altered in respect of fixed sums formally covenanted to the church for seven successive years. Where an individual covenanted money in this way, the income tax that he or she had paid to the Inland Revenue was transferred over to the church. With many people paying 10 shillings in the pound (50%) income tax, this meant their contributions were effectively doubled. Nine families immediately signed up to this long-term commitment and the additional income helped to swell the freewill offering fund[4]. Over the next few years, the fund was also boosted by the income from several legacies left for the purpose.

Finally, the war was over and the church counted the cost. The vicar listed the "church boys" who had been killed: Robert Graham Roberts, Archibald Dudley Middleton, William John Jarman, David Anderson Edwards, Thomas Challoner and John Cuthbert Stivey. A plaque was mounted within the porch as a memorial to everyone from the parish who had lost his life in the war – although it was not unveiled and dedicated until August 1948. The cost of the plaque was more than covered by generous donations from across the parish. There was a small surplus of just over £50, which was invested in a 2½% war loan, the income from which provided an annual wreath for Remembrance Sunday for many years. In early 1949, the two banners of the British Legion (Men's and Women's Sections) were dedicated and laid up in St Cadfan's Church.

POST-WAR PROBLEMS

The end of the war brought new problems. The country was struggling to get back on its feet and pay off the enormous debts incurred by the war. At Easter 1947 the vicar reported

"The year 1946/47 will go down in the annals of history as the most disappointing in many respects, and the grimmest perhaps so far as climatic conditions are concerned, ever experienced in Britain or in Europe. A disastrous harvest and intensely cold winter, culminating in a destructive blizzard and still more destructive floods in many parts of the country brought their heavy toll of loss and suffering. They took a heavy toll also from church congregations. Even the faithful were not able to attend Divine Service by reason of the snow and intense cold and the shortage of fuel made it impossible to heat the church adequately."

The harvest disaster resulted in the introduction of the rationing of bread, which had not been rationed throughout the war. The very cold winter led to the loss of many stored potatoes and, as a result, potato rationing was also introduced. On a brighter note, in the midst of this gloom a branch of the Girls Friendly Society (GFS) was founded in Tywyn under the direction of Mrs D. B. (Hilda) James.

By late 1949, manpower and materials slowly became available and the interior walls of the church were cleaned and rewhitened "after a period of 20 years". The £114 cost was met by the Women's Guild.

THE SUNDAY SCHOOL

Michael Edwards describes some of his earliest memories of the church in the late 1940s: "The Sunday School met in the south transept and the service, taken by the vicar, lasted about an hour starting at 2 o'clock. My collection was usually a silver threepenny piece with a cross on one side. A number of children attended the service including some of the school boarders from Brynarfor and Trefeddyg. As Christmas approached, attendance rose so that children could attend the annual Christmas party in Church House. Towards the end of the school year the vicar usually took all the children to the top of the tower and brought them safely back down. We used to look forward to this – there was no Health and Safety in those days! At the age of eleven I joined the choir of about 4 men and 6 boys. The choir stalls were in the chancel then and the boys sat in the front row. When I was 14 I was honoured to be asked to be the first to carry the processional cross given in memory of Dr Alban Davies by his wife. As one processed along the side aisles one had to lower the cross otherwise it would make a dreadful clang if it hit any arches."

After the war, the vicar had welcomed the return of the young people and expressed the hope that they would once more enter fully into the fellowship and service of the church. This hope does not seem to have been fulfilled by either the young or some of the older people. The vicar's 1949 report includes the comment "a large number of Church people are very indifferent and irregular in their attendance at Divine Service" and "We would be glad to see our young Communicants forming the definite habit of attending the early celebration of Holy Communion at least once a month… And not relegate that primary Service of the church to the dim background of their religious life." The next year he commented that "the church has always maintained the noble traditions of Sunday **morning** worship… in grave danger of being abandoned for the less estimable practice of Sunday **evening** worship".

Inadequate maintenance throughout the war and its immediate aftermath meant that much needed to be done at both churches and also at Church House. Dampness in the chancel was a major problem in St Cadfan's Church and, as a result, the large monument to Athelstan Owen was suffering from subsidence and dissilience[5]. Much of this was tackled in 1951-2, with repairs being done and exterior woodwork painted at both churches. The men of St Matthew's Church put in sterling work on painting both interior and exterior woodwork of that church and also rebuilding and repairing much of its churchyard wall.

[6]The Church in Wales continued to face serious problems of manpower and finance which were closely inter-related. Stipends had hardly increased since 1939. In real terms, they were worth only half as much as they had been before the war. England continued to draw clergy from Wales by offering better stipends and the attraction (for curates) of a curate's house – unheard of in Wales. The loss of Welsh-speaking curates was a particularly serious problem. The quota, although already a burden on the parishes, provided less than half the money needed by the church, while invested endowments provided limited income. Discussion by lay members of the Governing Body, in the absence of all clerical members, led to the launching in 1952 of a layman's appeal for half a million pounds to provide extra endowments. The target was exceeded within the year. The Parish of Tywyn was set a target of £703 towards the appeal and exceeded it by £300 thanks to many generous individual donations, a nativity pageant by people of Bryncrug and a major sale of work by the Women's Guild (plus an extra £100 from their funds).

It was probably at this time that Canon Thomas produced a booklet on the history of the church, since the appeal fund shows 14/- from sales of "vicar's booklets". In addition, the Women's Guild paid for the work on the Athelstan Owen monument (£107/6/2d) and gave a presentation gift to the vicar to mark his twenty-one years in the parish at a special "birthday tea". In an article full of praise for all of the above, there is a 'dig' at one group of people. After extending thanks to wardens and choir, Canon Thomas added "and sidesmen (who we should like to see more punctilious in their duties and oftener in church when not on duty)"!

King George VI died and the accession of Queen Elizabeth II was proclaimed in February 1952. The Coronation, to great rejoicing (and heavy rain), took place in June 1953. Another cause for celebration among the children of Tywyn and throughout the country was the ending of sweet rationing in February 1952.

The quota continued to creep upwards. In 1954 it was £237, or £1/1/6d for each person on the Tywyn Electoral Roll. The Church in Wales as a whole was now raising £145,000 per year in quota payments – only £51,000 less than the Church of England, which had fourteen times as many parishes[7].

In 1954 the Martha and Mary Window in the south aisle was dedicated as were a processional cross and a faldstool in memory of Dr Alban Davies who had been churchwarden for twenty-six years. He had also been a driving force behind the erection of the Tywyn War Memorial Hospital after the First World War.

In 1955, on "the Saturday before the Third Sunday in Advent", a very special event took place in St Cadfan's Church – an event thought to be unique in the annals of its long history and unusual for most ordinary parish churches. A service of ordination was held in the church when Mr Thomas Gomer Davies BA was admitted to Holy Orders and to the office of deacon in the church and licensed to serve in the Parish of Machynlleth. "The Lord Bishop was attended by six chaplains and the Service throughout was very impressive and dignified. The Eucharist was sung to Marbecke's setting. The Women's Guild kindly entertained the clergy and visitors to luncheon in Church House."

Canon Thomas had worked in the parish for twenty-five years and must have been about seventy-five years old. Following the example of his predecessor, in late 1956 he accepted the bishop's offer of the smaller living of Arthog where he would have only one church and fewer parishioners to care for. It also left him time to pursue his interest in ecclesiastical and other history, acting as a member of the Council of the Merioneth Historical and Record Society and contributing articles to its journal.

TUDDYD OWEN

The induction service for the Rev. Tuddyd Owen, successor to Canon Thomas, did not take place until March 1957, and for a number of months the parish was left without a vicar. During this time the church received considerable help from the chaplain of Tonfannau Camp "and the Ordinands stationed there" as well as from "Walter and Vernon Davies". The next year there was both good and bad news (depending on your viewpoint) about two of these: Vernon Davies was shortly to be ordained deacon to serve as curate in the Parish of St David's, Bangor, and the chaplain of Tonfannau Camp was to move away to "resume Parochial duties".

Maintenance at St Cadfan's Church is always ongoing and 1957 was the year in which improvements were made to the heating system. The next year there were improvements and repairs to the bells, partly paid for by the Women's Guild, who also gave £200 from their reserves for the redecoration of the church[8]. The nave roof was also treated, for which a grant had been obtained from the Provincial Churches Committee. Good work continued to be done at the Sunday school and GFS, and a Young People's Fellowship was started, although this latter received only limited support.

The two lay readers in the parish were soon to be joined by a third, Mr G. T. Heywood, who had offered himself for the work in 1959 and was licensed the next year. The vicar commented that "while the shortage of clergy persists their help will be greatly needed in the Deanery". (This was while the vicar still had only St Cadfan's and St Matthew's Churches to care for; how much more are they needed now!)

The old reed organ at St Matthew's Church had become unserviceable and the Bryncrug congregation had been working hard to raise £110 for its replacement. Their efforts were successful and the new instrument was dedicated at the end of March 1960. St Cadfan's organ was also in need of overhaul and repair, and an organ fund was started which, over two years, received a number of donations. The Women's Guild gave financial assistance and there was also help from the new Young Wives Club (which had recently formed at the request of the young wives themselves).

About this time the proposed development of large parcels of land for housing to the west of the railway also concerned the vicar. If fully implemented, it would bring hundreds of new residents to the town. The vicar saw that this would be a challenge, for which the parish needed to prepare. The pastoral and evangelistic work involved would require greater assistance and service from the laity. A particular area of concern for this, as in the past, was the number of people willing to help with the Sunday school. Although there was a faithful band of teachers, more would be required as it grew.

In 1960 it was concluded that the old system of dividing the church income into two parts – the freewill offering for the quota and the Sunday collections for the general running of the churches – was unsatisfactory. Apart from anything else, it meant that those who covenanted their freewill offering (so the church could reclaim the income tax) did not have any easy way to covenant their Sunday collections. As a result, it was decided to introduce an envelope scheme, with those taking part receiving an envelope to be put in the collecting plate for every Sunday of the year. The envelopes were individually numbered (and so anonymous to most of the congregation) and the amounts given were entered in a covenants book so the offerings could be totalled as the year progressed. Those who were covenanting their donations could be alerted in time if it seemed as though their contributions were falling short of the covenanted amount. Where possible, people were asked to pledge in advance the amount they would give each week to help the church budget for its expenditure. Those who did not want envelopes could still put their contributions in the open plate. This seems to have been very successful. The total income increased from £679 in 1960 to over £1000 from 1961 onwards.

The increase was needed, for not only was the quota continuing to rise, but also repairs to the two churches and to Church House were becoming increasingly expensive. It was at this stage that St Cadfan's Church Repair Fund was set up, funded by cash from the maintenance box and gifts of £95 and £300 from the Young Wives Club and the Women's Guild. In 1962 the bishop agreed to appoint a curate who would start in June. His appointment was particularly welcomed as G. T. Heywood, one of the lay readers, had been studying for the ministry at St Michael's College, Llandaff, and was shortly to be ordained deacon, when he would move to another parish. There was a downside to the news about the new curate: the parish had to find an additional £325 (more than the quota at that time) towards his stipend.

In the 1963-4 Parochialia, names which are still associated with the church fifty years later started to appear. The organist at the time (Miss Roberts) was ill and special thanks were given to Mrs Claudia Dawson (Charlton), Miss Susanna Yeomans and Mrs Janet Evans for their assistance during this illness.

Other changes were also in train. The bishop had asked the vicar to assist in maintaining the services and pastoral care at Abergynolwyn during the suspension of the incumbency of Talyllyn and Abergynolwyn. Meanwhile, the need for more helpers at the Sunday schools in Tywyn and Bryncrug was pressing and the leaders of the Girls Friendly Society also needed more support. The Young People's Fellowship was flourishing under the curate but again more assistance was needed. Perhaps as married women, even those with children, increasingly went out to work, they had less time and energy to help with activities outside the family – or perhaps television was beginning to exert its siren pull.

The next year showed how the parish inspired men for the ministry. Walter Davies of Bryncrug, who had assisted with services for over seven years and had been a lay reader for some time, had been studying at St Deiniol's Library, Hawarden, and was ordained deacon in June 1966. Sadly, like those ordained before him, this meant he would move away from the parish and take up a curacy elsewhere. Meanwhile, after three years in the parish, the Tywyn curate had moved to Penmaenmawr. These changes once more revealed the need for greater support, particularly for the Sunday schools. The vicar challenged his people: were they "content to see their church children being sent to Chapel Sunday Schools which, owing to greater interest and support, are more able to look after them"?

In 1966-7 a new heating system was installed in St Matthew's Church, Bryncrug. The improvement was greatly appreciated by those attending the church – despite an increase in the electricity bill from just under £7 in 1965-6 to over £60 in 1968. The tower was once more a problem at St Cadfan's Church. Estimates were sought for repair work, which took place the next year at a cost of over £1200. The vicar was also very concerned about vandalism both in St Cadfan's churchyard and also Church House premises and grounds, including the complete destruction of the outside toilets. Some of the vandals were very young children and it was known that some came from homes of churchgoers. The vicar appealed for help in keeping them from acting in this destructive manner and reminded parishioners that the cost of upkeep of Church House was already a problem.

For five years from 1965 the quota had remained unchanged at £475 while inflation had averaged over 4% a year – over the five years money had lost over one-fifth of its value. The result was two major increases: first to £529 in 1970 and then to £690 in 1971. However, the repair fund had received a boost of £160 net following a major flower festival. With the aid of a legacy and a major donation, St Cadfan's was able to replace the existing coal furnace with a gas boiler and carry out other heating improvements to the tune of £930. The following year £248 was paid to the gas board – a nasty shock – but this probably covered two years as payments fell to about half that amount in subsequent years. (The last full year with the coal furnace had cost £103 for coal plus £16 to the person who "rang the bells and stoked the boiler".)

18. FORTY YEARS: 1973-2013[1]

In the 1970s inflation was running wild. From just over 9% in 1973 it rose to a peak of 24% in 1975. After fluctuating for four years, it peaked again at 18% in 1980. In ten years money had fallen to less than one-third of its value. Change was becoming essential for the Church in Wales; money was very tight and the number of clergy and of ordinands in training had been falling for many years. The Church's funds (used not only for stipends but also for pensions, training, and the provision and maintenance of vicarages) could not keep pace. Inevitably, the financial burden had to fall on the parishes – at a time when many of the parishioners were themselves struggling with high mortgage rates.

It was against this background that, in March 1978, the Rev. Martin Riley with his wife and two sons moved to Tywyn as the new vicar of the parish and its two churches, St Cadfan's, Tywyn, and St Matthew's, Bryncrug. In addition to his pastoral work, he faced the financial problems of the quota and church repairs. There would also be further changes and challenges not foreseen on his arrival.

THE QUOTA

Rather than raise the quota as inflation started to rise, the Church in Wales had hoped that matters would improve and held the quota at the same level for each parish for five years. In 1975, the quota only contributed 7.3% of the money for stipends, wages and training, with the rest coming from investments. In that year, the church authorities set up a committee on inflation and in 1976 the quota was doubled – for Tywyn (including Bryncrug), it increased from £690 to £1380. It then increased every year and by 1982 stood at £2634. Worse was to come: two years later the quota had more than doubled to £5900. Fundraising to pay the quota, rather than to pay for repairs to the buildings, had become vital and Tywyn Parish was just able to meet its quota. It was, perhaps, unfortunate that the new Church in Wales Prayer Book was published the same year and all churches were expected to buy and start using them.

However, as the quota increased, the income from collections and special events soon became insufficient to meet the quota requirement for Tywyn Parish. At first, money from St Cadfan's reserve account was used to cover the shortfall. By 1993 the parish fell short of paying the quota by £1500 and the deficit increased each year. By the end of 1995 the parish was in arrears by over £11,000. Subsequently, the income from additional fundraising events enabled the quota to be paid in full and it became possible to make a small over-payment each year to reduce the arrears slightly.

As a millennium gesture, Bangor Diocese offered to write off 50% of the arrears for those churches that paid the remaining 50% in the first few months of 2000. By almost emptying St Cadfan's reserves, Tywyn Parish was able to take advantage of this offer and start the new millennium free from debt.

In early 1982, bitter snow hit Britain. Even Tywyn, which usually escapes the worst of the cold weather, was hit by snowstorms heavy enough to immobilise a train just outside the town so that the passengers had to be evacuated by helicopter. Martin Riley's decision to run the heating day and night during the bad weather probably saved the cast iron pipes and radiators from major damage. Snow had, however, blown in between wall and roof on the east side of the south transept, settling in the organ and badly damaging it. The insurance company covered the cost of the storm damage of up to £6900 and the PCC decided that, while the organ was stripped for repair, it should be converted from pneumatic to electric action at a cost of £1000.

From the 1980s for more than thirty years, St Cadfan's Church was fortunate to have a small maintenance group that worked in the church every week. The team, led initially by Bob Evans and subsequently by Jac Lemon, concentrated on preventative maintenance. By ensuring, for example, that gutters and drains were regularly cleared, that woodworm was treated at the first sight of a problem or that cracked floorboards were quickly replaced, they prevented small problems from turning into major crises. However, some problems were not small ones. Following the quinquennial inspection in 1986, the diocesan surveyor recommended provision of a new church roof. A roof appeal was launched but had only reached £800 by the start of 1987. The lowest estimate for the work was £36,308 – far more than had been raised. Applications for grants were made, including one to CADW[2]. Unfortunately, they were unwilling to accept the locally produced specification for the reroofing and sent their own architect to look at the situation. He estimated an overall cost of £60,000 (including replacing the downpipes and gutters with cast iron rather than plastic pipes) and CADW offered a grant of £36,000 towards this. The cost had gone up but the church now only needed to raise £24,000 rather than £36,000. A leaflet explaining the situation and asking for support was delivered by church members to every house in the parish. Donations started to come in, sometimes from surprising sources, while fundraising events continued. There was still a shortfall of £7000 when the work started in spring 1989 but, spurred by the sight of the work actually taking place, the final sum was raised.

In the 1990s, a skilled wood-carver, Tommy Davies, produced a number of carvings which he gave to the church, to the great delight of all. They included Noah's dove, the cock which crowed on Good Friday and the Stations of the Cross.

At that time most of the churchyard was in a completely wild state, with saplings and brambles growing through and covering most of the graves. The church could not afford to pay contractors to deal with the situation and did not have the manpower to tackle it with volunteers. Those concerned with finding work for offenders on community service/community pay-back orders agreed to tackle the problem. Their assistance has continued over many years, for which the church is deeply grateful.

In 2000, there was a fall of stone from a mullion of the north transept window[3]. At the suggestion of the then architect, an attempt was made to replace the stone with epoxy mortar but this proved to be ineffective. Close inspection revealed that the mullions of the windows in both transepts were in poor condition. A decision was made to replace the mullions in both and at the same time have the stained glass releaded at a total cost of £17,282. A 50% grant from CADW and grants of £2000 and £2500 from the W. G. Roberts and Piggott Trusts together with £2000 from the Listed Places of Worship Scheme left the church with only £3600 to find from its own resources. The work was completed by late 2001.

CHURCH HOUSE

St Cadfan's Church had been making use of Church House ever since the closure of the National School in 1913 with no formal agreement or lease. In 1981 the diocese urged that one should be put in place. The diocese wanted a full repairing lease requiring the church to put the building into "good and tenantable repair" and then maintain it to that standard. At the time, it was estimated that about £7000 would be required to put the hall into tenantable repair; there would then be ongoing costs especially as, after an initial three-year period, a "fair market rent" was to be charged.

From the time it had first been taken over by St Cadfan's Church, Church House had needed financing for improvements and for repairs. Only limited income was obtained by letting it, as there were other venues in the town in better condition. The church made little use of it, except for Parochial Church Council meetings and fundraising events, but there was always the hope that some children's or young people's work could be started in it. Many church members were keen to keep it.

Rather than face a future of continually repairing the building and paying rent on it, the Parochial Church Council decided to try to buy Church House but an offer of £5000 (just below the estimated market value) was rejected by the diocese. No further progress was made, and the problem of the building and its repairs was left in abeyance. St Cadfan's continued to make use of it as before, while putting off the problem of the lease.

By 1990, Church House needed a new boiler (£1250), an overhaul of its electrical system (£3500) and reroofing (£3500), all at a time when the church was struggling to find enough money to pay the quota. Rather than undertaking the necessary work, Church House was patched up – again – but even that cost £1500.

The diocese continued to press for a decision on Church House. In 1994 an impasse was reached as Ecclesiastical Insurance refused to insure the building any longer unless a formal lease was in place. While the policy for St Cadfan's Church covered third party risks for church events held in Church House, there would be no cover of any kind for when it was let or at other times. After once more considering the cost of putting the building into good repair (which had now risen to £30,000) and likely ongoing costs, the building was finally surrendered to the diocese in January 1996.

PARISHES AND PEOPLE

Martin Riley had originally been appointed to the Parish of Tywyn with its two churches, but in 1982 Tywyn was grouped with Aberdyfi. The parishes remained separate, but the vicar now had three churches. Provision of services became more of a problem, especially as it was hoped to maintain the pattern of Morning Prayer and Holy Eucharist services on alternate Sundays in all three churches. There were already two elderly lay readers in Tywyn, Freddie Fuller and John Gover, who helped by taking Morning Prayer. Shortly thereafter, Janet Evans and Bruce Morris were trained and licensed as readers, while Roy Barber was accepted as a candidate for ordination.

In 1991 the Church in Wales asked parishes for their views on the ordination of women as deacons. The congregation at St Cadfan's was already accustomed to Morning and Evening Prayer being taken by a woman since, by then, Janet Evans had been a lay reader for many years, but the matter was still hotly debated in the Parochial Church Council. A PCC recommendation in favour of the ordination of women was approved by nine votes to four. The ordination of women as deacons was finally passed at the Governing Body by bishops, clergy and people.

Numbers of clergy in the Church in Wales continued to fall and, in late 1994, the Tywyn and Aberdyfi group was augmented. The parishes of Llanegryn and Abergynolwyn were added, bringing with them four more churches. Two of these were in the two villages and had regular Sunday services. The other two, at Llanfihangel-y-Pennant and Talyllyn, were ancient churches whose farming congregations had now vanished; in these, services were held only occasionally.

By now there were only two readers at Tywyn to help in the ministry. Christiné ten Wolde (Aberdyfi) and Meryl Gover (Tywyn) were accepted to train as readers and were licensed the following year. Christiné ten Wolde was subsequently accepted for ordination. The parish was fortunate that the Rev. Malcolm Northall, a retired priest, was also willing to help by taking services frequently.

The small congregation of Abergynolwyn Church had, for many years, been looking after both Llanfihangel-y-Pennant and Talyllyn churches in addition to their own St David's Church. As "Mary Jones's church", St Michael's at Llanfihangel-y-Pennant had many visitors and their donations covered the cost of insurance and electricity for the church. St Mary's, Talyllyn, had few visitors and little income. With little manpower to physically care for all three churches, and with inadequate funds to cover even the insurance of St Mary's, it was sadly decided, at the turn of the century, that it must close and it was later sold.

CANON MARTIN RILEY

While vicar of the Tywyn group of churches, Martin Riley had been appointed Cursal Canon of St Deiniol's Cathedral, Bangor in 1990, and seven years later, in 1997, he was appointed as Prebendary Canon, one of the most senior canons, with his own stall in the cathedral.

At the end of August 2003 he retired after forty years in the ministry, twenty-five of them at Tywyn. He and his wife moved to Corris where they continued to be very involved with the local churches and with the Mothers' Union.

THE VACANCY

Although they did not know it at the time, the group of parishes faced a long vacancy when Martin Riley retired.

They were fortunate that the Rev. Nigel and Rev. Celia Adams had recently retired to Tywyn and joined the Rev. Malcolm Northall in taking services. There was also a retired deacon, the Rev. Alan White, and a non-stipendiary priest, the Rev. Christiné ten Wolde. The existing readers had been joined by Arthur Higgins who found himself involved almost from the moment he retired to the parish. All were happy to take services and be involved with the running of the various churches. In this way, the existing pattern of services in the five churches was maintained. The Rev. Dick France from Llangelynnin led Holy Eucharist regularly in Llanegryn but otherwise very little help was needed from outside the group.

ST MATTHEW'S CHURCH, BRYNCRUG

St Matthew's Church in Bryncrug was a daughter church to St Cadfan's. It had been built in 1882 because the older people and children of Bryncrug found the journey to St Cadfan's difficult and it had been a flourishing church for many years. However, with the almost universal decrease in church attendance and the ease with which those with cars could drive to other churches, the numbers in the congregation fell. By the mid-1990s the collections could do little more than cover the cost of insurance and electricity, with little left to contribute towards the quota. Numbers at services continued to fall until, by 2003, the average attendance was down to four.

To add to the problems, the fabric of the church needed considerable attention. Damp was penetrating the west wall, resulting in widespread green mould on the inside, and it was thought that it might also be necessary to rebuild the bell cote. Following a visit in 1993, the architect reported that most of the west wall needed repointing and the plaster inside replaced. The cost would be at least £10,000 – and St Matthew's had minimal reserves. Financially, there was no possibility that such major works could be attempted. The church was not a listed building and grants would have been very hard to obtain. In the event, no action was taken.

The fabric continued to deteriorate. There were numerous falls of plaster from the ceiling over the south side of the aisle and by the entrance to the church. By 2003, to ensure the safety of the congregation, both areas had been cordoned off with entry via the vestry at the back of the church. St Matthew's had very few members and, while each of them helped in some way towards the running of the church, there was little enthusiasm for retaining the building if too much money was required for repairs. An electrical inspection was required, with whatever costs that would highlight, and there were continuing problems with the west wall.

A circular explaining the situation and warning that without a larger congregation the church would close was sent to all who lived in Bryncrug. This brought some sympathy but nothing else. Regretfully, the small congregation decided that, although they would love to keep the church open, they saw no alternative but to close it and a final service, led by the Archdeacon of Merioneth, was held on 2 November 2005.

Some items were transferred from St Matthew's Church to St Cadfan's Church. They included the altar, which became the prayer table, the brass altar cross, the communion vessels and some plaques, including the relief of an angel which is now in the baptistry. No new home could be found for the font, so medallions on each of its four faces were mounted on wood and are in the south transept.

REPAIRS AND IMPROVEMENTS

The lighting in church had been of concern for some time. The high-level fittings, each containing two bulbs, were burning out, with the result that only two-thirds of the bulbs were working, and things could only get worse. The 2004 quinquennial inspection and the accompanying electrical inspection highlighted the need for the electrical circuitry to be updated (including the provision of a new distribution board in the vestry) and the lighting to be redesigned. Specific fundraising events were held so that it was possible – with the assistance of grants from the Piggott and W. G. Roberts Trusts – to meet the cost of the new lighting, which was designed by the architect, Adam Voelcker.

For many years, the plaster under the tower adjacent to parts of the nave and the south transept had been in a poor state of repair. Dust and pieces of plaster frequently fell – on several occasions actually falling into the organ and causing damage, which needed emergency repairs. Gwenda Graham, who had been organist since late 1986, expressed her concerns to the organ builders, Robert Edwards (Chester) Ltd, who carried out a thorough investigation during their next tuning visit. In the summer of 2005, they wrote to the PCC to warn of possible repair costs of between £40,000 and £100,000 if the problem was not addressed.

In his report on the quinquennial inspection the previous year, the architect had emphasised that the high-level plaster inside and outside the crossing, including the area above and beside the organ, was in a very bad state and needed urgent attention. In addition, the south wall of the vestry and the walls of the south transept were in a poor state of repair. CADW promised a grant and, with help from other sources, it was possible to carry out all the work at a cost of £28,300.

It was clear from the start that it would not be possible to use any part of St Cadfan's Church for services during the replastering. St David's Roman Catholic Church in Pier Road kindly took pity on the congregation and allowed the use of their church for all the services throughout the work. But there was a downside – after experiencing the warmth of St David's, the congregation was quite reluctant to return to the cooler environs of St Cadfan's!

The success of the work was celebrated with a flower festival which closely involved the children of Penybryn School and was organised by two of the mothers. The theme was from the Benedicite, "Oh all ye works of the Lord, praise ye the Lord". For the west wall, the children produced a great mural of the ocean with the fish, whales and all manner of marine animals and plants. The many flower arrangements took up the themes of other verses.

RICHARD VROOM

At long last, the vacancy came to an end after more than four years. All the churches in the Tywyn group were delighted to welcome the Rev. Richard Vroom and

Margriet, his wife, at his induction in late October 2007. He came to a busy group of four working churches plus St Michael's Church at Llanfihangel-y-Pennant. Most of those who had led services during the vacancy were happy to continue assisting, though the number was reduced by illness and house moves. However, Sue Whitehouse had been accepted for training as a reader and she was licensed in 2009.

REDEVELOPMENT

About 2007, it became clear that St Matthew's Church would be sold. As it was a daughter church to Tywyn, the money would be available for the development or improvement of St Cadfan's Church. There was a consensus that the most important needs were a toilet and a small meeting room that could be independently heated, and could also be used as part of the church if necessary. As Adam Voelcker was no longer available (having been asked to help complete the Gwynedd edition of *Pevsner Buildings of Wales*), Gruffydd Price was appointed as architect. The meeting room was constructed within the north transept by installing a ceiling, partially of glass, and sliding glass doors. A door from the meeting room led to a small lobby, a toilet suitable for disabled use and a very small boiler room for a new boiler. These had been provided inside the old boiler house by raising its roof and floor. Work started at the end of August 2010 and was completed the following spring. With carpets, comfortable chairs, good lighting and independent heating the "glass room" has proved a great asset to the church.

FULL CIRCLE

In 2013, Pennal was added to the Tywyn group of parishes and later that year the Ministry Area of Bro Ystumanner was constituted. The Ministry Area contained the churches of Tywyn and Aberdyfi, Pennal, Llanegryn and Llanfihangel-y-Pennant with Abergynolwyn in place of Talyllyn. Each church retained its autonomy but there was now an overarching Ministry Area Council.

The area once covered by "Tywyn and its three chapels" had been reunited. Perhaps Egryn would not have objected to Llanegryn, once the commotal centre of Tal-y-bont, being added to this ancient group.

And what of the future? That is in God's hands. We can only echo the words of the last line of *Canu Cadfan*:

Cedwid Duw Dewr-Doeth Cyfoeth Cadfan
May the valiant wise God guard Cadfan's domain.

APPENDIX A – THE BUILDING

St Cadfan's Church is a Grade I listed building. It is "as remarkable a church as any in Wales, despite the ravages of time"[1].

EXTERNALS

To get some feeling for how the building has been modified over time, it is helpful to look around the outside and compare areas of known date with those of uncertain date.

External areas for which the dates are thought to be definite are:

11/12th century Nave and clerestory (except west wall). Side aisles (except the rectangular windows). North transept except for the north window.
1880-4 Tower and tower stair. South and part of east wall of chancel. Centre section of west wall of nave. Vestry.
1911 Boiler house (extended 2010)
1920 Porch
2014 Sacristy

Areas which were, or may have been, altered at some stage:

Much of south transept after the fall of the central tower. The south wall may have been rebuilt in 1880-4.

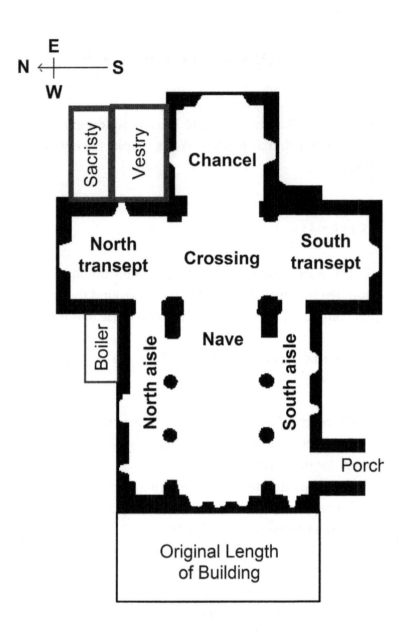

Plan of the church, 2014

West end of south aisle, possibly in 1735-7 when the west tower was built.

West end of north aisle This looks older than the west end of the south aisle but does not match the adjacent north wall of the aisle.

11TH AND 12TH CENTURIES

The building of the church took place over a number of decades. Its original form was much as the present building, with its cruciform shape and side aisles, but the overall length was greater by one arch of the nave (internally at least 109^2 feet against the current 93 feet).

The building probably started with the nave and side aisles in the latter part of the 11th century or earlier[3], and at that stage the internal floor would have been level with that outside. The arcades are of rough masonry merely plastered over and with no stone dressings. They have squat round drum pillars with no capitals, splaying out to a circular rim at the top with no decoration. The arches rising from them are of square cross-section with no ornamentation. The clerestory windows are tiny, with expanding splays internally; the windows at the lower level in the aisles and in the transepts and chancel would have been similar, though perhaps larger. The floor would have been of earth; rushes would have been strewn over it several times a year[4].

The arches to the crossing from nave, chancel and transepts were of very early first pointed work[5]. This style appeared in England in the latter part of the 12th century but, as sea communication to the continent was still important in the 12th century, it is possible that it reached Tywyn earlier. The external ground level rises from the nave to the chancel, which assisted the rise in floor levels to transepts and then to chancel.

The central tower would have been lower than the current tower and probably had a pyramidal roof like that at Penmon Priory. It must, however, have been of a reasonable height or it could not have caused so much damage when it fell.

If the building took place in stages over a long time it may be true, as has been suggested, that the chancel is on the site of the previous church building (which was most likely on the highest point of ground). The nave and side aisles could have been walled off and used as a church while the old church was demolished and the current transepts and chancel built. The implication from *Canu Cadfan* is that a building was substantially complete by the mid-12th century.

The octagonal font, which has spur or griffe mouldings at the base, was probably installed in the 13th century after the completion of the building[6].

Evidence

Dating of the nave[7]: Pevsner suggests 12th century while Davidson considers the clerestory windows to indicate a late 12th century date. Potter suggests that the spacing of the clerestory windows and the thickness of the wall above the pillars to indicate pre-Norman construction. The very plain and crude nature of the pillars indicate an early date.

Evidence for the extra length of the nave includes:

- The vestry minute, which was confirmed by the faculty, that "a steeple or stone Tower be made and raised at ye west, *and within ye west end* of ye Parish chch"[8].
- The westmost pillars are oddly tight against the west wall.
- There appears to be the start of another arch to the west of the south-west pillar.
- The clerestory windows at the west end of the nave are unusually spaced very close to the west wall.
- The side walls of the west tower would probably have been built on the nave side of the pillars. This fits with the west tower having been narrower than the nave. (It can, however, equally be argued that a narrow tower could have been built against the end of a short nave.)

An additional point in favour of the longer nave is the longevity of many Tywyn people[9] and that, for many, it was still a time of oral transmission of information. Between 1737, when the west tower was completed, and 1880 when the restoration started is less than 150 years. It is likely that there were those in the Tywyn area who had heard from great-grandparents or even grandparents what happened to the length of the church when the west tower was built.

Arches to the crossing: John Prichard's description of the church[10] states that the arches to the nave and north transept were of very early first pointed work, which suggests that they all were, although the others would have been destroyed by the fall of the tower in 1692.

During the installation of the toilet and glass room in 2010[11] the plaster on the lower parts of the walls of the north transept was removed. The report on the archaeological watching brief indicated that the stonework revealed was 12th century and it was constructed of fairly small flat schist stones. Put-log holes, which would have supported timbers during construction, were found in both north and east walls. The one in the east wall contained a thumb pot that could not easily be dated; it appeared to have been formed by working clay around a finger or stick. Its purpose was unclear as it did not show any signs of burning so it was unlikely to be a crude form of oil lamp. It is possible that it once contained a substance of which no sign now remains. A small schist stone, which had been shaped into a disk, and a rounded pebble, different in appearance from the stones which had been used to fill in the put-log hole, were also found. The practice of placing objects within walls is well known in Wales.

In addition, the beginning of an arch was found just to the left of the current vestry door and at the same height as its arch. There was not enough to identify it definitely, but it was likely to be the remains of a 12th century door out of the church.

THE 14TH CENTURY

When the plaster in the lower wall of the north transept was removed (see above)[12], in-filled apertures, with 14th century stonework around them, were found on both the east and the north wall of the transept. These were thought to have been part of large 14th century windows that replaced the earlier slit windows. The aperture in the north wall was about the same width as the current north transept window and the sill level of both windows would have been about 1.6 metres (5 feet) below the sill of the present window.

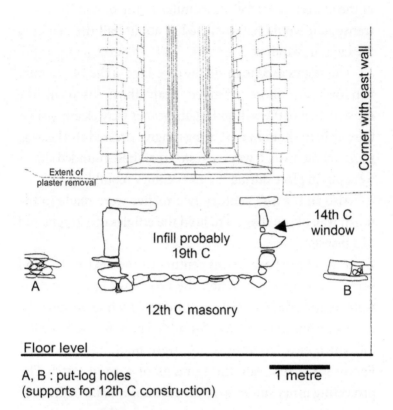

Corner with east wall

Extent of plaster removal

Infill probably 19th C

14th C window

A

B

12th C masonry

Floor level

A, B : put-log holes
(supports for 12th C construction)

1 metre

*12th & 14th century stonework, the north wall of the north transept
(from the archaeologists' report)*

Scrutiny of the existing masonry on the outside of the
northern wall suggested that the gable of the north transept
was rebuilt in the 14th century. It appears that the 12th
century masonry was capped (visible as a distinct line)
prior to the rebuilding of the gable, and the large window
was inserted with a relieving arch above it. The height of
the 14th century window is unknown as its top would have
been somewhere within the area of the current window.
However, if the south transept window visible in the picture

of the church pre-1880 was similar to the one in the north transept, it would have reached to about half the height of the current window.

The stones used to in-fill the openings of the 14th century windows are more rounded than those used in the construction of the wall and edging stones were clearly visible, the one in the bottom west being roughly dressed and bearing signs of limewash. It was suggested that these rounded stones were put in place during the 19th century rebuilding.

Also in the 14th century two niches were made in the north wall of the chancel to hold the effigies of a knight and of a priest[13].

It may have been in this century or the next that a rood screen was installed. When the box pews in the chancel were demolished in 1870, an antique screen separating the chancel from the nave was found[14]. There was also a rood loft since new "rooding seats" were made in 1729[15] and Fenton, in 1808, saw the remains of a rood loft[16]. The projecting inner surfaces on the eastmost pillars of the aisle may have formed part of the supports for this.

THE 15TH CENTURY

At some stage the timbers of the nave roof were replaced with the current ones. When the building was reslated in the 1980s the roof timbers were inspected closely for rot or worm and found to be sound. At that time, they were said to be 13th or 14th century "and second hand when they were put up"[17]. Pevsner dates the roof with its comparatively shallow pitch as late 15th century with arch-braced collar trusses with apex cusping.

The old corbels suggest the south aisle roof was once lower

Thin tie beams, some with one or more crude Tudor-style roses carved in the centre, were added later. This may have been an attempt to stop the roof spreading and causing movement of the nave walls, particularly the north wall.

A doorway in the south wall of the chancel was described as Tudor[18]. It may have been installed during that period or a much earlier door may have been 'updated' in the 15th century.

It may also have been at this time that the roof of the south aisle was raised. Evidence for this having been carried out at some time include the south aisle roof being higher than that of the north aisle, with the part abutting the nave being very close under the clerestory windows, and the existence of some corbels, all at the same level, on the south wall of the south aisle below roof level.

THE 17TH CENTURY

During the Civil War and the period of the Commonwealth, troops and fanatics were encouraged to break up and destroy images, pictures and stained glass as well as to destroy church registers. The rood screen itself would have had any figures defaced or destroyed but the supports and loft could have been left more-or-less intact. If the inside walls of the church had pictures painted on them, as was commonly done, they would have been defaced or whitewashed. What damage was done to the structure of the building is unknown and no registers exist from that period. The only damage to the effigies – deep score marks and the loss of the knight's nose – may date from that time or may be due to villagers over the centuries making use of them to sharpen their blades.

It was in 1692 that the central tower fell towards the south or south-east, taking with it the roofs of the chancel and part of the south transept[19]. It is difficult to determine exactly what was destroyed and rebuilt shortly after that time. However, if the repairs had not been completed before 1736 then surely that would have been done instead of erecting the west tower. In the extant picture of the church in the 19th century, the south transept walls appear similar to the present ones. When the restoration work took place in the 1880s there were periods when the work stopped. In one case, this was said to relate to plans being returned to the architect. It could be that the southern part of the south transept, originally thought to be sound, proved unstable and plans had to be drawn up to rebuild it. This would explain the use of dressed stone, especially on its south wall.

The remains of the original wall of the south transept can be seen on its west wall near the south aisle. Any similar remains in the east wall have disappeared with the building of the tower stairs. What damage had occurred to the south wall of the chancel cannot be determined as this wall was rebuilt in 1880-4.

THE 18TH CENTURY

Between 1735 and 1737 a tower with a short steeple was built at the west end of the church "within the west end", with a doorway to the west. From an etching, a painting and photographs, the line of the wall must have been along the inner side of the westernmost pillars and arches. The information about the tower in the churchwardens' book does not give any suggestion that the side aisles would be truncated but this would appear to have been done. This may be because the clerestory walls, which supported the inner end of the aisle roofs, became unstable during the building of the tower. Alternatively, the tower standing clear of the rest of the building looked more impressive than if it had just emerged "through the roof". There is a considerable difference in appearance of the two truncated aisles. The south aisle, which would have been visible as people walked to the main west door, is very tidily finished and has a window which looks like the current one. The end of the north aisle, perhaps because it was not so visible, has just been patched up with the stones from the demolished walls, although it is clear that there was once a door through it.

The full width of the west tower opened into the nave, and there was a stairway and platform on the south side of it to allow access to the bell ropes[20].

In 1773, flagstones were laid in the north and south aisles and across the back of the church from the current main door. Part of the south aisle was roofed (or reroofed) and plastered internally. The timber in the main roof was in a bad condition and was patched up. There was also an application to erect a gallery in the church, but there is no indication of whether the work was carried out[21].

Towards the end of the 18th century a vestry was built in the corner between the west tower and the west end of the north transept[22]. It can be seen in the 1808 etching of the church, which also shows a chimney for the vestry fireplace. The filled-in doorway, which can be seen from outside the current west end of the north transept, will have provided access from the body of the church.

It was probably during this century or early the next century that thick internal buttresses (one reinforced with steel straps) were inserted across the north aisle on the line of each pillar. This was probably an attempt to stop continued outward leaning of the north-west pillars which was causing cracking in the north-west wall of the nave. A small external buttress was built level with the easternmost of the pillars.

THE 19TH CENTURY

S. R. Glynne[23] (visit 1839) specifically referred to a gallery over the **eastern** portion of the nave – perhaps the remains or modification of the old rood loft. Information in the *Cambrian News* (1 October 1870 and 12 May 1871) referred to a west gallery, which was demolished in 1870. It was apparently called the "Aberdovey Gallery"[24] which may suggest it was at the west end of the church (closest to Aberdyfi). It is possible that at some stage the old dilapidated rood loft had been scrapped and a large west gallery installed, like those in many of the chapels being built at that time. Also in 1870, the box pews were removed and the three-decker pulpit lowered.

It was between 1880 and 1884, that the changes took place which produced most of the church as it is today.

The plans of the work are no longer available but the specifications of the architect (John Prichard, Diocesan Architect of Llandaff) have been preserved[25]. They were mainly concerned with detail of how work was to be carried out and did not necessarily repeat information that was clear from the plans. They did, however, show that the work was intended to include:

- Taking down the west tower and the west walls of nave and side aisles and building a wall across the whole of the west end. However, judging by the outside masonry of the west wall, it would seem that in practice the side aisles had already been truncated and the new wall was joined to existing masonry on either side. The internal buttress at the west end of the north aisle must have been built at this stage.
- Saving the window from the west wall of the tower to put into the new west wall. This was not carried out for some reason[26], possibly because stained glass to fit a larger window had been promised.

- Taking down and rebuilding the south wall of the chancel and "such other walls as may become necessary". From the outside one can see that increasing amounts of the old east wall of the chancel remain in place, from very little on the south side to almost half height at the north side. The east window was within the area replaced.

- Building the central tower with an external staircase at the south-east corner. A description of finding a vault with the coffin of Edward Corbet while working on the north-east pier of the tower[27] suggests that all four piers (pillars) of the tower were wholly or partially rebuilt with firmer foundations. The eight carved heads were also added at this time (Mary and Peter at the entry to the chancel, Cadfan and David at the entry to the nave and the four evangelists on the entries to the transepts)[28].

- Removing the existing floors (some were of slate and some of wood). Excavating to a depth of 2 feet (60cm) below the existing floors and building brick piers to hold oak sleepers that would support the new floors – wood where the seats would be and encaustic tiles for the aisles. This under-floor space was to be thoroughly ventilated.

- Building the vestry. It was to have a new door into it through the east wall of the north transept. The vestry was also to have a fireplace with the chimney coming out at the top of the tower.

- Laying drains round the chancel and transepts into which downpipes would run. The water was to be delivered "twenty yards outside the churchyard wall".

- Moving the font to its present position and raising it. It was to drain to a blind well.

- Lowering the ground for a distance of 6 feet (1.8m) from the church to a level of 6 inches (15cm) below the nave floor. (This was presumably to stop damp coming through the walls.) The only remaining sign of this is a trench along the wall of the south aisle.
- Installing 'heating apparatuses' on either side of the east end of the nave with chimneys built into the wall and with ventilation from below. (The squared off extensions to the two piers bordering the nave were to be their sites and the squared-off columns above them contained chimneys which led up the walls and through the tower to chimney pots on the parapet.) However, a postcard dated 1892[29] shows no sign of any fireplace or heating apparatus and the chairs are placed right up to the pillars.
- Replacing and then slating the roofs of chancel and transepts.
- Glazing the windows of chancel and transepts with ornamental quarry glass.
- Removing the plaster from all the walls including the nave and side aisles and replastering them. It would seem that the pillars were also replastered at that time thus "depriving them of their primitive appearance"[30].
- Repairing the buttresses of chancel and transepts as necessary.

There was no indication in the specification that the walls of the south transept, with its low 14th century window, were to be rebuilt but it would seem that this was done. The external walls show no sign of the old window and the inside of the south and much of the west walls are faced internally with cement rather than plaster. In addition, the window in the north transept was replaced by the current one[31].

It must also have been at this stage that both the tower roof and the floor of the bell chamber were laid with lead sheets with expansion loops between them. The bell frame rests on the sheets in the bell chamber

Almost certainly gas lighting was installed at this time[32].

The church reopened in 1884 and a new organ was installed in 1897.

THE 20TH CENTURY

1900 New choir stalls were placed in the chancel.

1902 Twenty-two pitch pine pews were placed in the nave "to match existing pews in the transepts".

1905 The current altar was installed at the request of the Rev. Titus Lewis instead of a retirement gift to him.

1908 A new lychgate was built, replacing the one demolished when the road was widened (architect Harold Hughes). The roof was at right angles to that on the old lychgate[33].
An oak reredos was installed.

1907-12 Installation of gas incandescent lights (i.e. with gas mantles) gradually took place as finance allowed[34].

1909-20 Panelling was gradually extended either side of the reredos and down the side walls of the chancel.

1911 The organ was moved to its current position, extended and cased (see Appendix C).
A "heating chamber" (i.e. the boiler house) was installed with a coal boiler. A flue was built through the west wall of the north transept to join

the flue from the old stove in the nave[35]. The hot-water pipes looped up through the tower before going round the church. This utilised the effect of hot water rising to drive the heat through the whole system.

To prevent the air in the church stagnating it was considered imperative to improve the ventilation. Inlet shafts were made under the west window and those in the two transepts. An outlet shaft went up through the floor of the ringing chamber and was led out through the floor of the bell chamber.

The choir stalls were moved from the chancel to the crossing where they would be closer to the organ and the congregation. In addition the pulpit was moved from the chancel to the crossing.

1920   The Memorial Porch was opened (architect Harold Hughes). Its walls bear the names of all those from the parish killed in the Great War (First World War).

1931   Two gifts were given to the baptistry: an oak and bronze lid for the font and a silver ewer (M. H. Minns of Willow Studio, Hampstead). A recess was made in the wall near the font to receive the ewer and given a metal ironwork gate that could be padlocked.

1934   The Cadfan Stone was erected at the west end of the north aisle.

1935   Tower restoration took place including repointing the south and west walls; louvres were installed on the bell chamber windows to reduce the amount of rain getting in.

1937-8 Electric light was installed.

1941 The baptistry was panelled in oak.

1948 A new plaque in the memorial porch was dedicated bearing the names of all those in the parish who had died in the Second World War.

1951 The church was declared a Grade I listed building

1968 Major repairs to the tower were again needed.

1989 The church roof was reslated and broken gutters and downpipes replaced.

1990s Stations of the Cross and other carvings donated.

2001 The mullions of the north and south transepts were replaced and their stained glass releaded.

2004 The lighting in the church was redesigned and upgraded. Special attention was paid to proper lighting of the Cadfan Stone so that the inscription could be clearly seen (architect Adam Voelcker).

2006 The plaster of the crossing, south transept and south wall of the transept were replaced and these walls limewashed. The organ was dismantled, cleaned and reassembled.

2010 The ancient prayer sundial (or mass clock) was installed in the church.

2010-11 A meeting room, separately heated and lighted, was created within the north transept with a glass front and doors and a partially glazed ceiling. The boiler house walls were slightly extended westwards, the floor raised to the same level as the north transept, the angle of the roof altered to give adequate headroom and a door broken through to the north transept. A toilet with lobby and small boiler room was installed in the extended boiler house (architect Gruffydd Price, builder G. & W. Wigglesworth).

2014 The church was extended by the provision of a sacristy alongside the vestry (architect Gruffydd Price, builder B. Shellis).

JOHN PRICHARD'S NOTES

To some extent we can only surmise what was present when changes were made in 1880-4. The description given at the beginning of the project by John Prichard, the architect of that work, is therefore of special interest[36]:

It seems that the upper part of the central tower fell in 1692, and instead of rebuilding it, a task which might have been readily accomplished, as the abutments of its arches are still sound, the men of that day thought proper to curtail the proportions of the nave, and to build an unsightly tower at the west end, and since then a still more modern vestry has been appended to the western end of the north aisle.

With these exceptions, the building retains its main original features, and most of its details belonging to different periods of mediaeval architecture, and is on the whole in substantial repair. What remains of the nave is of early Norman work extremely rude and simple. The arcades, though full of character and expression, are composed of rough masonry, merely plastered over, and are devoid of any stone dressings. They are surmounted by clerestory windows of very minute proportions, with the usual expanding splays internally, and I discovered windows of a similar date in the aisle walls which are mere slits externally.

The roofs of the nave and south aisle are of early second pointed work, and are capable of reparation, but that of the north aisle has been tampered with[37]. The west and north arches of the crux, which still exist, are of the same rude treatment as the arcades, but of a trifle later date, being of very early first pointed. Those of the east and south sides have shared the fate of the central tower, and have disappeared.

The windows in the end of each of the transepts differ from each other, and are as peculiar as they are perplexing, having late forms with early expressions but as they bear a strong analogy to the window in the east wall of the south transept[38], which I have no hesitation in pronouncing to be first pointed, I incline to the belief in their early character also, and propose to give them the benefit of the doubt by retaining them intact[39]. They evidently have their idiosyncrasies, which perhaps, for want of a more perfect knowledge of the archaeology of the neighbourhood, I may be wrong in attributing to the intractable nature of the slaty material of which they are partly composed.

In the east wall of the north transept, and in the north wall of the chancel, are narrow slits of early first pointed work, differing only from the Norman lights in having pointed instead of round or square heads. In the east end of the chancel there is a third pointed window, which has, with more ingenuity than honesty, been repaired, or rather renewed, in cement, and a modern window similarly treated, which has been placed over a mutilated Tudor doorway in the south wall of the chancel, disposes of the list of details, if I except two good recumbent effigies in their sepulchral recesses in the north wall of the chancel.

Prichard also stated that he was "not prepared to say that the building was not erected at an earlier period than the eleventh century".

APPENDIX B – THE MEDIAEVAL INSCRIBED STONES[1]

The first three stones mentioned below, the Cadfan Stone, the sundial and the cross-marked stone, are all made of Crystal Tuff (Ordovician)[2] and come from the igneous intrusion north of Tonfannau[3].

1. THE CADFAN STONE

What is now known as the Cadfan Stone has been dated to the 9th century from the linguistic forms inscribed on it, although earlier suggestions have also included the 7th and 8th centuries.

The four inscriptions are memorials to people who have died, showing its original purpose as a memorial stone or gravestone. They are of great significance as the earliest examples of written Welsh (Brittonic Period). They are also the only early mediaeval inscriptions, other than names, in Old Welsh rather than in Latin. The stone is deeply incised but the characters are unevenly carved, words run together and abbreviations have been used. Wear by the weather, and other damage over more than a millennium, have added to the problems of reading and interpreting it.

Since the mid-19th century many attempts have been made to identify all the lettering, helped by old drawings and by a cast made in 1902. In 2007-8 rubbings were made

The Cadfan stone

of the four sides of the stone by the University of Bangor to aid the latest interpretation.

The wordings and translations of the four inscriptions are now thought to be:

Tengr(um)ui cimalted gu(reic) / Adgan // anterunc du But Marciau
Tegrumui wedded wife of Adgan (lies) near to But Marciau

M(ortici)c / ar tr(i)
The mortal remains of three

Cin ben Celen // tricet nictanam
Cin woman (or wife) of Celyn, a mortal wound remains

Mort/cic pe/tuar
The mortal remains of four

The later history of the Cadfan Stone

The stone was first recorded by Lhuyd in a letter in 1698 when it was standing at "the west end of the churchyard" and he or a helper made drawings of all four faces, copies of which survived[4]. It was obviously a useful-looking monolith as some time subsequently it disappeared from the churchyard and, it is said, became a gate post. If so, it must have been the latch end as the holes drilled into the stone are only long enough to hold a pole, not to take the weight of the hinges of a farm gate. It is said to have been brought back to the churchyard "from its position as a gate post"[5] in 1761 by Dr Taylor who also made drawings of the lettering as he saw it[6]. Both Taylor's and Lhuyd's drawings show that at this stage the stone was intact.

In the churchyard at Tywyn, about 25 yards to the west of the nave, there are four low, small stones set vertically. These are said to have been the place where the stone rested horizontally and, at one stage, they were thought to mark the position of Cadfan's burial place. In 1740, Mr Vaughan obtained permission to open the grave to look for any remains, for which he made a payment to the churchwardens of 2/6d on 15 July[7]. There is no record of any remains being found and a later vicar, the Rev. Titus Lewis, said that it was reported that there had never been an interment of any kind in that particular place[8].

Exactly where the stone was placed after its return is unknown, but it had not yet finished its travels, although quite what they were is uncertain. Fenton, on his 1808 tour, says it was removed to a small building meant to be a mausoleum for the late Mrs Scott but never finished[9]. In 1921, an Editor's footnote in Cambro-Briton[10] reported that "this ancient relic now decorates a grotto belonging to a neighbouring gentleman, who took the liberty of removing it".

The Rev. David Pugh spent considerable time in the 1920s working on his interpretation of the stone and included in his notebook the following information:

In 1796 it was in a gentleman's garden in the neighbourhood, probably at Bodtalog, and an extract from a newspaper published in 1884[11] confirms the local tradition to this effect:
'A writer, referring to the Cadvan Stone in 1796, said if it is to be seen it must be by the light of torches and tapers, for a gentleman of the

neighbourhood, stimulated by a most eccentric taste, sacrilegiously removed the Tomb-stone from the Churchyard, with the consent of the Vicar, to decorate his own grotto, which is as dark as Erebus and situate in an almost impenetrable wilderness.'

Sometime after 1796 the stone was returned, it is said, under the will of Edward Scott of Bodtalog[12] but there is no mention of the stone in the body of the will[13]. It was presumably back at the church by 1844, as a report of the Cambrian Archaeological Society meeting that year refers to Mr W. W. E. Wynne arranging for plaster casts of the four faces of the stone and also for rubbings of each face.

At some stage, it was erected on a small mound to the right of the south door of the church[14]. Following the 1880-4 rebuilding, it was moved to lie on the floor of the north aisle before eventually being erected in its current position in 1934.

2. THE SUNDIAL

The sundial/prayer dial/mass clock dates to the 8th or 9th century.

It is one of only two Irish-style sundials known in Wales, the other being at Clynnog Fawr which, like Tywyn, was the site of an ancient *clas*. It would have been used to mark the times of services, both for the *clas* community and for laity wanting to attend a service. Usually, as at Clynnog Fawr, the time was divided into four periods of about three hours each but the Tywyn sundial has six periods of about two hours marked. (Does this mean they had more services – and were more 'holy' – than Clynnog Fawr?)

The prayer sundial

The top part of the stone is missing but the central circle at the top has been completed in modern times to show where the peg or gnomon would have been. In addition to the sundial markings there is also an inscription slightly lower down reading "From Towyn 1 mile" in an 18th century hand.

The church has no extant records that mention the sundial and it only came to light following the demolishing of Ynysymaengwyn Hall in 1968 when Thomas Lloyd, a member of the British Sundial Society, was examining the rubble[15]. It is said to have stood by the gate of the Hall and subsequently to have been built into an outbuilding.

The following is a possible re-creation of its travels:

Carved for, and used by, the *clas* at Tywyn in the 8th or 9th century, it stood near the entrance to the church or churchyard throughout mediaeval times. Even when multiple services no longer took place it could be used to mark the time of one or more Sunday services. Following the erection of the west tower, a clock was installed on its south face in 1776[16], and the old prayer sundial was regarded as old fashioned and ugly. Ynysymaengwyn Hall was the centre of the greatest estate in the area and its owner offered to use it as a milestone, since the hall gates were about a mile from the town. Many years later, when its link with the church had been forgotten, outbuildings were being erected at Ynysymaengwyn and so large a monolith would have been ideal as a lintel. Quite possibly this is when the top was lost, especially if the stone was deliberately squared off at that end. Following the destruction of the hall by fire and the increasingly unsafe nature of all the buildings, the sundial joined the rubble as the place was demolished.

The town council, to whom the building and its environs belonged, offered the sundial to the church. Unfortunately, for various reasons, it was not possible to obtain a faculty within the necessary time and, as a temporary measure, it was put in the flowerbed by the Leisure Centre (facing east…!). Life was busy – and it was once again forgotten.

Twenty-three years later the churchwarden of St Cadfan's Church was contacted by Mike Cowham[17] enquiring about the whereabouts of the sundial. On hearing of its position he expressed concern and recommended that it should be under cover, either in the church or in a museum, to reduce erosion of the inscription. Tywyn Town Council agreed to the move to the church and very kindly assisted in funding it. A faculty was obtained and in

February 2010 it was moved to a site adjacent to the Cadfan Stone at the west end of the north aisle.

3. THE CROSS CARVED STONE

In 1863, the local Guidebook[18] to the area recorded that "a long stone with an early cross carved upon it" was to be seen on the west side of the "comparatively modern" (i.e. 18th century) tower. This, presumably, is the stone which was built into the central tower in 1880-4. It can be seen laid horizontally on the south side of the tower to the left and below the belfry window. The shape of the cross suggests that the stone was originally erected as a pillar. It is dated as 7th to 9th century and may have marked the extent of church land or of its *nawdd*[19].

Westwood reported that the stone was brought "from a place a quarter of a mile from the town called Bryn Paderau, which may be translated the Hill of Pater Noster. From this spot persons coming in one direction to Towyn would obtain the first view of the church, as well as of the chapel of St. Cadvan"[20]. It is said to have been found buried some feet underground, near the present entrance gate to the hospital[21].

There is a very similar stone to be seen on the east wall of the tower, but the visible face is not inscribed. Could this stone also have marked a limit of the church's protection at one time?

4. THE PASCENT STONE

In 1698 Lhuyd recorded a stone "pitch'd on end on ye southeast of Towyn Church". It was about 4 feet by 1 foot (1.2m x 30cm). Lhuyd's drawing of the stone, which was copied and eventually appeared in Gough[22], has PASCENT (with the S back to front) written along its length. Pascent was a fairly common Roman Christian name.

The whereabouts of this stone have been unknown for very many years. When one considers the travels of the Cadfan Stone and of the sundial it is easy to imagine that a smaller stone, easier to handle, would be taken away as building material – it may even have been built into the church itself.

In the absence of the stone, dating is very uncertain. Nash-Williams and Professor Edwards both suggest the capital letters point to 5th or 6th century. This means that it may have been one of the earliest gravestones in the churchyard.

APPENDIX C – THE MUSIC

In the early years of the 19th century, music in the church was provided by a small number of instruments, possibly only a flute and a bass viol.

At some stage these were replaced by a harmonium; this was put in the gallery with the choir to enable its limited sound to carry to the greatest extent. When the gallery was demolished in 1870 the harmonium was succeeded by a small organ which was placed against the south wall of the chancel. After the restoration it was installed under the arch between the crossing and the south transept.

THE 1897 ORGAN

This new organ was installed under the arch between the crossing and the north transept. The area used for its supports may be seen as wooden stretches in the tiles of the north transept passage. The whole of the following description was copied by the Rev. Titus Lewis[1] from the specification:

The organ was built by Messers Ingram and Co, organ builders, Hereford at a cost of nearly £365. It is a double manual of a very superior tone, the specifications of which were approved by Mr T Westley Morgan, organist of Bangor Cathedral, who suggested some of the stops. The following particulars of the two manuals, and independent pedal organ, will be interesting.

	Material	Feet	Pipes

Great organ (Five Stops) CC to G

		Material	Feet	Pipes
1. Open Diapason		Metal	8	56
2. Clarabella		Wood	8	56
3. Dolciana		Metal	8	56
4. Principal		Metal	4	56
5. Wald Flute		Wood	4	56

Swell Organ (7 stops) CC to G

		Material	Feet	Pipes
6. Violin Open Diapason		Wood & Metal	8	56
7. Leiblich Gedacht		Wood	8	56
8. Salicional	Derived	Metal	8	56
9. Voix Celeste	Bass	Metal	8	56
10. Gemshorn		Metal	4	56
11. Oboe		Metal	8	56
12. Cornopean		Wood	8	30

Pedal Organ

	Material	Feet	Pipes
13. Bourdon (Large scale)…	Wood	16	30

Couplers:

14. Swell to Great	Two double-acting
15. Swell to Pedals	composition pedals to
16* Swell super Octave	Swell organ and two
17. Great to Pedals	to Great Organ

* To act through swell to Great as well as on the Swell Manual

According to the specifications the lower notes of Open Diapason (Great Organ) are to be architecturally arranged to form a speaking front. The swell box is three inches in thickness, and of compound construction. The front is fitted with Venetian shutters, activated by a new and improved method, and ensuring the production of the best possible crescendo and diminuendo effects. The bellows are of ample size, and supply the organ with a good and steady wind, blown by two feeders.

The whole is solidly constructed, double leathered, and panelled within and without, to afford access to all parts. The sound boards are of ample proportions, to allow free and proper speaking room for all pipes, and are fitted with the most improved noiseless pallets. All the fittings and action are of hardwood, and coated with French polish, to prevent absorption of moisture. The drawing-up action, composition, and all parts requiring great rigidity are of iron, coated with enamel. The coupler and all actions throughout the organ are constructed on the most advanced principles, and guaranteed to produce a light, elastic, and absolutely noiseless touch. All the pipes are of good and durable material, and of substantial thickness. The keyboard, pedal board and key fittings, are arranged in their relative positions, in accordance with the recommendations of the Royal College of Organists. The key fittings are of solid oak. The pedal boards are concave, with radiating sharp keys (College of Organists model). The keyboard is of the best ivory, and strong, and both sets of keys are of the latest overhanging pattern, supplied with patent oval pins. The diapasons, and foundation stops of the organ throughout, are of good seal, and of grand and full tone. The voicing throughout the instrument is of the highest artistic standard, preserving in a marked degree the peculiar characteristics of each individual stop, without sacrificing the sonorous diapason effect of full organ, so essential for church purposes. The case is of yellow deal and pitch pine, and in accordance with the design submitted and approved.

The whole of the above have been executed with the best materials and workmanship, and were open to the examination of any fully qualified referees.

It is justly due to add, that this organ was obtained by the good offices of Mrs Lewis, the Vicarage, and her daughter, Mary Emmeline Lewis, at a cost of £364/7/6d.

THE CURRENT ORGAN

The original specification at its installation in 1911 is as shown in Table B1[2].

The bellows were placed on the floor of the south transept, with the water engine at its side on a concrete base about 2 feet square. This had a lead drip tray, which drained through the wall. The weight of this section was about 1½ tons and the floor had to be strengthened to carry it.

The organ itself weighed 4 tons and required a platform 17½ feet long and 6 feet wide raised 8 feet above the ground on steel uprights and RSJs. The console was as at present, the platform allowing controls to be led to the organ.

It was suggested that the casework should be on the lines of the chancel screen at Llanegryn.

In 1941 the hydraulic engine of the organ was replaced by an electric blower at a cost of £110/9/8d, and ten years later the organ was overhauled and cleaned[3].

Over the winter of 1981-2 snow blew under the roof of the south transept and got into the organ causing

Table B1.   The current organ specification

Specification

| Manuals | CC to G | 56 notes |
| Pedals | CCC to F | 30 notes |

Great Organ

	Length & material	Number of notes / pipes
Violone (New. Bottom octave of wood, remaining of zinc & metal)	16 ft wood & metal	56 / 56
Open Diapason	8 ft wood	56 / 56
Clarabella	8 ft wood	56 / 56
Dulciana (New bottom octave of zinc)	8 ft metal	56 / 56
Principal	4 ft metal	56 / 56
Wald flute	4 ft	56 / 56

Swell organ

Violin Diapason (New bottom octave of wood)	8 ft wood & metal	56 / 56
Lieblich Gedact	8 ft	56 / 56
Salicional (bass gro.)	8 ft metal	56 / 44
Voix Celeste (Ten.C)	8 ft metal	56 / 44
Gemshorn	4ft metal	56 / 56
Horn	8 ft metal	56 / 56
Oboe	8 ft metal	56 / 56
Tremulant (New)		

Pedal Organ

Violone (New. Derived from No 1 by pneumatic transmission)	16 ft wood & metal	30 / ---
Bourdon (Scale increased by adding 4 new pipes)	16 ft wood	30 / 30
Echo Bass (New.)	16 ft wood	30 / 30

Couplers

Swell octave	Pneumatic	new
Swell sub-octave	Pneumatic	new
Swell to great	Pneumatic	new
Swell to pedals	Mechanical	new
Great to pedals	Mechanical	new

Accessories

Three composition pedals to the Great Organ.

Three composition pedals to the Swell Organ.

One double-acting piston to the Swell to pedal coupler.

One double-acting piston to the Great to pedal coupler.

Balanced Swell pedal.

257

considerable damage. The insurance company paid what it would cost to restore the organ to its previous condition. While it was stripped down for this, the action was changed from pneumatic to electric by Robert Edwards (Chester) Ltd, which resulted in a better organ and also made it easier to maintain. This company has continued to maintain the organ for over thirty years.

By 1996 all the organ sliders had finally been replaced with electronics.

In 2006 the organ was dismantled while work was done on the plaster of the church. Before reinstalling it was cleaned and serviced.

APPENDIX D – SCHOOL AND CHURCH

[1]In 1717 Vincent Corbet, owner of the Ynysymaengwyn estate, is said to have given land producing £4 per annum for a free school in the Parish of Tywyn. The money was passed yearly to the schoolmaster from an agent as a charge on Hendy Farm. Seventy years later no documents could be found concerning it and neither could Vincent Corbet's will.

Parliamentary returns for 1786 state that Lady Moyer of London by Trust gave £200 in 3% Consols for teaching poor children in the Parish of Towyn. Again, there is no deed relating to it. A letter from Lady Moyer concerning money for Towyn Charity School mentions Vincent Corbet's donation but not her own gift. Instead it refers to £10 a year to be given by Athelstan Owen and his heirs to teach twenty children – boys and girls – to read and write; whoever copied the letter refers to the £200 in an addendum. As Athelstan Owen died in August 1731[2], the letter must have been written between 1717 and 1731.

Lady Moyer was most specific about certain aspects of the school and schoolmaster. No one in holy orders was to be schoolmaster so that "no Romish priest may ever poison them" and "his whole time may be spent for the good of the children in his charge". He had to go to church with them twice every Sabbath day and every day that prayers were read, and pray with them in the morning before he started teaching and also at the end of the school day. The hours were to be 8am (or 7am in summer) to 11am and 1pm to

5pm. If he asked any fee or reward from the parents of the poor children he was to forfeit £5.

So, for most of the 18th century, there was a school in Tywyn and provision for the education of the poorest children. Those parents whose children did not qualify for free education could pay for them to attend. There was, however, no financial provision for a schoolroom.

In the early 19th century, official reports described educational facilities in Wales as an "educational desolation". In 1808 the non-denominational "British and Foreign School Society for the Teaching of Children of the Poorer Classes" had been founded with a view to giving scriptural education to the whole population of England. Its "British Schools" were non-denominational. They must have been seen as a threat by the established church, for three years later the Church of England founded "The National Society for Promoting the Education of the Poor in the Principles of the Established Church". Its "National Schools" were closely linked with the local Anglican church, and for many years the two societies dominated the Welsh educational scene[3]. Although Lady Moyer's School was not a church foundation, it specified that its free scholars must attend church twice on Sunday, which would not have been acceptable to many non-conformists.

By 1834 some of the endowment money seems to have been going astray, with only the £4 from Vincent Corbet and part of the interest from Lady Moyer's £200 reaching the schoolmaster. He was teaching twenty-one poor children free of charge and accepting others at a rate of 2/6d for English reading and 3/6d for writing and arithmetic. Numbers in the school fluctuated from thirty-five in summer to sixty in winter.

In 1840 the Lady Moyer's Gift Charity was formally established with three trustees and with £420 at 3% standing to its credit. In 1858 the sole surviving trustee applied for further trustees to be appointed, stating that the schoolhouse had fallen into decay, that there were no funds to repair it and that the school had been discontinued for many years. New trustees were appointed but did not take up their work and the dividends began to be sent to the vicar of the parish. It would seem that it was at this stage that the church became directly involved with the school. Meanwhile Vincent Corbet's £4 per year continued to be paid annually by the owner of Hendy Farm.

Exactly when the school became a National School is difficult to determine. The foundation stone of the building reads "National School free for 21 poor children" and "rebuilt 1861 by public subscription". It was endowed by the Lady Moyer and Vincent Corbet charities. In addition, one-third of the Rev. Lewis Lloyd's Abergroes charity was transferred to the school[4]. The public subscription must have been inadequate, for in 1864 "a tea meeting was held in the National School, the proceeds to go towards the liquidation of the debt now standing"[5].

In 1879 the Charity Commissioners appointed the vicar and churchwardens of the Parish of Towyn and their successors, together with two others, as trustees of the school with respect to the Vincent Corbet Charity, Lady Moyer's gift and real estate vested in the Official Trustee. From 1878 the dividends were not paid to the trustees but accumulated and they were not handed over until 1887. Throughout this time the vicar, Titus Lewis, had paid £12/12/0d annually to the schoolmaster out of his own pocket. At last, it was refunded to him.

The Forster Elementary Education Act 1870 required partially state-funded board schools to be set up to provide elementary (primary) education in areas where existing provision was inadequate. Board schools were managed by elected school boards and remained fee-charging, but poor parents could be exempted and the boards could pay for poor pupils even if they attended church schools. Non-board schools could have 50% of their running costs met by a grant and this was received by Tywyn National School.

In the summer of 1874 Her Majesty's Inspector of Schools examined the Tywyn National School for the first time in three years. The result was highly satisfactory to all concerned. The discipline and manner of the children deserved high praise. The elementary subjects were taught with great success, 100% of the children passed their standards and the singing was good[6]. Perhaps it was just bad timing that at the beginning of the autumn term 1874 the Tywyn school board wrote to ask if the managers of the National School intended "to place their school under the control of the board". They respectfully declined to do so[7]. The British Schools in the area did, however, either close or hand over to the board.

The Great School Fete at Ynysymaengwyn in August 1875 reveals that, at that time, the area contained British Schools at Bryncrug, Tywyn and Aberdyfi but a National School only at Tywyn. This probably reflects the high non-conformist population of the area[8].

In 1891 provision was made for state payment of school fees up to 10 shillings per pupil. This meant that the money from the charities, which had paid for the education of poor children, could be used for the school in general. Two years later the Charity Commissioners looked carefully at the school accounts, with special reference to the charity income. Some figures are:

Income: Education Dept. Grant £53; Charities income £34/15/6d; Fee grant £26/19/2d; voluntary contributions £8/5/2d; concerts etc £8/12/2d.

Expenditure: Teachers & assistants (day & evening) £112/15/7d; Books etc £5/10/6d; fuel, light & cleaning £3/0/6d; other 18/4d.

Already the income from the charities was considerably less than the cost of running the school.

The managers' minutes for 1900 to 1910 still exist[9]. From them it would seem that the managers had an increasingly 'hands-off' approach, with meetings four or fewer times a year. On a number of occasions either there was no quorum, so no meeting, or all that was recorded was "there was no formal business to complete". With hindsight, it is possible to see in this limited information seeds of the problems that were to arise later.

A new Education Act in 1902 abolished school boards and replaced them with Local Education Authorities (LEAs) under the overall control of the Board of Education. It allowed for all schools, including denominational schools, to be funded through the rates. Because of their larger size compared to the school boards and the number of schools they covered, LEAs would have a wider overview of education in their area and how it should best be carried out. One way they could influence the schools was by limiting the number of teachers they were prepared to pay.

By 1908 the numbers in the National School had dropped considerably. When the assistant teacher resigned, the LEA maintained that the attendance was not sufficient to warrant a replacement. A report from His Majesty's Inspector from the Board of Education detailed the unsatisfactory condition of the school. It stated that this was due to the headteacher being single-handed, and recommended the appointment of an assistant with a knowledge of Welsh for the lower classes. This recommendation was sent to the LEA with the request that an assistant teacher be appointed, but by May 1909 matters were no better and the headteacher was still single-handed. The LEA was obdurate that an assistant teacher was not needed, but a sewing teacher was appointed on a very part-time basis.

In November 1909, the vicar had to report that an attempt was being made to divert the Lewis Lloyd Abergroes charity money from the National School towards secondary education. A motion was passed that such an action was unjust and that legitimate resistance should be offered to the carrying out of the scheme but lack of interest in the school by the managers is revealed in that the next meeting, four months later, failed to achieve a quorum. It was not until 11 April 1910 that they decided to see what could be done to put the school in a more satisfactory condition as regards both the condition of the building and the attendance of the children.

Then, on the night of Sunday 19 April 1910, the headteacher disappeared. This was apparently because of the arrival of a summons or warrant for his arrest for the non-maintenance of his wife[10]. The teaching was quickly shared between the vicar and curate, and Merioneth Education Committee notified. Their reply revealed what was in store.

The reply pointed out that the average attendance in 1909 had been only 17.25 and in the first three months of 1910 only 15. "The present occasion appears the most favourable for the Board of Education to determine whether the School is necessary or not." Meanwhile the board would not be responsible for paying any head or assistant teacher and the positions should not be advertised. In reply, the managers asserted that as soon as the headmaster departed (only ten days before) the parents sent their children to the school and the number on the register immediately increased to sixty with an average attendance of forty-nine. They then advertised for both head and assistant teachers, and at the end of May decided to make an appointment. It is at this stage that the minute book ceases to show further meetings.

What was behind all this? The closure of Towyn Church School seems to some extent to have been orchestrated by the Local Education Authority, as revealed in a report of a meeting by the Church Schools Emergency League, reports of the House of Commons education debate on 13 July 1910 and letters in The Times[11]. The report on the parliamentary debate included a remark from the President of the Board of Education that "the closure of the church school... will serve the interests of secular education". A letter in The Times from W. Ormsby-Gore, MP for Denbigh, quoted Winston Churchill (then a Liberal) telling the House of Commons that "it is the hope of the Liberal party to free Wales from its alien church".

Until three years previously the attendance at the school had been between fifty and sixty. The headteacher subsequently "became unsatisfactory" and because of his conduct, parents did not want their children in a school where he taught. He had sent in his resignation some time before and the managers had accepted it but it was rejected by the LEA and he had continued in his post. He had even been summoned by the police in Dolgellau on a charge of drunkenness, later dropped; this information was known to the LEA but not communicated to the managers. Directly he left and the clergy took up the teaching, the numbers in the school increased considerably and the attendance for May 1910 was fifty-seven.

At the time the church school had a capacity of 102 and the council school of 310. The Board of Education had recently approved plans by the LEA to increase the accommodation at the council school by eighty, even though its attendance was only 220. It was after this approval that the move was made against the church school. Although the letter read at the managers' meeting of 22 April gave a strong indication that the grant to the school might be withdrawn "as the school was not necessary", which would be expected to result in its closure, the formal notice of grant withdrawal was dated 16 June and stated that the grant would be withdrawn from 30 June – only fourteen days later.

Arguments in the House of Commons included reference to a request by the LEA in 1904 that an extra classroom should be built and made much of the fact that this had not been done, although even without it the church school had accommodation for 102 children. Accusation was made by Mr Haydn Jones, MP for Merionethshire, that the clergy had gone from door to door of church households, compelling them to send their children to the church school. This accusation was denied in the vicar's letter to *The Times*. It is clear that there was considerable disquiet in the papers, both locally and nationally, about what happened to the school.

Meanwhile by 25 July 1910[12] the managers had gone ahead in faith and appointed two new teachers, committing themselves to expenditure of £140 per annum. They had also let the contract for a new schoolroom at a cost of £300 (with only £160 so far in the bank). There were sixty-nine pupils on the roll and they confidently expected eighty by September.

An application to be reinstated on the grant list was made and a sad note from the vicar outlines what happened. Only a few days after the application was made the LEA lodged an objection putting forward reasons why the school was unnecessary, reasons to which the managers replied. However on 19 January 1911 the Board of Education decided that "the school is not necessary within the meaning of... the Act". Then, quietly, it began to make arrangements for the school's remaining endowments to be transferred to scholarships for council school pupils who wished to proceed to intermediate school.

The matter came up for lengthy debate in the House of Commons on 23 March 1911 but there was no change of mind and the school remained without grant support.

Even though it would now have to educate its pupils free of charge, and without any income from the Board of Education, the school remained open. Early in 1913 an application was made for grant status to "re-open" the school. Only a week before the final date for objections the LEA wrote to say that they were opposing the application. When the details of the objections were received, they were refuted in detail. The National Society put David Pugh, the vicar, in touch with a vicar in Halifax who had successfully argued for the reinstatement of the church school and recommended that the managers insist on a public inquiry. Despite all attempts the application for the grant was once more refused. Faced with the need to depend solely on donations from supporters to cover all the costs of the school, support which could not be expected to continue in the long term, it was decided reluctantly that it must close.

APPENDIX E – INCUMBENTS

The year given is the start year where it is known.
If the year is starred it means "known to be present that year".
R = rector, V = vicar, C = curate, Chap = chaplain

Year	Name		Notes
1147*	Morfran	Abbot	
1291*	Gruff: de Towyn	Dean	
1291*	David ap Llewellyn		
1291*	David Crach		
1291*	Ade Capellani (Adam the Chaplain)	Chap	
1397	David ap Ieuan ap Tuder Nicholas Harwold		1426 exchanged with Beuchamp for Llanveir
1426	Reginald Beuchamp (Bechamp, Beauchamp)	R	
1448*	Richard Fowey (Fowy), Bachelor of Canon Law of Oxford	R	1451 exchanged with Brugge for Lanreythowe
1451	John Brugge (Bruge)	R	
1461	Owen Lloit (Lloyd)	R	
1504*	Mag. Mathew Pole	R	
1504*	Dom. Hugh ap Rees	C	
1504*	Dom. Gruff ap John Velewyth	V	
1504*	Dom. Edmund ap John	Chap	
1504*	Dom. John Penyall	Chap	
1504*	Dom. Gruff ap Rynallt	Chap	

	William Tofte (Toste, Tost)	R	Resigned 1523
	John Tona (Touna)	V	Died about 1513
1523	Dom. Humphrey Thomas	R	1524-34 Master of Battlefield College, Shropshire
	William Tofte (Toste, Tost)	R	Died 1528
1528	John Coole MA	R	Resigned 1529
1529	John Griffithe, clk	R	Uncle of Bishop of Rochester. Said to be dying July 1536
1537	Mag. George Woolsell LLD (Wulfet, Wulflet, Wolflete, Wolfet, Wellifed)	R	1546 refused to pay ecclesiastical subsidy and replaced by Poynte
1544*	Mr Acrod, Parson of Towyn	V?	Executor of the will of William Clarke, 14 June 1544
1546	Mag. John Poynte (Ponett, Poynet), clk	R	Prebendary of Canterbury Cathedral 1550. Bishop of Rochester – allowed to keep rectorship of Towyn (1551 became Bishop of Winchester).
1547	The Rectory of Tywyn, with all its emoluments, was granted to the Bishop of Coventry and Lichfield by Edward VI.		
	John Kymm		Died 1555
1555	Arthur Hughes, clk (Arthur ap Huw)	V	Died 1570
1570	Gruffith ap Morgan, clk	V	1606

1606	Robert Parry MA	V	1623
1623	Richard Nanney MA	V	Died 1633
1634	Robert Price LLB	V	Resigned 1636 to become chancellor of Bangor Cathedral (subsequently Bishop of Ferns & Leighlin and then Bishop of Bangor).
1636	Richard Johnes MA	V	Resigned 1636
1636	John Hughes MA	V	Also held Llanaber from 1638. Ejected from Tywyn as a pluralist some time between 1650 and 1658.
1658	John Swayne	V	Had been curate of Pennal
1662	John Hughes STP	V	Reinstated at the Restoration
1681	William Lewis	V	
1717	Edward Morgan BA	V	
1749	William Lloyd BA	V	Resigned 1753
1753	Jeremiah Griffith MA	V	Died 1784
1784	John Pierce BA	V	Ceased (resigned?) 1785
1785	Pryse Maurice	V	Died 1803
1803	Robert Davies MA	V	Died 1827
1827	John Maurice Edwards BA	V	Died 1841
1841	Owen Jones	V	Died 1869
1869	Titus Lewis BD	V	Had been Stipendiary Curate from 1861. Retired 1905

1906	David Richard Pugh MA	V	Had been Stipendiary Curate from 1901. Resigned 1932. Became vicar of Penstrowed.
1932	Henry Thomas BA	V	Resigned 1957. Became vicar of Arthog.
1957	Tuddyd Owen BA	V	Retired 1978
1978	John Martin Riley BA	V	Retired 2003
2003	Vacancy		No vicar September 2003 to October 2007
2007	Richard Adriaan Vroom STL	V	

BD – Bachelor of Divinity
clk – clerk (cleric)
LLB – Bachelor of Laws
LLD – Doctor of Laws
STL – Licenciate of Sacred Theology
STP – Professor of Sacred Theology (equivalent to DD – Doctor of Divinity)
Mag. – *Magister* (Master e.g. MA)
Dom – *Dominus* (equivalent to Reverend)

APPENDIX F – CANU CADFAN
(Song to Cadfan)
Llewellyn Fardd I

Translated by Professor Catherine McKenna, Harvard University

Supreme divinity, God, succour to me,
Worthy possessor, lord of deliverance,
Since he is ruler to me, may he give me inspiration,
An ode fair of destiny, of superior loyalty.

5   I long to love the song of community
Since my lord gave me the gift of desire,
Since the lord gives me a sufficiency of pleasure, for my part,
In praising Cadfan, the refuge of warriors.

He upheld the right of his land and its tribute,
10   The warrior hero upheld the fair dwelling,
God upheld dignity, as man and as boy,
For the son of Eneas, excellent man of honour.
The chief, son of Gwen, whom it was fortunate to see, is upheld;
May the strength of the one powerfully protective on the battlefield uphold me.

15   May the help of God be the solace of my nature —
Wise, pleasant teaching of special work,

To undertake labour which is no fatigue,
Where violence dares not go,
Where no man dares carry off a necessity from the
church
20   Near the edge of the blue sea, because of its due.

Where no one dares constraint of its revenues,
Where I shall dare to visit for a while.

There are three potent altars, famous for miracles,
Between sea and wood and mighty tide:
25   Mary's altar of the Lord, trustworthy sacred relic;
The altar of Peter in his authority which should be
praised;
And the third altar which was bestowed by
heaven —
Blessed is its dwelling because of its hospitality.

Blessed is he who is willingly
30   Where dwells the lord of Ednyfed's land;
Blessed is his spirit who is exalted therein,
Like Dewi's church it was made.

Church of fair Cadfan, brilliant to behold,
Bright whitewashed church proudly whitened,
35   Church of faith and devotion and belief and
communion,
As though it had been fashioned by God himself.

He fashioned for the Godhead a choice residence
When he came from Brittany to the community of
Christendom.

The blessed youth nurtured no sin:
40   May God bless the devout servant.

The blessing of the nine orders of heaven upon his
dwellings,
Blessed region of a silent one's prerogative.

Blessed the voyage of his company
When he came to the realm night by night, day by day,
45   When there came to the issue of Emyr the desire to
gaze upon
Aber Menwenfer in the evening and in the morning.

A noble panegyric is this to Meirionydd,
A noble bard shapes it as a poet,

The noble country of Cadfan where there coexist
always
50   The noble gospel, humble guide,
With the fair precious crozier of new miracles,
Which prevents the enemy from killing his
opponent;
And its country-prospering lord, joy of the country,
Who makes his refuge good and happy,
55   Like loud Osfran piercing the enemy's shield,
A generous, magnificent shield prevailing over
counterclaims;
And its giver-abbot dispenses favour;
To us he distributes from his church a multitude,
He arranges battle with the Lord's consent,
60   Morfran flowing with gifts, pride of a day's
entertainment.

God has made two elders for its sake,
They are fortune-favoured, genial priests;
Being under the celebrated one does not trouble
The happy, devout valley,

65 And guarding the rood and the tribute and the
wood and the choir
And the sea and the coast and the highlands.
How beneficial is my protection, in the forefront of
many,
On a path pleasant because of the high season.

A noble place is this before a stout lord,

70 The noble church of Cadfan by the shore of the blue
sea.

There is not lost of its land nor of the strength of its
dwelling
A foot because of war, difficult to avoid.

No one dares violence over its wall,
No one contemplates the treachery of piercing its
door,

75 The lord of the host has not tolerated cowardice in
conflict,
He has not taken up a shield in the same way
Nor does he speak falsely with the wrath of Hector,
The shield on the lord's shoulder has not been
reproached,
I shall not reproach my lord in the dreadfulness of
his rage.

80   The lofty church of Cadfan's flock, like Bangor,
        Its renowned relics are heard of widely,
        Its music, its leaders, its marble,
        Its manifest miracles are seen daily,
        Its precious dwelling is observed,
85   Its uplands, the justice within its bounds,
        Its fame, its situation on its seacoast.

How fitting for me because of my talent and my
fortunate understanding
To remember the lord by my new song,
Since he gave me a share of castoff white horses,
90   Since he remembered me when he distributed
favour.

To remember Jesus is the intention in my verse
And to praise Cadfan with his permission.

The guardian of the host merits praise:
It is right to praise a king who is a giver.

95   Praiseworthy is the one God, he is the one defender,
        To Meirionydd he gives continual gifts.
        Its choir and its liturgy are praised
        And its music and its warriors and its sea and its ale
        And its church near the sea, near the tide bank too.

100   Let its ground prosper and its grain and its seed,
        Let truth and land prosper in its dwelling,
        Let feast and mead and goodly wealth prosper,
        Let every mixture of grain and mixture of seed
        prosper in it,

Let it prosper me to praise the strengthener of
warriors.

105 My poem is exhausted by the condition
Of hosts and riches on your part.

Glad was the Lord God on the day that Cadfan was
begotten,
Open to the weak was his blessed hand.

He performed miracles by his permission,
110 Setting fire here in clothing.
He relieved plague and want and denial,
Blessing Gwynnyr and his men and his land.
He sustained him like an acknowledged judge,
He took heaven for his patrimony.

115 Two men I praise, as the lord permits me,
Two fair ones, two blessed ones, two liberal givers,
Two wise in dominion, in harmony,
Two dear ones, two compatriots, two holy ones,
Two who perform miracles for the sake of
enlightenment before them,
120 Two unstinting of their favour to the satisfaction of
the suppliant,
Two cousins they were who plotted no treachery:
Cadfan to guard the church with Lleuddad.

Powerfully Cadfan guards the shore of the blue sea,
Fair son of Eneas, supporter of prayer.

125 A fair hill is Tywyn, it is not right to be silent about it,

Like the fair abode of heaven its dwellings.
Powerfully he guarded, near Dysynni,
Beauty and liberality and liberal giving.

Powerful proud pomp is the increase of strength,
130 The powerful bulwark of the coast: there is
contentment therein.
The intention in my mind is to compose for it,
I intended, I came to the Dyfi valley.
Whoever desires God, it is no futility for him
To venture to cross beyond Eryri.

135 It was a great plan, in order to claim it
Arms from the south, the furies of spears;
Splendid was his welcome before he died,
Guarding against the public the riches of Enlli.

One monastery there is by the brine,
140 Lleuddad and Cadfan guarding it,
Sea-land of a host's valour,
Strong, much-visited, of gentleness and courtesy.

There is a church fully fair to describe
In the land of Meirionydd, good to praise it.
145 I praise the supreme God, I ask a petition of him,
To visit before death and before silence.

Much-visited church of Cadfan of fair dwellings,
Haunt of generous ones more generous than the
three,
And because of devotion, renegades near it are not
the rule,

150   And neither is there want therein,
       Only beautiful things and poets and poetry,
       Only peace and mead in vessels,
       Only easy discourse, exchange with a poet,
       And fine men without shame, without hardness,
155   And a treasure house and talent and goodness,
       And a properly arrayed relic as excellent as itself,
       And craft and song and cheerful singing,
       And our hangings are superior to Llanddewi's,
       And around its dyke its honourable community,
160   And the drinking horns in fists, adornment of the
       lodge,
       And the circle of the floodtide filling the river
       mouth,
       And at the time of vespers the order of service.

       A minister is my song for grace, for a share,
       Ministers on his behalf the cantors of Cadfan,

165   Warriors from beside the sea, from beside the high
       coast,
       Maintaining their warfare, which they do not conceal:
       The nobility of Meirionydd, Elfan's land,
       God be with them to their advantage as regards us.
       I chose my poetry in the ferocity of battle
170   Beside flood and current and cry of the sea.

       I praise a valiant man whom the world's poets praise,
       Valiant men who remove the penance of every weakling,
       A mightily gifted one of perfection,
       Of unquestionable gifts, of John's customs.

175   So long as he is in heaven in his brilliant white throne,
       When he speaks as a chief, as a fair lord,
       My song is preserved in his monastery church;
       May the valiant wise God guard Cadfan's domain.

C.McK.

NOTES BY THE AUTHOR[1]

The breaks in the above have been inserted by the author of this book to separate thoughts or sentences. They were not inserted by the translator and do not reflect the structure of the poem.

8. Cadfan, the refuge of warriors. The link with warriors may come from *cad* – battle, *man/fan* – place. There may be a pun on his name in line 14 – "battlefield".

12-13. Cadfan is said to be the son of Eneas and Gwen.

30. Ednyfed Meirionydd was a descendant of Meirion who was traditionally the founder of the *cantref* of Meirionydd.

32. This suggests that Tywyn Church was already substantially complete at the time the poem was written.

45. Emyr Llydaw was the father of Gwen, and so Cadfan's grandfather, according to *Bonedd y Saint*.

95-99. The clear implication is that Tywyn is the pre-eminent church of Meirionydd, i.e. its mother church.

115-22. The traditional relationship between Cadfan and Lleuddad is a spiritual one. Cadfan appointed Lleuddad as his successor on Ynys Enlli (Bardsey).

132. The Dyfi (River Dovey) was the southern boundary of the *cantref* of Merionydd.

134. Eryri – Snowdon

167. Elfan. *Cantref* Meirionydd was associated with Powys until about 1120, so this might refer to Elfan Powys.

Nothing is known about Aber Menwenfer (46), Osran (55), Gwynnyr (112).

GENERAL NOTES AND GLOSSARY

Merioneth/Meirionydd

Following the usage in *The History of Merioneth Vol. 2*, Meirionydd has been used for the early Middle Ages *cantref*, which lay between the Mawddach and the Dyfi. Merioneth has been used for the county and also for the archdeaconry.

Money

Currency is shown as used at the time. Pre-1972 this is in pounds, shillings and pence (£ s d.); £10/2/4d represents £10, 2 shillings and 4 pence. There were 20 shillings in a pound and 12 pence in a shilling. From 1972 decimal currency is used and the format is £10.11 – £10 and 11 pence.

Spellings of Cadfan

During the last 200-300 years the spelling "Cadvan" was almost invariably used. The spelling "Cadfan" was introduced in the 1970s.

In mediaeval times, 'u' and 'v' had not been differentiated, and 'd'/'t' were sometimes confused. Spellings recorded for Cadfan of Tywyn (and Cadfan, king, a century later) include: Catuan/Catuanus, Catman, Catvan, Catamanus.

GLOSSARY OF WELSH TERMS

ap/ab   Son of

cantref   A mediaeval land division, particularly important in the administration of Welsh law. Cant – hundred, tref – town/settlement. (cf English "Hundred").

capel-y-bedd   Chapel of the grave or memorial chapel

clas   A community associated with a major church, led by an abbot.

claswyr   Men of the *clas*. They had hereditary rights which, while probably clerical in origin, were frequently non-clerical by the 12th century.

commote   An administrative division of land. There were usually two or more commotes in a cantref. The cantref of Meirionydd was made up of the commotes of Tal-y-bont and Ystumanner.

castell   Castle

eisteddfa   Seat

llwybr   Path, track

llys   Residence/court of a local lord or a prince

mab/fab   Boy or son

maerdref   Administrative centre of a commote. Pennal was the *maerdref* of Ystumanner.

merch/ferch   Girl or daughter

nawdd	Protective power. Unlike the English right of sanctuary in a church (recognised in English law 4-17th centuries), it could apply over an extended area from a church or from a person (depending on their status).
noddfa	Place of protection, sanctuary place
pererini	Pilgrims
pistyll	Spout, well, waterfall
tywyn	Seashore, sand dune

GENERAL GLOSSARY

advowson	The right to present a nominee for a position in the church.
appropriation	Taking all or part of the income of a benefice.
archdeaconry/ archdeacon	An archdeaconry is a division of a diocese. The Diocese of Bangor has two archdeaconries: Merioneth and Bangor. An archdeacon is in charge of an archdeaconry.
benefice	A benefice is the description given to the area over which a cleric has responsibility; it can comprise one or more parishes.
bishop	A bishop is in charge of a diocese.
bishopric	Office or diocese of a bishop.
bondman	Similar to villein (English Middle Ages).

canon — Each cathedral in Wales is managed by the dean of the cathedral and a number of canons, who are chosen from amongst the clergy serving in the diocese.

canonical hours — The canonical hours mark the divisions of the day into fixed times of prayer at regular intervals.

chantry — A chantry is a monetary trust fund established for the purpose of employing one or more priests to sing a specified number of Masses during a stipulated period of time for the spiritual benefit of a deceased person. A chantry might include an altar within a church or even a dedicated chapel either within the church or on private land but neither was actually necessary; the Masses could be sung at the church altar.

church rate/ church tax — The church rate was a tax on the occupier of a house or of land in a parish for the benefit of the parish church. It was used for costs associated with carrying on divine service, repairing the fabric of the church and paying the salaries of the officials (not clergy) connected with it.

collation — The presentation of a clergyman to a benefice by a bishop, who has it in his own gift, i.e. is in effect the patron of the parish.

crosier/crozier — The pastoral staff or crook of a bishop or abbot.

curate — A curate is a cleric appointed to assist another cleric – a role traditionally taken in the early stages of their ministry.

cure of souls — Care for souls (people), originally by the parish priest and curates, including provision of services, instruction (sermons etc.), encouragement, counselling and outreach.

deanery/dean Every benefice is part of a deanery which is a grouping of several benefices. Deanery activities are co-ordinated by an area dean who also has responsibility for any vacant benefices within the deanery.

diocese A diocese is an extended area containing a number of parishes under the care of a bishop. The Church in Wales has six dioceses.

faldstool A portable folding chair, used by a bishop when not occupying the throne in his own cathedral, or when officiating in a cathedral or church other than his own. It can also mean any movable folding stool used during divine service.

farmer/
tithe farmer When there was an absentee rector, the rectorial tithes might be collected by a "farmer" who paid a fixed sum to the rector for the privilege and then kept all the tithe above this amount. It meant that the rector did not have to employ an agent nor to supervise the tithe collection.

faculty Permission from the diocesan chancellor to carry out alterations to a church.

impropriator Another word for tithe farmer.

incumbent Rector or vicar of a parish or group of parishes.

induction Formal installation of a vicar or rector in a new benefice at a special service.

institution	The presentation of a cleric to a benefice by someone other than the bishop of the diocese.
living	Another word for benefice.
Mass	The name given by the Roman Catholic and some other churches to what most Protestant churches call "Eucharist", "Holy Communion" or "Lord's Supper".
obit	Another word for a chantry.
office	A service of worship in a prescribed form.
parish	Wales is divided into parishes. Each parish covers a specific geographic area and is looked after by a cleric assigned to it (who may also look after other parishes). A parish usually includes one or more church buildings. Historically, parishes were also the units of civil administration.
parochial	Of, or relating to, a parish.
parochial church council	The members of the parochial church council (PCC) are elected by the annual vestry meeting of the church. In conjunction with the incumbent, the PCC is responsible for the finances and administration of the parish.
paten	A small plate, usually of silver or gold, which holds the bread to be consecrated at a communion (eucharist) service.
patron/ patronage	The patron of a parish had the right of patronage to nominate the incumbent of a parish. In theory, the bishop could reject the nominee, but in

practice, this seldom happened especially if the patron was the king (as at Tywyn in the 16th century).

pluralism   The holding of more than one benefice by a cleric; they received the income of all the benefices which they held. (This is not the case where a modern Anglican clergyman is appointed to a group of churches or parishes, since clergy stipends are now from central finances, not from the individual churches.)
The clerics were said to be holding the benefices in plurality.

Poor Law   The Poor Laws made each parish legally responsible for supporting the legitimate needy in their community. Taxes to provide this support were decided at an annual vestry.

portioner/   A portioner was a person entitled to a share of
portionary   the income of a church (which often was, or had been, a *clas* church). Churches with portioners were portionary churches.

preferment   Promotion.

present to a   Nominate as an incumbent.
living

procuration   Procuration was the provision of necessities for bishops and archdeacons during their visitation of any parish church in their diocese or archdeaconry. Procurations originally took the form of meat, drink and accommodation, but gradually changed to a sum of money. Sometimes the amount demanded for procurations was excessive.

province	A group of dioceses under an archbishop or a member church of the Anglican Communion.
quinquennial	Every five years; used to refer to an architect's five-yearly inspection of church buildings.
reader/ lay reader	A person who has received training from the church and is allowed to preach. Nowadays, in the Anglican Church, they can take non-eucharistic services.
rector	Originally an incumbent who received all the tithes and the income from the glebe land of a parish.
rectory	1. The value of the tithe and glebe income received by a rector 2. A house provided for a rector.
return	Information sent to the bishop of a diocese concerning income, church attendance, state of the building etc., usually on an annual basis.
sanctuary	1. A sacred place, such as a church, in which fugitives formerly were immune from arrest (recognised by English law from the 4th to the 17th century) 2. The area within a church closest to the altar.
see	Diocese.
stipend	Clerical pay. An NSM (non-stipendiary minister) is ordained but works on a voluntary basis.
synod	A Church council, usually convened to decide an issue of doctrine, administration or application. The Church in Wales refers to its

ruling body as the Governing Body, while the Church of England's ruling body is usually called the Synod.

terrier — Inventory of the church, its buildings and its contents.

vestry — 1. Historically, vestries were responsible not only for the church affairs of the parish but also for much of the secular administration of the area of the parish (like a town council).
2. Nowadays, the Annual Vestry (or Easter Vestry) is the Annual General Meeting of the benefice.
3. A vestry is also the name given to a room, in or adjacent to the church building, where the incumbent robes for services.

vicar — Where a rector was non-resident (but received the money from a parish), he was supposed to appoint a vicar to look after the parish and its people in his place. The vicar usually received the small tithes of the parish as his payment. Except for historical interest, there is now no difference between a rector and a vicar.

vicarage — 1. The value of the small tithes and any other income going to a vicar
2. The house provided for a vicar.

visitation — An inspection or inquiry by an archbishop or bishop, or by an archdeacon on his behalf.

BIBLIOGRAPHY

Abbreviations used in endnotes

Aber Obs   *Aberystwyth Observer*
AIP16   *The Diocese of Bangor in the 16th Century*, A. I.
             Pryce (Bangor, 1923)
AIP3C   *The Diocese of Bangor During Three Centuries*, A.
             I. Pryce (Cardiff, 1929)
Arch Camb   *Archaeologica Cambrensis*
Arch EMCC   *Archaeology of Early Medieval Celtic Churches*,
             ed. N. Edwards (Leeds, 2009)
B/   Documents of the Diocese of Bangor in the
             National Library of Wales
Baring-Gould *The Lives of the British Saints Vol. 2*, S. Baring-
             Gould (London, 1908)
Bartrum   *Early Welsh Genealogical Tracts*, P. C. Bartrum
             (Cardiff, 1966)
BHO   British History Online
Bowen Settlements   *Settlements of the Celtic Saints in Wales*,
             E. G. Bowen (Cardiff, 1956)
Browne-Willis *A Survey of the Cathedral Church of Bangor and
             the Edifices Belonging to it*, Browne-Willis
             (London, 1721)
CCEd   Clergy of the Church of England Database
CinW20   *A History of the Church in Wales in the 20th
             Century*, D. T. W. Price (Church in Wales, 1990)
DRO   Merioneth Records Office, Dolgellau
DRP   Manuscript Notebook, D. R. Pugh, Vicar 1905-
             32 (St Cadfan's Church safe)
ECW&W   *The Early Church in Wales and the West*, ed. A.
             Lane & N. Edwards (Oxford, 1992)
Fenton   *Tours in Wales (1804-1813)*, R. Fenton, ed. J.
             Fisher (London, 1917)

Gerald   *Journey through Wales*, Giraldus Cambrensis

H Thomas 1485 *A History of Wales 1485-1660*, H. Thomas (Cardiff, 1972)

HCPP   House of Commons Parliamentary Papers

HM1   *History of Merioneth Volume 1*, E. G. Bowen & C. A. Gresham (Dolgellau, 1967)

HM2   *History of Merioneth Volume 2*, J. & L. Beverley Smith (Cardiff, 2001)

JMHRS   *Journal of the Merioneth Historical and Record Society*

Kettle   The Kettle Family Tree (1683-1984), David Anand (printed Artists Valley Press, privately circulated)

NL&Ch   *Native Law and the Church in Medieval Wales*, Huw Pryce (Oxford, 1993)

NLW   National Library of Wales

P Jenkins   *A History of Modern Wales 1536-1990*, P. Jenkins (London, 1991)

RCAHMW   Royal Commission on Ancient and Historic Monuments of Wales, Vol 6, Merioneth

Roads   *Paterson's Roads*, 17th edn, E. Mogg (London, 1824)

RRDavies   *Conquest, Coexistence and Change: Wales 1063-1415*, R. R. Davies (Oxford, 1987)

S&S   *Saints, Seaways and Settlements in Celtic Lands*, E. G. Bowen (Cardiff, 1969)

Samson   *The Life of St Samson of Dol*, T. Taylor (London, 1925)

SPB   *The Story of the Prayer Book*, V. Johnstone & E. Evans (London, 1949)

TL   Manuscript Notebook, Titus Lewis, Vicar 1869-1905 (St Cadfan's Church safe). Transcript at DRO

T-o-S&MCT   *Towyn-on-Sea and Merioneth County Times*

Victorian Vet   *The Several Lives of a Victorian Vet*, J. Hunt & S. Hunt (London, 1979)

Victory   *The Celtic Church in Wales*, S. Victory (London, 1977)

WCC   Welsh Church Commission (documents in NLW)
WEMA   *Wales in the Early Middle Ages*, W. Davies
        (Leicester, 1982)

ADDITIONAL BIBLIOGRAPHY

1. Books etc.

Bartrum, P. C., *A Welsh Classical Dictionary* (NLW, 1993)

Bramley, K. A. (ed.), *Gwaith Llewellyn Fardd I ac...* (Cardiff, 1994)

British & Foreign Bible Society, *The Bible in Wales* (London, 1906)

Cartwright, J. (ed.), *Celtic Hagiography and Saints Cults* (Cardiff, 2003)

Davies, J., *A History of Wales* (Penguin, 1993)

Davies, D. E., *Christian Schools* (Evangelical Library of Wales, Wales, 1978)

Dwyers, J. O., *St Cadfan's Route*, Manuscript NLW 20083C

Edwards, N., *A Corpus of Medieval Inscribed Stones and Stone Sculptures in Wales Vol. III* (Cardiff, 2013)

Evans, D. S., *A Medieval Prince of Wales: Gruffudd ap Cynan* (Llanerch, 1990)

Evans, J., *Description of North Wales* (London, 1810)

Evans, D., *The Sunday Schools of Wales* (London, 1883)

Gildas tr J. A. Giles, *De Excidio et Conquestu Britanniae* (London, 1881)

Gough, *Britannia* (London, 1789)

Gresham, C. A., *Medieval Stone Carving in North Wales* (Cardiff, 1968)

Haslam, R., Orbach, J. & Voelcker, A., *Pevsner: The Buildings of Wales, Gwynedd* (London, 2009)

Henken, E. R., *Traditions of the Welsh Saints* (Cambridge, 1987)

Jenkins, G. H., *The Foundations of Modern Wales 1642-1780* (Oxford, 1993)

Jenkins, D. (trans.), *The Law of Hywel Dda* (Llandysul, 1986)

Jones, D., *The Tourist's and Visitor's Hand-book and Guide to Harlech, Barmouth,….,* (Barmouth, 1863)

Jones, J. G., *The History of Wales* (Cardiff, 1998)

Jones, F., *The Holy Wells of Wales* (Cardiff, 1954)

Leland, J., (ed. L. T. Smith), *Itinerary in Wales (c1536-39)* (London, 1906)

Lewis, T., *St Cadvan's Stone* (Aberystwyth, 1927)

Lewis, S., *Topographical Dictionary of Wales Vol. 2* (London, 1842)

Lloyd, J. E., *History of Wales Vol. 1* (London, 1911)

McKenna, C. A., *The Hagiographic Poetics of Canu Cadfan in A Celtic Florilegium*, (Massachusetts, 1996)

Morgan, K. O., *Wales 1880-1980: Rebirth of a Nation* (Oxford, 1981)

Pethick, J., *Shoreline Intervention Proposals: The Dyfi Estuary and the Aberdyfi Coast* (Countryside Commission for Wales, 1996)

Potter, J. F., *Searching for Early Welsh Churches* (Oxford, 2013)

Price, D. T. W., *A History of the Church in Wales in the 20th Century* (Church in Wales, 1990)

Richards, M., *Welsh Administrative and Territorial Units* (Cardiff, 1969)

Wade-Evans, A., *Welsh Medieval Law* (Oxford, 1909)

Westwood, J. O., *Lapidarium Walliae* (Oxford, 1876-9)

Williams, G. H., *Wales and the Reformation* (Cardiff, 1997)

Williams, G. H., *The Welsh Church from Conquest to Reformation* (Cardiff, 1976)

2. Articles from journals

Arch Camb, 1878: 'Cistfaen at Abergynolwyn', R. Prys Morris

Arch Camb, 1886: 'The Portionary Churches of Medieval North Wales', A. N. Palmer

Arch Camb, 1901: 'The Older Churches in the Four Welsh Dioceses', S. R. Glynne

Arch Camb, 1922: 'The Register of Benedict, Bishop of Bangor 1408-1417', A. I. Pryce

Arch Camb, 1989: 'An Early Sundial from the Towyn Area', W. Gwynn Thomas

Arch Camb, 1997: 'The Western Seaways, myth or reality', Pierre-Roland Giot

Arch Camb, 2000: 'Ecclesiology and Ritualism in Wales', N. Yates

Cambro-Briton, 1820-21: 'Walks around Dolgellau', "Mervinius" J. Welsh Religious History, 2002: 'The Rise and Fall of Llandeilo Fawr', W. A. Strange

J.Historical Soc. of Church in Wales, 1947: 'The Welsh Medieval Dioceses', A. Hamilton Thompson

J.Historical Soc. of Church in Wales, 1953: 'Educational Activity in the Diocese of St Asaph 1500-1650', D. Eifion Evans

J.Historical Soc. of Church in Wales, 1955: '18th Century Background of Church Life in Wales', Bishop of St David's

J.Historical Soc. of Church in Wales, 1956/7: 'Royal Briefs for the Restoration of Churches in Wales Parts 1&2', Gwynfryn Richards

J.Historical Soc. of Church in Wales, 1961: 'Disputes concerning Seats in Church', W. T. Morgan

J.Historical Soc. of Church in Wales, 1970: 'The Origins of the Non-Conformist Disestablishment Campaign', R. Tudur Jones

J.Historical Soc. of Church in Wales, 1970: 'Welsh Disestablishment and Welsh Nationalism', W. B. George

J.Historical Soc. of Church in Wales, 1973: 'The Distribution and Proportion of Celtic and non-Celtic Church Dedications in Wales', W. N. Yeates

J.Historical Soc. of Church in Wales, 1976: 'Clandestine Marriage in Wales', R. Brown

JMHRS, 1953: 'An Old Vestry Book', H. Thomas

JMHRS, 1954-6: 'Merioneth in the Dark Ages', E. G. Bowen

JMHRS, 1962: 'Edward Corbet, Ynysymaengwyn', H. Thomas

JMHRS, 1962: 'Cipolwg ar Ynysymaengwyn a'i Deuluoedd', B. Owen

JMHRS, 1963: 'Archbishop Baldwin's Journey through Wales', C. A. Gresham

JMHRS, 1967: 'Tywyn of a Century and a Half Ago', H. Thomas

JMHRS, 1971: 'St Cadfan's Church, Tywyn', H. Thomas

JMHRS, 1973: 'Educational Charities in Merioneth before 1837',
    T. Ellis

JMHRS, 1978: 'The Quakers of Merioneth Part 2', J. Gwynn
    Williams

JMHRS, 1989: 'Was there a Borough of Bere?', E. D. Evans

JMHRS, 1999: 'A Tywyn Brief of 1694', E. D. Evans

JMHRS, 2005: 'The Church Bells of Merioneth', J. C. Eisel

Journal of Welsh Ecclesiastical History, 1988: 'The Diocese of
    Bangor in the late 16th Century', M. Gray

Transactions of the Anglesey Antiquarian and Field Club, 1939:
    'Reformation in the Diocese of Bangor', A. I. Pryce

Transactions of Cymmrodorion, 1991: 'Poets & Pilgrims in the
    15th & 16th Centuries', G. Williams

Welsh History Review, 1966-7: 'Crown and Community in the
    Principality of North Wales', J. Beverley Smith

Welsh History Review, 1968-9: 'Marriage and Politics in Wales
    1066-1292', A. J. Rodrick

Welsh History Review, 1986-7: 'In Search of a Medieval Society',
    H. Pryce

Y Cymmrodor, 1910: 'Parochiale Wallicanum', A. W. Wade Evans

Y Cymmrodor, 1918: 'Taliesin Appendix I, the Stone of Cingen',
    J. Morris-Jones

Y Cymmrodor, 1927: 'Merioneth Notes', T. P. Ellis

3. Newspapers

Aberystwyth Observer
Cambrian News
Carnarvon and Denbigh Herald
Llangollen Observer
Towyn-on-Sea and Merioneth County Times
Wrexham Guardian

ENDNOTES TO CHAPTERS

CHAPTER 1

[1] HM1, pp. 61, 132 & 142ff

[2] HM1, p. 2, and deduction from the geography of the Mawddach, Dysynni and Dyfi, coupled with information about draining of the Dysynni marshes

[3] S&S, pp. 2, 14, map p. 5, Victory, p. 7

[4] Deduction from need to grow crops before their first winter

[5] St Cadfan's Well, sourced by the spring, has been known since early times.

[6] Children are always children!

[7] HM1, p. 265

[8] Bryneglwys is up the small valley that runs south-eastwards from Abergynolwyn

[9] HM1, p. 276

[10] Baring-Gould, *The Lives of the British Saints*, Vol. 2, London, 1908. Baring-Gould worked mainly from the *Iolo Manuscripts*, a collection made in the 19th century, which was said to be of ancient Welsh texts; some of them are of questionable origin.

[11] S&S, p. 2, map p. 4

[12] Victory, p. 7

[13] P.-R. Giot, 'The Western Seaways – Myth or Reality?' in *Arch Camb*, 1997, p. 1ff

[14] S&S, p. 19

[15] S&S, p. 7

[16] HM1, p. 3 & p. 56ff.

[17] Wikipedia, "Desert Fathers"

[18] S&S, pp. 62-63 ff

[19] S&S, p. 52

[20] S&S, pp. 67-69

[21] J. Pethick, Report to the Countryside Commission for Wales: 'The Dyfi Estuary and the Aberdyfi Coast', 1996

[22] British Geological Survey, 2001

[23] Archaeological watching brief for building of sacristy, 2014

[24] From excavation for a lightning conductor earth. The rods also went down 4 metres without reaching rock or water.

[25] Fenton, p. 110

[26] HM1, pp. 61-62

[27] HM1, p. 153

[28] HM1, p. 142ff

[29] Source: Mrs Pugh of Eisteddfa, Tan y Coed Farm, Abergynolwyn

[30] Extract received from RCAHMW. The pathway was included in an upland survey conducted in 2005.

[31] HM1, p. 264ff

[32] Latter half of the 12th century

[33] Originally composed in the 12th century; earliest surviving incomplete copy 13th century

[34] Bartrum, *Welsh Classical Dictionary*, p. 75

[35] Peniarth, Hafod and Cardiff genealogies

[36] HM1, p. 273ff

[37] HM2, p. 266 and JMHRS, 1954-6; E. G. Bowen, *Merioneth in the Dark Ages*

[38] Bartrum

[39] HM1, p. 275

[40] 'Parochiale Wallicanum', *Y Cymmrodor*, 1910, p. 22

[41] Aber Obs, 1 October 1896. Various websites give 516 AD as a date associated with Cadfan – for his birth, death, move to Bardsey or arrival at Tywyn. I cannot find any indication of the source of any of their statements.

CHAPTER 2

[1] Possibly written in the early 6th century and certainly by the mid-9th century

[2] Gildas, *De Excidio et Conquestu Britanniae*, c500-570

[3] See Chapter 3

[4] Victory, p. 15

[5] WEMA, p. 148

[6] Victory, p. 53ff

[7] WEMA, p. 149

[8] Samson, Part 1 XIV & XIX

[9] Victory, p. 59

[10] Victory, p. 60

[11] WEMA, p. 151; Samson XII, XXI

[12] Samson, XVI

[13] Victory, p. 24

[14] 1908 faculty. NLW, B/F/470

[15] N. Edwards, *A Corpus of Medieval Inscribed Stones and Stone Sculpture in Wales*, Vol. 3, North Wales

[16] NL&Ch, pp. 41 & 43

[17] See Appendix B for details

[18] NL&Ch, p. 211

[19] H. Pryce, 'Ecclesiastical Wealth in Early Medieval Wales' in *The Early Church in Wales and the West*, ed. N. Edwards, pp. 27-31

[20] HM2, p. 261

[21] NL&Ch, p. 165

[22] N.Edwards, *A Corpus of Medieval Inscribed Stones...*, Vol. III, North Wales

[23] NL&Ch, p. 179

[24] NL&Ch, p. 186/7

[25] Davidson, Arch EMCC, p. 46

[26] Arch EMCC, p. 46

[27] Gough's edition of *Camden's Britannia*, p. 172

[28] Arch EMCC, p. 47

CHAPTER 3

[1] Arch EMCC, pp. 48, 50

[2] The only known mediaeval churches in the *cantref* are Tywyn, Llanegryn, Llangelynnin, Dolgellau, Talyllyn, Llanfihangel-y-Pennant and Pennal.

[3] It has been suggested that at some stage the church became an Augustinian canonry, but there seems to be no evidence for this.

[4] RRDavies, pp. 172, 174

[5] *Domesday Book* quoted in HM2, pp. 6, 7

[6] WEMA, p. 2

[7] HM2, p. 11. At that time Gwynedd did not include Meirionydd, which was only added about 1124.

[8] J. Potter, *Searching for the Early Welsh Churches*

[9] See end of Appendix A

[10] RRDavies, pp. 187-8

[11] Pevsner, Gwynedd, p. 719

[12] HM2, p. 368ff

[13] J. Potter, *Searching for the Early Welsh Churches*

[14] Canu Cadfan. The wording of the poem may mean a gospel book or the preaching of the gospel.

[15] NL&Ch, p. 43

[16] HM2, p. 263 & S&S, p. 197

[17] Bowen, *Settlements of the Celtic Saints*, p. 94

[18] Gough's edition of *Camden's Britannia*, p. 172

[19] HM2, p. 14

[20] RRDavies, p. 176

[21] HM2, p. 262

[22] This section relates to Giraldus Cambrensis, *The Journey Through Wales* Book 2, Chapters 4 & 5

[23] C. Gresham, 'Archbishop Baldwin's Journey', JMHRS, 1987/8

[24] C. Gresham, 'Archbishop Baldwin's Journey', JMHRS, 1987/8

[25] HM2, p. 262

[26] HM2, p. 256

[27] HM2, p. 255ff

[28] HM2, p. 259

[29] J. Cartwright (ed.), *Celtic Hagiography and Saints Cults*, p. 57

[30] This section is based on C. McKenna, 'The Hagiographic Poetics of Canu Cadfan' in *A Celtic Florilegium*, Massachusetts, 1996, and on HM2, pp. 262ff and 324ff.

[31] Henken gives an alternative translation: "renowned relics, loud are they heard" – a suggestion that it may refer to bells. E. R. Henken, *Traditions of the Welsh Saints*, Cambridge, 1987, p. 175

[32] Dewi is David, Llanddewi is St David's.

[33] WEMA, p. 16

CHAPTER 4

[1] HM2, p. 297ff

[2] HM2, p. 309

[3] HM2, p. 531. She may have been a niece of Hywel ap Cynan, but this is not documented.

[4] HM2, p. 30

[5] E. D. Evans, 'Was there a Borough of Bere?', JMHRS, 1989

[6] 'Extent of Merioneth 1284', HM2, p. 709

[7] BHO Gazetteer of Markets and Fairs in England and Wales

[8] HM2, p. 262

[9] HM2, p. 45

[10] HM2, p. 49

[11] HM2, p. 51

[12] HM2, p. 53

[13] HM2, p. 54

[14] HM2, p. 55

[15] E. D. Evans, 'Was there a Borough of Bere?', JMHRS, 1989

[16] HM2, p. 56

[17] HM2, Appendix I, p. 702ff

[18] HM2, p. 233

[19] HM2, p. 707ff

[20] This section is based on HM2, pp. 267-70

[21] RRDavies, p. 187

[22] RRDavies, pp. 206-7

[23] HM2, pp. 57-59

[24] HM2, p. 403

[25] HM2, p. 59

[26] HM2, p. 229

[27] HM2, p. 229

[28] HM2, p. 262

[29] HM2, pp. 65-66

[30] RRDavies, p. 382

[31] HM2, pp. 68-69

[32] Entries in the Close Rolls of Edward I for May 1295 show four missives sent from Tywyn to the sheriffs of Westmoreland and Bedford and to the escheators this side and beyond Trent on 17 and 18 May.

CHAPTER 5

[1] HM2, pp. 271-2

[2] Benedict's register of clerical appointments is the earliest extant register; it is only partial and contains no information of appointments to Tywyn.

[3] AIP16, x

[4] A rectory was not a building but the incumbency – with all its emoluments – of a parish.

[5] Browne-Willis, *A Survey of the Cathedral Church of Bangor and the Edifices Belonging to it*, London, 1721

[6] An obit was a mass sung annually on the anniversary of a death. A chantry usually implied more frequent masses and might also include the provision of a separate altar at which they were sung.

[7] RCAHMW, p. 170, quoting PRO Chantry Certificates no. 76

[8] HM2, p. 292. When part of the floor of the north transept was lifted to allow pipes to be laid under it, in 2010, two ulna bones (elbow bones, both right side) were seen lying on the earth beneath.

[9] HM2, p. 294

[10] 1724 Vestry book, DRO

[11] 1724 Vestry book, DRO

[12] S. R. Glynne, 'The Older Churches in the Four Welsh Dioceses', Arch Camb, 6th series, vol. 1, p. 141

[13] HM2, p. 249

[14] RRDavies, p. 425. Murrain usually referred to infectious diseases of cattle.

[15] HM2, p. 291

[16] C. A. Gresham, *Medieval stone carving in North Wales*, Cardiff, 1968, item 155

[17] The rhaglot, rhingyll or rhaglaw was the officer responsible for rendering the fiscal liabilities of a community. He often bought the office in a deal allowing him to make a profit. HM2, p. 63

[18] C. A. Gresham, *Medieval stone carving in North Wales*, Cardiff 1968, item 180

[19] RRDavies, p. 425

[20] RRDavies, p. 427

[21] RRDavies, p. 426

[22] HM2, pp. 262 & 284

[23] AIP3C, p. 179, and *Calendar of Patent Rolls, Richard II*, Vol. 6, 1397

[24] Advowson is the patronage or ability to present to the bishop a nominee for a vacant ecclesiastical benefice.

[25] National Archives 8/25/1209 from *Parliament Rolls of Medieval England: Henry VI*, February 1426

[26] HM2, p. 290 says he successively held Llanfair-juxta-Harlech and Tywyn.

[27] Lateran Regista, 395:1442-1443

[28] *Calendar of Papal Registers*, 17 September 1448, BHO, and HM2, p. 290

[29] *Calendar of Patent Rolls, Henry VI*, 14 October 1451

[30] *Calendar of Papal Registers GB & Ireland 1447-1455*, BHO. Brugge had been given Papal permission to hold for life with Lanreythowe any benefice of a value not exceeding £26 sterling, so would not have been expected to want the exchange.

[31] HM2, p. 290 footnote

CHAPTER 6

[1] The following two paragraphs are based on AIP16, p. xi ff

[2] AIP16, p. xii

[3] AIP16, p. xiii

[4] HM2, p. 289

[5] AIP16, p. xxxii

[6] Mostly Hugh Thomas, *A History of Wales 1485-1660*, p. 80ff

[7] G. Williams, *Wales and the Reformation*, Cardiff, 1997, p. 21

[8] AIP16, p. 5

[9] Henry VIII May 1528: Letters & Papers Vol. 4, BHO

[10] Henry VIII June 1509: Letters & Papers Vol. 1, BHO

[11] Henry VIII March 1520: Letters & Papers Vol. 3, BHO

[12] Henry VIII February 1510: Letters & Papers Vol. 1, BHO

[13] Henry VIII May 1519: Letters & Papers Vol. 3, BHO

[14] Henry VIII April 1513: Letters & Papers Vol. 1, BHO. Cowen is thought to be a mistranscription from the manuscript capital T of Towen. Vol. 14, BHO

[15] Henry VIII January 1522: Letters & Papers Vol. 3, BHO

[16] Henry VIII February 1523: Letters & Papers Vol. 3, BHO

[17] *History of County of Shropshire*, Vol. 2, pp. 128-31, BHO

[18] Referred to in NLW. Bangor Diocesan Papers. 25 Welsh Commission 124014

[19] Henry VIII May 1539: Letters & Papers Vol. 7, BHO

[20] HM2, p. 289; Valor Eccl, iv, 427

[21] G. Williams, *The Welsh Church from Conquest to Reformation*, Cardiff, 1976, p. 286-7 and his Appendix A

[22] Ibid, p. 287

[23] Remains seen later. Gough/Camden, Vol. 3, p. 172

[24] Cymmrodorion, 1991, p. 73

[25] Henry Thomas, 'Some Features & Episodes in the History of the Church of Saint Cadvan Towyn, Merioneth', JMHRS, 1971

[26] Henry VIII April 1529: Letters & Papers, BHO

[27] Henry VIII July 1538: Letters & Papers, BHO

[28] Henry VIII May 1539: Letters & Papers, BHO. Letters relating to the likelihood of the two Griffiths being the same man are now at the Merioneth Records Office, Dolgellau.

[29] G. Williams, *Wales and the Reformation*, Cardiff, 1997, p. 61

[30] G. Williams, *Wales and the Reformation*, p. 65

[31] G. Williams, *Wales and the Reformation*, Cardiff, 1997, p. 65

[32] Henry VIII Jan 1536: Letters & Papers, BHO

[33] G. Williams, *The Welsh Church from Conquest to Reformation*, Cardiff, 1976, p. 341

[34] Henry VIII July 1538: Letters & Papers, BHO

[35] Henry VIII Index U-Z 1546-47: Letters & Papers Vol. 21, Part 2, BHO

[36] Henry VIII September 1546: Letters & Papers Vol. 21, BHO

[37] Henry VIII November 1546: Letters & Papers Vol. 21, Part 2, BHO

[38] Henry VIII November 1546: Letters & Papers Vol. 21, Part 2, BHO

[39] Separate Wills 1544-1547 (nos 200-45), London Consistory Court Wills 1492-1547, BHO

[40] SPB, p. 19

[41] SPB, p. 19ff

[42] *The Bible in Wales*, 1906, p. 16

[43] *History & Topographical Survey of County of Kent*, Vol. 12; *Canterbury Cathedral: Canons*, BHO; *Fasti Ecclesiae Anglicanae 1541-1857*, Vol. 3, BHO

[44] NLW, Diocese of Bangor Records 24106 File 25 (25 Welsh Church Commission 124014)

[45] NLW Peniarth Estate (33) NA4

[46] SPB, p. 21

[47] *The Bible in Wales*, p. 16

[48] G. Williams, *Wales and the Reformation*, p. 159

[49] RCAHMW, p. 170

CHAPTER 7

[1] AIP16, p. 12ff

[2] HM2, pp. 680-685; *Wales and the Reformation*, p. 213

[3] M. Gray, 'The Diocese of Bangor in the late C16', *Journal of Welsh Ecclesiastical History*, 1988, p. 41

[4] M. Gray, 'The Diocese of Bangor in the late C16', *Journal of Welsh Ecclesiastical History*, 1988, pp. 61-2

[5] Browne-Willis, p. 270

[6] G. Williams, *Wales and the Reformation*, p. 247

[7] G. Williams, *Wales and the Reformation*, p. 247

[8] G. Williams, *Wales and the Reformation*, p. 298

[9] HM2, p. 685

[10] CCEd

[11] AIP16, p. 44

[12] *Charles II Calendar of State Papers*, Vol. 146, 23-31 January 1666, BHO

[13] AIP3C, p. xxii

[14] NLW, Peniarth Estate (33) NA85

[15] P. Jenkins, p. 132ff; H. Thomas 1485, p. 218ff

[16] AIP3C, p. xxvi

[17] Written in Latin. Registers are at DRO

[18] CCEd

[19] AIP3C, p. 162

[20] Lactuals were the payments made on the number of cows owned, as a 10% tithe on cattle would be impractical.

[21] J. Gwynn Williams, 'The Quakers of Merioneth During the Seventeenth Century', Part 2, JMHRS, 1978, pp. 127, 138

CHAPTER 8

[1] SPB, pp. 64, 67, 68

[2] Churchwardens' accounts 1724-45, DRO

[3] Canon Thomas, 'An Old Vestry Book', JMHRS, 1953, p. 40

[4] TL

[5] Gough/Camden, pp. 172-3

[6] I am unable to find a source for this.

[7] Deduction from J. C. Eisel, 'The Church Bells of Merioneth', JMHRC XIV, 2005, p. 315, which states it is probably 17th century.

[8] The architect for the Ecclesiastical Commissioners in 1875 reported the south wall of the chancel as 13th century. Letter, Tywyn Safe. Now DRO

[9] NLW, 25 (24016) Lichfield Bishopric Tywyn Account

[10] E. D. Evans, 'A Tywyn Brief of 1694', *JMHRS*, 1999, p. 184

[11] *Journal of the Historical Society of the Church in Wales*, 1956, pp. 65-67

[12] E. D. Evans, 'A Tywyn Brief of 1694', *JMHRS*, 1999, p. 184

[13] 'An Old Vestry Book', JMHRS, 1953, p. 41

[14] *Alumni Oxonienses 1500-1714*, BHO

CHAPTER 9

[1] *Journal of the Historical Society of the Church in Wales*, 1953, p. 90

[2] End date not known

[3] i.e. R. Prys Jones

[4] £1 in 1724 would be worth about £130 in 2014. 6d would be worth £3.25.

[5] H. Thomas, 'An Old Vestry Book', JMHRC, 1953, p. 41

[6] All dates after 1767 were in the second vestry book which went astray in the early years of the 20th century and were reported by Robyn Frych in his articles in the *Cambrian News*.

[7] DRP notes

CHAPTER 10

[1] *History of the Church in Wales in the 20th Century*, p.1

[2] AIP3C, p. lvi

[3] Clergy appointed to more than one benefice and receiving the income from all of them

[4] TL

[5] Churchwardens' book

[6] Recorded on a vellum in Tywyn church safe. Now at DRO

[7] TL, 'The Vicars of the Parish'

[8] TL, 'The Vicars of the Parish'

[9] AIP3C, p. 29

[10] TL, 'The Vicars of the Parish' (written 1905)

[11] J. C. Eisel, 'The Church Bells of Merioneth', JMHRC, 2005, p. 315

[12] Gough's edition of *Camden's Britannia* Vol. 3, London, 1810, p. 172. This also includes copies of the engravings.

[13] Aber Obs, 15 December 1881. The information comes from the missing vestry book and had appeared in another newspaper from which it had been copied.

[14] NLW, B/CC/(G)/164

[15] S. R. Glynne. *Arch Camb*, 6th Series, Vol. 1

[16] *Oswestry Advertiser*, 29 December 1880 quoting from the second (now missing) churchwardens' accounts book

[17] W. Gwynn Thomas, 'An Early Sundial from the Towyn Area', *Arch Camb*, 1989, pp. 111-3

[18] NLW, Bangor Diocesan Records B/Misc Vol. 1

[19] NLW, B/TERR/1382

[20] Privy

[21] Claude's details from Andrew Lacey, *The Cult of King Charles the Martyr*, Rochester, NY, 2003

CHAPTER 11

[1] This may have been in the churchwardens' book that followed the only one which is still extant.

[2] NLW, B/TERR/1382

[3] NLW, 25 (24016) Lichfield Bishopric Towyn Account

[4] This letter, and those that follow, are all from NLW, 25 Welsh Church Commission 124017.

[5] NLW, 25 Welsh Church Commission 124017. Reference in a letter from Curate of Pennal dated 8 August 1718

[6] NLW, 12014 Welsh CC 25

[7] William Salt Library, Stafford: 'Case and Opinion on title to tithes at Towyn, county Merioneth', 1808 [WSL Ref: M101]

[8] WCC, 25 ECE/EL/B420 0 438

[9] NLW, 124,017

[10] NLW, 124,017

[11] William Salt Library, Stafford: 'Case and Opinion on title to tithes at Towyn, county Merioneth', 1808 [WSL Ref: M101]

[12] HCPP, 1847-8 (298)

[13] Very simplified!

[14] HCPP, 1856 (2039)

[15] The following all relate to letters etc. in Tywyn safe, now at DRO.

[16] These were the money rents that replaced the corn rents, which themselves had replaced the payment of tithe in kind in 1836.

[17] This was the current Tywyn parish only, and did not include the three "chapels". The figures for them were Llanfihangel-y-Pennant £100, Pennal £223, Talyllyn £250 (HCPP 1887 (214)).

[18] Although Robert Pugh had reported in 1787 that Llanfihangel-y-Pennant, Talyllyn and Pennal functioned as separate parishes there seems no record of when separate parish boundaries were formally instituted.

[19] Aber Obs, 6 November 1886; *Cambrian News*, 14 January 1887

[20] *Cambrian News*, 9 & 16 March 1888

[21] Aber Obs, 23 June 1888

[22] These two paragraphs: *Carnarvon and Denbigh Herald*, 6 July 1888

[23] *Cambrian News*, 13 December 1889

[24] *Carnarvon and Denbigh Herald*, 24 January 1890

[25] A different family from the Corbet (single 't') family

CHAPTER 12

[1] Rev. J. Evans, *Description of North Wales*, London, 1810, pp. 892-3

[2] *Cambrian Quarterly*, 1829, quoted in JMHRS, 1962, p. 142 (Edward Corbet, Ynysymaengwyn: Henry Thomas)

[3] CambroBriton, 1820-21, p120: "Mervinius", 'Walks around Dolgellau'

[4] *Cambrian Quarterly*, 1829, op cit

[5] E. Mogg, *Paterson's Roads*, 17th edition, 1824, p. 170

[6] JMHRS, 1962, p. 144: H. Thomas, 'Edward Corbet, Ynysymaengwyn'

[7] JMHRS, 1962, p. 115: Bob Owen, 'Cipolwg ar Ynysymaengwyn a'i Deuluoedd',

[8] Fenton, *Tours in Wales*, p. 110

[9] AIP3C, p. 45

[10] NLW, B/LET/54

[11] NLW, BMisc Vol. 2. Among other things, this contains lists of benefices with incumbent, patron and the value of the living for each.

[12] NLW, BMisc, Vol. 2. This is dated 1800 but is either misdated or was updated at intervals later.

[13] NLW, B/PDM/326

[14] NLW, B/OC/8

[15] HCPP, 1861 (2792)

[16] AIP3C, p. 69

[17] S. R. Glynne, 'The Older Churches in the Four Welsh Dioceses', Arch Camb, 1901, p. 141

[18] Victorian Vet, Chapter 1

[19] See Appendix D

[20] 'Tywyn Past and Present', Aber Obs, 12 September 1874

[21] This section and next two paragraphs, 'Tywyn Past and Present', Aber Obs, 17 October 1874

[22] Also quoted by Fenton after his 1804 visit. Fenton, p. 53

[23] 'Tywyn Past and Present', Aber Obs, 17 October 1874

[24] National Archives. The will was proved "with a codicil" in 1842 but

does not mention the stone; it may, however, have been mentioned in the codicil.

[25] HCPP, 1847-8 (216)

[26] HCPP, 1850 (4) and 1850 (186)

[27] NLW, B/Misc/117

[28] HCPP, 1856 (323)

[29] HCPP, 1856 (319)

[30] Although it is in theory still legal in England to request a voluntary tax

[31] Victorian Vet, p. 22

[32] NLW, B/MISC/106

[33] Kettle, pp. 21-22

[34] Aber Obs, 22 June 1867

[35] NLW, B/S/219

[36] Victorian Vet, p. 22. The dates of that chapter are wrong but Evans was in Tywyn in 1869 (p. 100) and may have confused the two.

CHAPTER 13

[1] This is not the well-known Baptist minister, whose dates were 1773-1811.

[2] Kettle

[3] This was probably Mary Cooke Allen (nee Kettle), daughter of Rupert Kettle.

[4] Kettle

[5] This must have been written before the 1880-4 rebuilding.

[6] *Cambrian News*, 23 June 1871

[7] *Cambrian News*, 28 April 1871

[8] *Cambrian News*, 31 July 1869

[9] St Cadfan's Church safe, now DRO

[10] St Cadfan's Church safe, now DRO

[11] NLW, B/Misc/186

[12] *Cambrian News*, 1 October 1870

[13] *Cambrian News*, 18 February 1871

[14] All letters from the Ecclesiastical Commissioners from St Cadfan's Church safe, now DRO

[15] There is still considerable cement between the south window and the east end of the chancel (found when replastering, 2006).

[16] Aber Obs, 2 December 1876

[17] Except where otherwise noted, all information about the restoration comes from NLW, B/F/469.

[18] TL

[19] TL

[20] His notes on the building at that time are at the end of Appendix A.

[21] This meeting is reported in detail in the *Aberystwyth Observer*, 27 July 1878.

[22] The *Aberystwyth Observer*, 9 August 1878, published a letter from W. W. E. Wynne of Peniarth, a noted amateur archaeologist. He made known his objection to Prichard's design as being over-elaborate and urged much greater fidelity to the original.

[23] Aber Obs, 28 September 1878

[24] *Wrexham Guardian*, 1 February 1879

[25] Aber Obs, 1 February 1879

[26] At that time this would have paid for about forty years' work from one skilled craftsman/builder (on a six-day week with no holidays). Inflation calculators vary but £4000 would be between a quarter and a third of £1 million now (2014).

[27] Dolgellau notes – possibly from *Cambrian News*

[28] T-o-S&MCT, 9 November 1905 (under Towyn Charities)

[29] *Cambrian News*, 22 October 1870: "it was said that the roofing of some of the vaults was insecure and there was a danger of the congregation descending quick among the dead". When part of the floor of the north transept was lifted in 2010, two ulna (elbow bones, both right arm) were found lying on the earth beneath.

[30] *Llangollen Observer*, 16 July 1880

[31] *Carnarvon and Denbigh Herald*, 16 April 1881

[32] Aber Obs, 31 December 1881

[33] Aber Obs, 4 February 1882

[34] Aber Obs, 16 September 1882

[35] Aber Obs, 30 September 1882

[36] TL

[37] Ecclesiastical Commissioner's letter 1875, Tywyn safe now DRO

[38] NLW, B/C/113 and Titus Lewis

[39] NLW, B/QA/32

[40] *Cambrian News*, 27 December 1889

[41] *Cambrian News*, 28 December 1888

[42] Details – Titus. Position – postcard and extant markings on floor

[43] T-o-S&MCT, 25 February 1904

CHAPTER 14

[1] All references in this chapter are from the paper except where otherwise specified. The earliest copy in NLW is marked No. 102 Vol. 2 (probably August 1897). The last copy is from November 2005.

[2] 10 August 1899

[3] 15 August 1901

[4] 14 February 1898

[5] 23 February 1899

[6] 10 August 1899

[7] 19 July/16 August 1900, 17 July 1902

[8] 6 April 1899

[9] 10 May 1899

[10] 12 October/30 November 1899

[11] 19 April 1900

[12] 8 November 1900

[13] 6 September 1900

[14] 8 and 22 November 1900

[15] 23 July 1903

[16] 19 April 1900

[17] 19 June 1902

[18] 30 April 1903

[19] 25 February 1904

[20] 16 February 1905

[21] 9 November 1905

CHAPTER 15

[1] Letters and plan. Black box, Tywyn safe, now DRO

[2] Possibly because a faculty was required – one was granted in May 1908. NLW, B/F/471

[3] Where not otherwise specified the information given in this chapter is from the Parochialia for the appropriate year.

[4] Parochialia, 1907-8

[5] NLW, B/F/471

[6] NLW, B/F/471

[7] The old lychgate and part of the bier house can be seen in a painting hanging in the south aisle.

[8] Black box, Tywyn safe plus NLW, B/F/474 plus Parochialia

[9] Black box, Tywyn safe and NLW, B/F/473

[10] Actually the current main door, which is on the south of the building but towards the west end. There was no door in the west wall after the 1880-4 rebuilding.

[11] Black box, Tywyn safe and NLW, B/F/477

[12] Tywyn safe, now DRO

[13] Rev. David Pugh's notebook, Tywyn safe

[14] The bulk of the information below comes from notes in Pugh's notebook or from letters he had pasted into it.

[15] Possibly the Thomas Edwards who objected to the extension of the church at the 1878 vestry meeting

[16] BHO, Henry VIII: April 1529, 26-30, *Letters and Papers, Foreign and Domestic, Volume 4: 1524-1530*, 1875, pp. 2427-37

[17] NLW, B/F/478 & Parochialia, 1927

[18] Apparently no faculty was needed for repainting walls in those days…

CHAPTER 16

[1] Much of the information in this chapter comes from *A History of the Church in Wales in the 20th Century*.

[2] NLW, B/Misc Vol1. See Chapter 10, "A bishop's visitation"

[3] The village near Llangelynnin

⁴ All dates of registration from NLW, B/PDM
⁵ HCPP, 1910 (5432). Also notes for the survey in black box, Tywyn safe (now DRO)
⁶ See Chapter 6, "Edward VI"
⁷ £1 million in 1920 would be the equivalent of £44 million in 2014.
⁸ 1906 terrier. Tywyn safe

CHAPTER 17

¹ Most of this chapter is based on the Parochialia.
² T-on-S&MCT, 23 April 1903
³ Information about this restoration is in Tywyn church safe.
⁴ The modern version, Gift Aid, which does not require a long-term commitment, is of great help to the current church.
⁵ Dissilience means bursting apart or bursting open (as seed pods do).
⁶ This paragraph: CinW20, p. 29
⁷ CinW20, p. 29
⁸ It is thought that it was at this time that the exciting new vinyl paint was used on the walls. A horror to modern thinking but, on the other hand, it has now lasted over fifty years while it used to be necessary to repaint every ten years.

CHAPTER 18

¹ Most of the information in this chapter comes from the minutes of the Parochial Church Council.
² The Welsh equivalent of English Heritage
³ It fell between two of the maintenance team, a churchwarden and the secretary, who were working on the wall about 5 feet apart. Church opinion was divided between it being God's grace that neither was hit and a suggestion that God had a bad aim!

APPENDIX A

[1] Pevsner, p. 718

[2] NLW, B/TERR/1382; Terrier 1776

[3] See Prichard's notes (last paragraph) at the end of this chapter, also Potter

[4] AIP3C, p. lviii

[5] TL and Prichard's notes

[6] Pevsner dates it as 13th century, Coflein suggests 14th century.

[7] See also John Prichard's notes at the end of this appendix.

[8] See chapter 10

[9] In 1808 there were thirty-six people in good health over the age of eighty within two miles of the church. *Cambrian News*, 26 November 1808

[10] See end of this appendix

[11] Gwynedd Archaeological Trust report on the watching brief, 2010

[12] Gwynedd Archaeological Trust report on the watching brief, 2010

[13] In 1808 Fenton looked for an inscription on the base "but could not see low enough down to find out if there was any". See chapter 5, "The effigies"

[14] *Cambrian News*, 1 October 1870

[15] Churchwardens' book

[16] Fenton, p. 121

[17] Recollection of verbal description only, as the report on the reslating cannot be found

[18] John Prichard's notes at the end of this appendix

[19] The architect for the Ecclesiastical Commission in 1875 reported the south wall of the chancel as being 13th century, so it had, presumably, not been demolished in the fall of the tower. Letter, Tywyn safe, now DRO

[20] From a painting in church marked as painted before the restoration

[21] NLW, B/CC/(G)/164

[22] Prichard – see end of this appendix

[23] 'The Older Churches of the four Welsh Dioceses', Arch Camb, 6th Series, Vol. 1, p. 141

[24] *Cambrian News*, 10 December 1870

[25] NLW, B/F/469

[26] Compare 19th century picture and current west window

[27] T-o-S&MCT, 9 November 1905

[28] TL

[29] Frith, Ref 30227

[30] Aber Obs, 1 October 1896. Cambrian Archaeological Society

[31] Coflein says that a new south door and the aisle windows were added at the same time, but they are clearly shown as already existing on a photograph of the church before its restoration.

[32] See photographs of the interior in 1885, chapter 13

[33] The old lychgate can be seen on a postcard dated 1892 (Frith, 30226).

[34] RCAHMW, Plate 138 (visited 1914)

[35] Stones and a brick were found infilling the area when the plaster was removed for the 2010 development.

[36] Quoted in *Aberystwyth Observer*, 19 April 1884

[37] This does not make sense as the south transept roof would surely have been damaged in the fall of the tower but not the north one. Could he have got north and south back to front? Or had there been other changes at an earlier time which are not recorded anywhere?

[38] This must have disappeared when the tower stair was built.

[39] Sadly, in the end he filled in the lower parts of these windows and put new ones at "Victorian" height (i.e. so you could not gaze outside during the sermon…). See photograph in 19th century, chapter 12.

APPENDIX B

[1] Unless otherwise specified, this appendix draws heavily on *A Corpus of Early Medieval Inscribed Stones and Stone Sculpture in Wales, Volume III, North Wales*. Professor Nancy Edwards of the University of Bangor very kindly sent me a copy of the catalogue entry from her book.

[2] N. Edwards

[3] Quinquennial report 1999

[4] N. Edwards

[5] D. R. Pugh reported that it was the gatepost of a pigsty at Caethle. Note in church safe, now at DRO.

[6] *Camden's Britannia*, Gough's 2nd edition, 1806, Vol. III, p. 172

[7] Churchwardens' book

[8] DRP, p. 15

[9] Fenton, p. 121

[10] Cambro-Briton, 1820-21, 'Walks around Dolgellau', Editor's footnote.

[11] I have been unable to find this article or letter in Welsh Newspapers Online any time between 1880 and 1890. However, there were numerous small local papers which were not preserved and it may have been in one of them.

[12] Note by D. R. Pugh in church safe. He also noted that "the horse shied and the stone fell and broke as it was transported back from Bodtalog".

[13] Proved 1842, National Archives. I have not been able to find a copy of a codicil that might have contained the instruction.

[14] Kettle, p. 27

[15] He reported it to the Royal Commission on Ancient and Historic Monuments in Wales.

[16] *Oswestry Advertiser*, 29 December 1889

[17] Editor of *Sundials of the British Isles*, Cambridge 2008

[18] D. Jones, *The Tourist and Visitors Handbook and Guide to Harlech, Barmouth, etc.*, Barmouth 1863

[19] N. Edwards, *A Corpus of Medieval Inscribed Stones…*, *Vol. III, North Wales*

[20] Westwood, J.O., *Lapidarium Walliae*, Oxford 1876-9

[21] D. R. Pugh, note in church safe

[22] Gough's edition of *Camden's Britannia*, Vol. 3, p. 173 in the second edition, 1806

APPENDIX C

[1] TL

[2] Tywyn safe/DRO

[3] Parochialia

APPENDIX D

[1] HCPP, 1895 (419) Endowed Charities (County of Merioneth) re Vincent Corbet & Lady Moyer and the subsequent setting up of trusts. The date of Vincent Corbet's donation is referred to as Midsummer 1717 in the letter from Lady Moyer.
[2] Monument in St Cadfan's Church
[3] D. Eryl Davies, *Christian Schools*, Association of Christian Teachers of Wales, 1978, pp. 1-2
[4] Foundation stone now in St Cadfan's Church
[5] Aber Obs, 25 August 1864
[6] Aber Obs, 18 July 1874
[7] Aber Obs, 31 October 1874
[8] Aber Obs, 20 August 1864
[9] Now at DRO
[10] Letter to Board of Education 3 May 1913
[11] Copies of all these from Tywyn church safe, now DRO
[12] Vicar's letter in *The Times*, 25 July 1910

APPENDIX E

[1] Notes on lines 8, 30, 115, 167 were outlined by McKenna